The Colonial Politics of Global Health

The Colonial Politics of Global Health

France and the United Nations in Postwar Africa

JESSICA LYNNE PEARSON

Harvard University Press
Cambridge, Massachusetts
London, England
2018

Printed in the United States of America

First printing

Library of Congress Cataloging-in-Publication Data

Names: Pearson, Jessica Lynne, 1984– author.
Title: The colonial politics of global health : France and the United Nations in postwar Africa / Jessica Lynne Pearson.
Description: Cambridge, Massachusetts : Harvard University Press, 2018.
Identifiers: LCCN 2018004945 | ISBN 9780674980488 (alk. paper)
Subjects: LCSH: Health services administration—Africa, French-speaking—History—20th century. | Medical policy—Africa, French-speaking—History—20th century. | Medical care—Political aspects—Africa, French-speaking—History—20th century. | United Nations. | Africa, French-speaking—Politics and government—20th century. | Decolonization—Africa, French-speaking.
Classification: LCC RA395.A35 P43 2018 | DDC 362.10966 /0917541—dc23
LC record available at https://lccn.loc.gov/2018004945

For my grandmother, D'Orsay W. Pearson

Contents

Abbreviations

ADLC	Archives diplomatiques du Ministère des Affaires Etrangères, La Courneuve
AEF	Afrique Equatoriale Française
AMI	Assistance médicale indigène
ANF	Archives nationales (France)
ANOM	Archives nationales d'outre-mer
ANS	Archives nationales du Sénégal
AOF	Afrique Occidentale Française
CCTA	Commission de coopération technique en Afrique au sud du Sahara
CFLN	Comité français de libération nationale
CIDEF	Archives du Centre international de l'enfance
CIE	Centre international de l'enfance
CMR	Comité médical de la résistance
DGSP	Direction générale de la santé publique
FAO	United Nations Food and Agriculture Organization
FIDES	Fonds d'investissement pour le développement économique et social
HCI	Hôpital central indigène
IME	Inspection médicale des écoles
IMTSSA	Archives de l'Institut de médecine tropicale du Service de santé des armées
MEP	Malaria Eradication Program
NUOI	Nations Unies—Organisations internationales
OIHP	Office international d'hygiène publique
OMS	Organisation mondiale de la Santé
ONU	Organisation des Nations Unies

ORANA	Organisme de recherches sur l'alimentation et la nutrition africaine
RF	Rockefeller Foundation
UN	United Nations
UNESCO	United Nations Educational, Scientific, and Cultural Organization
UNICEF	United Nations International Children's Emergency Fund
WHO	World Health Organization
WHOL	World Health Organization Library

The Colonial Politics of Global Health

Introduction

In his opening address to the second annual meeting of the World Health Organization's (WHO's) Regional Committee for Africa in 1952, Liberian president William V. S. Tubman described a rapidly changing postwar world that was coming together in previously unimagined ways:

> Thanks to the invention of the airplane and other forms of quick and comfortable transportation, the world today appears to be shrinking. While in the past it took weeks or even months to travel from one country to another, now a few hours or a few days suffice to access any country, whatever its latitude or longitude. While the spirit of isolationism may still exist, it must be radically eliminated by any nation or group of nations concerned with assuring their security and their well-being. No country can therefore fail to take interest in the general conditions of health and well-being in the other members of our family of nations.

In the context of this shifting global landscape, Tubman extolled the virtues of new international organizations such as the United Nations (UN) and the WHO, and the new modes of cooperation that they facilitated. It was in response to this "shrinking" world, he claimed, that the UN "wisely established the World Health Organization . . . charged with the task of helping those nations in need ameliorate their level of health." Tubman went on to explain that he considered the WHO to be fulfilling the "primordial needs of humanity." Attributing the "sterile peace" of previous eras to the "egotistical isolationism" of both families and countries, Tubman argued that only by rejecting this attitude of "indifference toward the future of humanity" could peace be achieved. The role of the WHO and the UN, he asserted, was to facilitate this process. He recommended that all the member states give themselves over fully to the "principles that are at the hearts of these institutions" in order to show their solidarity with this quest for justice.[1]

Tubman was correct that in certain regards, the postwar world was indeed coalescing. In other respects, however, old rifts were widening and new divisions were forming. Perhaps the biggest gulf was between people who continued to believe in the legitimacy of imperial rule and those who found themselves championing the cause of self-determination for Europe's colonial empires. Parties on either side of this divide held starkly different views about the role that international institutions should try to play in shaping the postwar world. At a time when colonial structures were becoming increasingly tenuous, the sense of possibility surrounding the creation of new international organizations was palpable. Tubman's statements, for example, signaled an important shift in thinking about how global institutions could promote health in the newly termed "developing world."[2] His country's engagement with the UN and its specialized agencies was a testament to the optimism that certain nations held about internationalism's transformative potential.[3] Liberia was the first country in the African region to seek technical assistance from the WHO, and starting in the early 1950s, WHO experts worked closely with the Liberian government to train sanitary inspectors, draft public health legislation, and launch programs to fight diseases such as malaria and yaws.

Tubman's enthusiasm for UN development programs, however, was not shared by all the delegations present at the African regional committee meeting, where the majority of attendees hailed from European countries that controlled territories in the region. Indeed, in many ways, Tubman's speech struck at the very heart of the tensions between the colonial governments and the WHO. While Liberia—one of two independent countries in the African region—would eagerly build a relationship with the WHO over the course of the 1950s, the colonial administrations responsible for other territories in Africa approached this UN agency with hesitation, if not outright suspicion.

The WHO was founded in the aftermath of the Second World War, at a time when the process of global decolonization was just beginning to unfold.[4] Many new states enthusiastically embraced UN and WHO technical assistance programs as they began the process of establishing their own national health systems.[5] But as Indians and Indonesians were reimagining themselves as citizens of independent nations, francophone Africans and the French were embarking on a very different project. In 1946 they worked together to create the French Union, a new association of France and its overseas territories that—in theory—had shed all the trappings of colonial inequality in favor of new rights and expanded access to social services, broadly conceived. More easily outlined on paper than put into practice, however, this newly envisaged union encountered myriad difficulties as Africans and their counterparts in metropolitan France worked to recast relationships that had been built on decades of inequality.[6]

Justifying the French Union to a broad international audience proved equally challenging. Over the course of the 1950s, the UN became an important forum for debating the fate of European empires, and French officials saw the expanding reach of UN agencies as a threat to the incipient French Union. If the WHO presented newly independent peoples with a vision of health that Sunil Amrith describes as both "a responsibility of government and a right of citizenship," the French government worried that the organization could serve as a rallying point for anticolonial voices, both African and international.[7] Fears about the potentially dangerous outcomes of global cooperation led French officials and doctors to reject WHO involvement in their colonial health systems just as fervently as newly independent countries embraced it.

If the WHO has come to represent a certain brand of postwar international cooperation, it is very telling that it was on the African continent that it had the hardest time implanting itself. Although many doctors who had worked in Africa felt that it was the region most in need of international assistance in the field of health, colonial officials used every diplomatic tool at their disposal to keep the WHO out.[8] The WHO Regional Office for Africa was the last regional branch to be established, and initial efforts to control malaria, for example, were piloted in Europe and the Far East, not in Africa.[9] In the wake of the 2014–2015 Ebola epidemic in West Africa, numerous scholars, medical practitioners, and political commentators have traced the crisis of health in this region back to the ways that colonial governments underdeveloped health services for African patients.[10] But if colonial governments underinvested in disease control programs or family health clinics, they also actively worked to keep international health organizations out of

Africa. In this book I ask, what was it about the WHO and its mission—and the mission of the UN more broadly—that struck fear in the hearts of colonial administrators and doctors from Paris, Brussels, and London to Dakar, Brazzaville, Léopoldville, and Kampala? And how did this resistance to global cooperation shape the landscape of public health on the African continent?

I make three interconnected arguments in response to these questions. First, I contend that French politicians and colonial administrators took the potential threat of anticolonialism at the UN very seriously. When it came to the empire, the UN did not represent for France a simple re-creation of the now-defunct League of Nations, which its founders created, in part, to keep the world safe for imperialism.[11] French officials and diplomats saw in the UN a potential forum for global debates and discussions about colonialism that could ultimately contribute to empire's undoing. They paid particularly close attention to the ways that anticolonial delegations to the UN were using health and social problems as evidence in their arguments about the ongoing dangers of colonial inequality.[12]

Second, in this book I argue that this fear of anticolonialism at the UN easily extended into France's engagements with other UN bodies—the WHO, the United Nations International Children's Emergency Fund (UNICEF), and the UN Food and Agriculture Organization (FAO), to name only the three that are the most relevant to this book. Colonial administrators and local doctors in the colonies feared that by allowing UN personnel to work in Africa under the aegis of a WHO regional office or under the rubric of UN technical assistance programs, they would open up the inner workings of their empire to international criticism and allow the UN to gain firsthand knowledge about conditions in Africa. In the interest of preventing international "interference" in their colonial empire, French diplomats did what they could to keep UN agencies and international health personnel out of Africa, severely limiting the access that Africans had to global health programs. In other words, broader trends of anticolonialism and decolonization impacted health in postwar Africa in surprising—and sometimes negative—ways. This study demonstrates that the pushback against internationalization shaped the landscape of public health as much as, if not more than, the international organizations themselves.

Third, I assert that French administrators and doctors were not immune to the arguments that expanding cooperation in the field of health could bring real benefits to their African constituents. Still desirous of limiting international involvement on the ground in their empire, however, French doctors and administrators sought new channels for cooperation with representatives from neighboring colonial empires. Between the conclusion of the Second World War and the advent of African independence in the late 1950s and early 1960s, French, British, and Belgian colonial governments had built an impressive intercolonial network for cooperation in the fields of health and development, a network that they believed could stave off UN interference and keep Africa safe for empire. This inter-European alliance quickly unraveled after independence, however, as European doctors turned their energies towards building new relationships with medical personnel from their former colonies.

While this battle between colonial governments and the UN involved British, Belgian, and Portuguese administrators and doctors as much as their French counterparts, there are certain aspects of this story that remain decidedly French. At a time when the Belgians were zealously battling accusations of rampant human rights abuses in the Belgian Congo and the British were focused on devolving authority in certain areas of their empire, the project of creating the French Union was a rather unique one. It was in French Equatorial Africa (Afrique Equatoriale Française; AEF), moreover, that the WHO would install its African headquarters, further embroiling this UN agency in French colonial affairs. Focusing on the clash between postwar internationalism and postwar imperialism, this book tells the story of a group of French doctors and officials who were as concerned with stemming the tide of decolonization as they were with stopping the spread of epidemic disease.[13] This tale of the slow and uneven evolution of international health cooperation in Africa illuminates important aspects of postwar colonial reform as well as the complex role that UN institutions played in the end of empire. Finally, it highlights the centrality of public health in the imagining of an independent Africa and the important role that bodies, medicine, families, and food played in the process of decolonization.

The UN and the End of Empire in French Africa

The immediate postwar period was a time of rapid political change both in metropolitan France and in France's overseas empire. Most exemplary of the changing relationship between France and its colonies was the creation of the French Union and the passage of the Lamine Guèye law in 1946. The law—named for its author, a socialist representative for French West Africa (Afrique Occidentale Française; AOF) to the French National Assembly—stipulated that "beginning on 1 June 1946, all people in the overseas territories will be considered citizens . . . with the same status as French nationals."[14] The French Constitution of 1946 clarified the law further. It stated, "France forms, with its overseas peoples, a Union founded on the equality of rights and obligations, without distinction of race or religion, overturning all systems of colonization founded on arbitrary impulses, [and this Union] guarantees equal access to all public positions as well as the individual and collective exercise of all the liberties proclaimed below."[15] Although on paper these principles sounded quite revolutionary, decades of racism and colonial violence in sub-Saharan Africa would make them difficult to implement.[16]

As French officials were attempting to preserve the empire by recasting it as something new, other members of the international community were striking out on a mission to forge an international organization that could facilitate the demise of colonialism.[17] In April 1945, delegates from fifty nations gathered in San Francisco to draft the charter for the new "United Nations Organization." Although many delegations were animated by a spirit of hope and optimism about the role that this new organization could play in heralding a new era of peace, prosperity, and equality, others approached the negotiations with hesitation. When it came to mapping out the role that the UN would play in overseeing Europe's colonial empires, French anxieties ran high. One memo from the French Ministry of Foreign Affairs explained that at San Francisco, the French empire was "gambling its definitive fate."[18] Some representatives at the conference, such as South African delegate Jan Smuts, had confidence that the UN, like the League of Nations, could serve as a force to preserve empire. The French delegation, however, took seriously the threats to extend the principle of trusteeship to all of the world's colonies.[19]

When the UN Charter was ratified at the close of the conference, it was still unclear exactly what the new system of international colonial oversight would look like or what role the organization could play in dismantling colonial empires. Chapter XI of the UN Charter, the "Declaration regarding Non-self-governing Territories," stipulated that all colonial governments should take steps to develop self-government in their territories, in addition to ensuring the fair treatment of colonial populations. Additionally, the charter required them to submit yearly reports to the UN Secretary-General on social and economic conditions in their overseas territories.[20] By contrast, the UN had direct supervisory powers over the governance of trust territories (the successors to the League of Nations mandates), including the ability to send visiting missions to and field petitions from inhabitants of those territories.[21] While it remained uncertain in 1945 just how much leverage these two systems would give the UN over the norms and forms of colonial governance, many anticolonial delegations left San Francisco feeling confident that they had opened the door to substantive reform in the colonial world.[22]

Over the course of the next two decades, the fiercest advocates of human rights across the globe would often find themselves disappointed by the UN's failure to bring about radical and immediate change.[23] In this book I argue, however, that the ambiguous structures of international oversight that the charter established would ultimately become a very real check on the previously unfettered powers of colonial governments. Recent scholarship on the UN has encouraged historians to view the UN Charter as the result of intense debate and evolving tensions between many actors, rather than as a unitary document that emerged from a postwar consensus about the desirability of peace and the means to achieve it. Historian Mark Mazower argues that it is possible to understand the UN Charter and the Universal Declaration of Human Rights "as promissory notes that the UN's founders never intended to be cashed."[24] I argue, however, that the charter's stipulations about the gathering of information from dependent territories created an opening that would ultimately unveil the inner workings of colonial empires across the globe, exposing imperial rule to unprecedented global scrutiny. In this sense, the UN's founding document can be understood to contain the seeds of a veritable revolution in international colonial oversight.[25]

Taking this argument as a starting point, this book focuses on an often overlooked arena of debate about decolonization: the UN Special Committee on Information from Non-self-governing Territories. This committee was responsible for assembling the data on colonial education, social conditions, and economics required by Chapter XI of the UN Charter.[26] It also served as a crucial forum for debating the legitimacy of colonial rule and for discussing the kinds of services and resources to which people living in dependent territories should be entitled. While some colonial officials saw the requirement to provide information to the UN as an unprecedented propaganda opportunity, others feared that this expanding system of oversight had the potential to undermine the legitimacy of imperial rule. The tensions that emerged in this committee would ultimately color the relationship between the French colonial administration in Africa and other UN bodies, such as the WHO.

Reimagining Global Health in the Postwar World

If the establishment of the UN at San Francisco in 1945 was an attempt to create a more peaceful and equitable world, the creation of the WHO was an effort to achieve the same aims by improving health conditions across the globe. Although the scope of this organization was certainly unprecedented, the WHO built on almost a century of international cooperation in the domain of health, as well as a century of political battles that played out in the domain of medicine. In 1851, representatives from twelve European countries gathered in Paris for the first of eleven International Sanitary Conferences.[27] The French foreign minister opened the proceedings with a speech that sounded very much like the one President Tubman would give at the inaugural meeting of the WHO Regional Committee for Africa almost a hundred years later: "Dear Sirs, new means of locomotion, on water and on land, compete each day to lower the obstacles, to reduce the distances that separate nations from one another; but, in order to complete this magnificent work of human genius, no effort would be more productive and more powerful than sage regulation and the just and reasonable limitation of sanitary obstacles."[28] Gathered to discuss the possibilities of harmonizing quarantine policies throughout Europe, these doctors and diplomats spent almost three months debating the nature of contagious disease and how best to contain it without hampering trade. Participants at the first conference could not agree on even the most basic principles, such as what diseases the conference should cover or whether cholera was even contagious. Delegates debated the role of insalubrious environments in spreading disease, and trade interests often trumped the relatively scant knowledge about the ways illness could be spread.[29] The French government, for its part, used the conference as an opportunity to promote a certain vision of France, one capable of playing by the rules of the European state system and eager to shed its recently revolutionary past in favor of new cooperative efforts.[30] If these meetings represented the possibilities for collectively addressing what were inherently transnational problems, they also foreshadowed the role that politics would play in limiting those possibilities.

It took almost six decades for the governments gathered at the International Sanitary Conferences to devise a formal organization to support international cooperation in the field of health. In 1907 they founded the Office international d'hygiène publique (the International Office of Public Hygiene; OIHP). While certainly unprecedented in terms of its cooperative mission in the field of health, the OIHP was limited by its narrow mandate. It served primarily as a centralized agency for collecting and disseminating epidemiological information among states but had little reach beyond basic information sharing. The first international health organization to actively combat disease was the League of Nations Health Organization. With an expanded mandate, the latter took the OIHP's mission a step further, advising members on domestic health policy, promoting research in preventative medicine, and facilitating expert exchanges between member countries. Other projects included studies on nutrition, infant mortality, tuberculosis vaccines, and rural hygiene.[31] Also active in the interwar period were private philanthropic organizations such as the Rockefeller Foundation, which initiated important health campaigns to fight diseases such as hookworm and malaria.[32] While all of these initiatives succeeded in breaking new ground in international health cooperation, they fell decidedly short of establishing a truly universal health organization.

The experience of the Second World War and the creation of new forms of international cooperation under the aegis of the UN provided both the motivation and the structure for achieving the level of global health cooperation that the League of Nations never reached. Building on previous efforts to coordinate public health efforts, representatives from across the globe gathered in the Henry Hudson Hotel in New York City in June 1946 to begin sketching out the parameters for a new organization. Wishing to reflect their commitment to universality, the delegates chose the name World Health Organization for the new body, conferring on it the ability to work in a wide range of fields, from the standardization of medical technology to the implementation of disease control programs.[33] The Constitution of the WHO reflected a revolutionary approach to thinking about global health. Health was not, it stated, simply "the absence of disease or infirmity" but was rather a "state of complete physical, mental and social well-being." It emphasized the importance of children's health and stated very clearly that the provision of medical services was a responsibility of the state to its people. Clearly a product of the world's collective wartime experience, the WHO Constitution also noted that health was inextricably tied to questions of human security and peace.[34]

Despite the early successes of the WHO's new global approach to health, the organization would fall short when it came to confronting one of the most significant health threats of the twentieth century: malaria.[35] But while the failure of the Malaria Eradication Program (MEP, 1953–1969) is perhaps the most visible blemish on the WHO's record, this was not the only area in which this new postwar global organization struggled. And while historians have provided useful accounts of the shortcomings of the MEP, what they have not fully explained are the reasons that this new global health organization had such a difficult time in its earliest years working in the one region of the world where it was needed most. In this book I argue that many of the WHO's shortcomings in the 1940s and 1950s—including the failure of the MEP—were due not only to poor planning and unreliable funding sources but also to the resistance of colonial governments. Many French officials felt that international development programs posed a significant threat to colonial expertise and worried that these programs would ultimately force local administrations in Africa to commit to projects that they would be unable to afford in the long term. Most importantly, however, they feared that by allowing international organizations to work in France's colonial territories, they would be providing opponents of empire with an unprecedented opportunity to bring their critiques to bear on African soil.

French Colonial Politics at the WHO

In 1946, the French government had enthusiastically supported the creation of a universal global health organization and, in the early stages of negotiation, even suggested headquartering it in France.[36] With its long history of fostering international health cooperation and as an important center for medical and scientific research, Paris would have been a logical choice for the WHO's headquarters. Even after Geneva was chosen as the site for the new organization, French doctors and government officials continued to support the WHO's mission enthusiastically. But as the WHO began to extend its reach beyond Europe, Latin America, and Asia, hopes that it could avoid the kinds political entanglements that had plagued the League of Nations Health Organization quickly dissolved, as two competing visions of postwar Africa collided in the WHO Regional Committee for Africa.[37]

Discussions about health and medicine in the postwar period were inextricably linked to debates about sovereignty, empire, and human rights in the developing world. Health provisions—according to delegations from recently independent states such as India and Indonesia—should no longer be simply concerned with the efficacy of vaccines or the need for mobile health services in rural Africa. Rather, they should focus on preparing colonial territories for self-sufficiency and, ultimately, independence. While colonial health reforms in postwar French sub-Saharan African aimed to bring France's overseas territories closer under the umbrella of the French Union—making Africans more French—many delegations at the UN were advancing a very different policy, one that would ultimately render the metropole-colony relationship obsolete. While some countries eagerly embraced new resources available through the WHO, enthusiasm for global health initiatives was far from universal.[38] As the broader political significance of postwar health programs became increasingly clear, the French administration in Africa began to look toward the WHO with more trepidation than optimism. If the WHO represented a new chapter in the history of global public health, it also represented a new window for international organizations to insert themselves into broader political debates about the fate of empire.

The most controversial feature of the WHO's structure was its system of regional offices.[39] Regionalization, according to a 1947 French Ministry of Foreign Affairs memo, was capable of serving as a bridge between the work of the Trusteeship Council and the looser framework of accountability that the UN Charter put in place for other colonial territories, offering a "new mode of administration for dependent territories allowing them to be held accountable to international criteria and standards."[40] Beyond their role in helping the centralized WHO implement its agenda on a more local level, regional organizations also gave dependent territories an opportunity to reimagine themselves as part of new geographic entities—the "eastern Mediterranean" rather than "the British Empire," for example.

Although colonial governments were allowed to serve in WHO regional committees on behalf of the territories they administered, regional offices had the ability to bring together dependent territories and independent states and put them in dialogue about important issues in the fields of health and social development. They also sent representatives from newly independent states to advocate on behalf of those still living under colonial rule. The Southeast Asia Regional Committee, for example, passed a resolution in 1948 stating that nonautonomous territories should be allowed to participate in the activities of the regional offices and that "the representatives from Associate Members should be chosen among the local population and, whenever possible, by the local population, not by the [colonial] government." These anticolonial maneuverings did not go unnoticed by the French government, who accused them of "playing with their new region the way that a child plays with a new slingshot."[41] While French authorities noted in the same memo that it "went without saying that representatives for regional offices would be drawn from local populations," they continued to select predominantly European medical personnel to fill these positions through the late 1950s.[42]

When it came to assigning colonial territories to WHO regions, perhaps the most contentious case was the placement of French North Africa. These territories were left unassigned until the early 1950s, and the French government worked tirelessly to have them included in the European Region. French officials clashed with delegations from the Middle East, who argued that the only connection between these territories and Europe were the decades of colonial violence and inequality that had characterized European rule.[43] In sub-Saharan Africa, the French conceived of a different kind of danger. A WHO regional office, according to French officials, would give this UN agency the ability to do something that the UN could only do in the context of the trust territories: gain entry into these territories and begin an

ongoing dialogue with their inhabitants about health and social conditions. French officials feared that allowing the WHO to establish itself in Africa would be akin to *inviting* an international agency to criticize French colonial rule, especially because opponents of empire at the UN were already framing their critique of colonialism in terms of health and social problems. According to French officials, the extension of the WHO's reach into the African continent posed the risk of provoking a "crisis of imperialism."[44] Although political constraints would ultimately force the French government to accept the installation of the WHO Regional Office for Africa in Brazzaville, the possibilities for genuine international cooperation would remain tenuous at best. Instead, resistance to global cooperation encouraged new modes of technical cooperation between colonial empires, which colonial authorities hoped would help to stave off UN involvement in their overseas territories.

Envisioning Intercolonial Medical Cooperation

Even as the body of scholarship on empire and colonialism continues to grow, few studies have considered the way that governments embraced intercolonial cooperation as a strategy to forestall decolonization. In the period leading up to the Second World War, colonial doctors and scientists transcended traditional colonial rivalries to build a transnational network based on shared interests at a moment when this subfield of medicine was working to carve out its own professional identity.[45] After the war, colonial governments capitalized on these relationships, and looked to intercolonial cooperation in technical fields such as health as a way to safeguard European sovereignty on the African continent. A colonial regional organization could, in the minds of colonial officials, serve as a stand-in for the kinds of regional organizations that were being proposed by different UN agencies. In response to what French officials and experts perceived as a growing threat from the UN and the WHO, the French government embraced this alternative approach to cooperation. Rather than working with foreign personnel who aimed to use global health programs to hasten empire's demise, colonial experts would collaborate to preserve their authority and cement the bond between Europe and European empires in Africa.

This book explores two different venues where intercolonial cooperation took place: the International Children's Centre (Centre international de l'enfance; CIE), founded in Paris in 1950 under the leadership of French pediatrician Robert Debré, and the Commission for Technical Cooperation in Africa South of the Sahara (Commission de coopération technique en Afrique au sud du Sahara; CCTA).[46] Both of these organizations provided a setting where French colonial doctors could engage with experts from outside the French empire while shielding their African territories from UN "interference." They also served as a means of promoting French medical and scientific expertise in a world where the relevance of French science appeared increasingly threatened. Debré, in particular, was committed to reclaiming a place for France in the world of science and medicine. While Paris had been an important capital of the scientific world in the nineteenth century, it had long been eclipsed by medical centers in the United States and Germany.[47] Alongside Paris, the capitals of France's African empire would serve as crucial nodes in France's global network of scientists, researchers, and clinicians.[48] Together, the CCTA and the CIE sponsored a variety of collaborative efforts in the field of health, ranging from social pediatrics courses to conferences on sleeping sickness and nutrition.[49]

Colonial authorities and doctors hoped that by preempting the kinds of health cooperation that UN agencies could sponsor in Africa, they would be able to keep organizations like the WHO out and keep the continent safe for empire. Gustave Moutet, the French delegate to the 1947 Franco-Anglo-Belgian talks, explained that if a UN agency wanted to create a regional office in Africa, "and if we can respond that one already exists, they will be forced to go somewhere else in the world."[50] Within this context of intercolonial cooperation in the field of health, the French administration in Africa worked to recast the civilizing mission as a project of development, a project that could best be achieved collaboratively, by those with decades of technical experience on the African continent.[51]

Ultimately, neither the CIE nor the CCTA would succeed in keeping the UN out of colonial Africa. In the early 1960s, the European-dominated CCTA dissolved almost in tandem with European empires themselves, while the CIE remained active in Africa through the 1970s, providing an ongoing venue for French medical personnel to continue to cultivate a relationship with France's former colonies. By the late 1970s, it would turn its attentions

to other regions of the world, finally dissolving in the late 1990s. Rather than dismiss these organizations as failed experiments in intercolonial and Franco-international cooperation, however, this book explores the possibilities they offered as alternatives to the UN model of international development in the 1940s and 1950s and considers the role that that cross-colonial endeavors played in the reenvisioning of empire after 1945.

Decolonizing African Health?

As the scope of scholarship on decolonization continues to expand, historians are moving away from approaches that paint the end of empire as a process that involved political institutions and practices above all else. Indeed, decolonization shaped people's lives in ways that went far beyond the ballot box and the legislative assembly, touching the minds and bodies of former colonial subjects in intimate ways.[52] If globalization and decolonization were powerful forces in shaping the broader philosophies and structures of health cooperation in postwar Africa, they also played an important role in defining the reach—and the limits—of those health services on the ground. Public health interventions throughout history have always served a variety of goals and have been shaped by a wide range of ideologies and political agendas. A maternity clinic in Africa, for example, could represent an attempt by medical missionaries to serve God and to recruit new followers. The same maternity clinic could be an effort by a colonial administration to bolster its population, guaranteeing a steady pool of soldiers and workers. Alternatively, it could represent an endeavor by a newly independent government to look toward a new future, protecting the well-being of its youngest citizens. Health programs in the context of this book are crucially important because they served as a tool both to reimagine empire after the war *and* to envision an independent Africa in the era of decolonization.[53]

Since the earliest European ventures in Africa, medicine and public health were integral to the broader imperial project. They were cornerstones of *la mission civilisatrice,* inextricably connected to the violence and political, social, and economic inequality that accompanied colonial endeavors.[54] Efforts to control disease were as much about protecting the colonizer as they were about saving the lives of the colonized. Diseases such as malaria, yellow fever, sleeping sickness, tuberculosis, and plague hampered the ability of colonial governments and European economic entities to effectively secure their dominance over subject populations. Health services in European colonial empires thus worked to control African bodies at the same time as they controlled the spread of illness.[55] Oftentimes, medical programs blatantly disregarded ethical standards, and the turn toward social medicine in other parts of the world remained a pipe dream for many Africans, especially those living in rural areas.[56] In many locales, infant and maternal health care services were oriented more toward the economic and political agendas of the colonial administration than toward the needs of African women and children.[57]

As colonial territories across the globe moved toward self-government and independence, and as new international institutions extended their reach into the African continent, health programs began to take on new political meanings. At first glance, the goals and structures of colonial and global health programs in the 1940s and 1950s appear strikingly similar. Both the French government and the WHO, for example, advocated for the expansion of family health services, vaccination campaigns, programs to control epidemic diseases, and social programs to promote nutrition. Both favored the expansion of training opportunities for African medical personnel and supported the growing trend in medicine to treat people as physical *and* social bodies in need of care. But if international institutions and colonial health services often found themselves promoting the same kinds of health programs, the political motivations at the heart of these programs remained starkly different.

In the wake of the war, French doctors working in the empire found themselves needing to justify their work to a wide international audience. In order to show their commitment to a more equitable union of France and Africa, they had to demonstrate that they were making a good-faith effort to ensure a level of well-being for the French citizen in Dakar that was equal to that which a French citizen in Paris would enjoy. While one of the UN's and the WHO's ultimate goals for medical training programs and eradication campaigns was to help inhabitants of colonial territories to stand on their own, for the French administration these programs were about making Africans more French and about demonstrating the ongoing need for *French* expertise at a time when the availability of international experts and development programs was growing rapidly. Through an exploration of the politics of health, this book situates the history of postwar French Africa within the broader context of the imperial world and explores the collision between that world—in many ways firmly anchored in the past—and the brave new world of postwar international institutions born under the umbrella of the UN.

Structure and Sources

The Colonial Politics of Global Health tells the story of two very different institutions attempting to embed (or reembed) themselves on the African continent amid the rapidly changing political currents of the postwar world. On one hand, through the creation of the French Union, the French government was seeking to cement the relationship between metropolitan France and its African territories, both through wide-reaching political reform and through services such as health care. On the other hand, the WHO—with its ties to the newly founded UN—proposed an alternative model for African health, one that would be linked to an evolving notion of universal rights rather than to decades of colonial violence and inequality.

The story begins in AOF and AEF at the close of the war, where years of fighting had all but completely severed the link between the French medical establishment in Paris and health services in the colonies. I first explore the ramifications that the war had for the colonial health administration's ability to provide services to its constituents after the war. I also consider how broader political changes fundamentally altered the way colonial populations engaged—and in some cases refused to engage—with those services. I argue that the multifaceted "crisis" in public health that resulted from the war would become an important liability for the French in an era of increasing international involvement in overseeing colonial governance. The focus then shifts from sub-Saharan Africa to San Francisco, New York, and Geneva, where opponents of empire from across the globe would use poor health outcomes and deplorable living conditions as a way to talk about the fundamental injustices of colonial rule. As critiques of empire mounted, anticolonial delegations worked to use the UN Special Committee on Information from Non-self-governing Territories as an unofficial oversight body for the world's colonial empires.

In response to growing international pressure at the UN to decolonize, colonial governments looked suspiciously not just toward the special committee but also toward other UN agencies. As discussions took off about establishing a WHO Regional Office for Africa, the French joined forces with diplomats and doctors from the Belgian and British empires in an effort to defend European sovereignty in Africa. The CCTA—an intercolonial technical organization—was created as a means of preventing international meddling in their African territories. When the CCTA failed to prevent the establishment of a WHO office in Africa, the discussions turned to the ways that the office's reach could be limited by careful diplomatic maneuvering. The story then moves back to Africa, where in the early 1950s the WHO set out to establish its regional headquarters in Brazzaville. As French doctors and government officials attempted to mediate the influence of the WHO on their African constituents, they found themselves embroiled in a public relations crisis that would test the limits of the French empire's postwar colonial reforms.

While diplomats and doctors continued to wage the battle between colonial and global visions of Africa, they were also working to expand existing health services and augment the body of available knowledge about health in the tropics. A third postwar health organization—the CIE—shaped the landscape of public health in postwar Africa with its different teaching and research initiatives. For French doctors and scientists, health cooperation was as much about staking a claim for French expertise in the postwar world as it was about defending colonial sovereignty from new international initiatives. The last part of the book focuses on two of the most important public health projects in postwar Africa: disease eradication programs and campaigns to fight malnutrition. It explores the way that this complex web of colonial, intercolonial, and international initiatives both facilitated and constrained efforts to promote African health. While the French ultimately failed in their efforts to keep international organizations out of Africa, they did succeed in drastically limiting the WHO's ability to put its agenda in action. Political debates about empire at the UN thus had the unintended consequence of constraining truly global medical action on the African continent, the region most in need of the kinds of programs the WHO aimed to provide.

This book draws on a variety of sources—including colonial health reports, proceedings of medical conferences, and minutes of UN and WHO committee meetings—to examine how the unraveling of empire touched sick and healthy bodies, shaped the intimacies of family life, and impacted the ways in which colonial doctors engaged with the broader global community. The lack of African voices in these documents is palpable and echoes their absence in some of the most important debates of the 1940s and 1950s. Despite the rapidly evolving political relationship between Africans and the French in the postwar era, the former remained largely excluded from shaping the policies that would govern their health care. When possible, I have read archival documents against the grain to draw out acts of resistance to the expanding reach of European medicine. I have also explored the moments in which colonial governments made explicit decisions to exclude African patients and medical personnel from their cooperative endeavors. Indeed, the dearth of African perspectives in the UN Special Committee, on French delegations to the UN, and in crucial meetings about the sanitary fate of the continent is, in itself, an important component of this history. If this book is a story of reform, movement, and evolution, it is also a story about the limitations of change, the enduring nature of colonial violence and inequality, and the silencing of African voices in a domain that touched one of the most intimate aspects of their lives—the care of the body.

CHAPTER ONE

War, Citizenship, and the Limits of French Civilization

> In 1939, the situation wasn't brilliant. At the beginning of 1946, it was catastrophic. This scenario urgently calls for a complete overhaul of the [colonial] health system based on a freer, more flexible, and more efficient foundation. The native population is wasting away, disappearing. Our doctors are ready. Give them arms.
>
> —Médecin-Colonel Lotte, director of health services, Guinea, 1946

THE FRAGILITY OF LIFE in wartime France has become a well-known story. The word *occupation* conjures up now-familiar images of the mass exodus from Paris in 1940, of French families trudging slowly along the roadside with all of their worldly possessions, and of French citizens weeping as they observed German armies taking control of their cities.[1] In this context of defeat and occupation, physical well-being became more precarious—not only on the battlefield but also at home, where hunger was ubiquitous and food shortages compounded other health problems. By December 1943, the average daily calorie intake for adults had dropped to 1,200. As a result, health services in France saw a rapid increase in rickets, digestive problems, and even tuberculosis, as weakened bodies found themselves increasingly unable to fight off infections. In addition to food scarcity, doctors and patients faced a shortage of medical supplies and hospital beds, which in many cases were requisitioned by German occupiers for their own use. Resistance leaders quickly connected these problems to the larger issue of national survival. In its reports, the Comité français de libération nationale (French Committee of National Liberation; CFLN) highlighted the precarious nature of life on the home front, comparing death by starvation to execution by the Nazi army or the Vichy government.[2]

Less familiar is the story of how half a decade of war shaped the daily lives of families—especially children—in France's overseas empire.[3] In 1946, a medical report from the director of health services in French Guinea evoked an ongoing battle to fight the effects of epidemic disease and malnourishment, which had been aggravated by wartime conditions. The "arms" that Médecin-Colonel Lotte referred to, however, were not rifles or grenades but rather rat poison to fight the spread of plague and microscope slides to perform blood analyses in malaria-endemic zones. Beyond the colonial government's inability to fight disease, Lotte's report also pointed to the French administration's failure to ensure the basic welfare of African families. While noting that social services were "a primordial component of medical action," he stated that without "method, continuity, and understanding," such programs were a "mere façade" in the empire.[4] Colonial health services had expanded rapidly during the interwar years, with the construction of hospitals and maternity clinics, the institution of mobile vaccination teams, and the establishment of protocol to combat endemic diseases, such as sleeping sickness and yellow fever. The onset of the Second World War, however, brought the expansion of public health services to a standstill. The occupation drained French budgets and cut off the normal supply of personnel and materials to the colonies, hindering the ability of medical services to reach the people who needed them most.

If ordinary people in the empire suffered alongside their counterparts in metropolitan France during the war, the colonies also served as a lifeline, supplying soldiers, workers, and raw materials and providing a home for resistance movements. In the war's aftermath, the demands made by imperial subjects for equal political rights thus became all the more compelling. So, as French officials struggled to address the more immediate tasks of postwar reconstruction, they were also embarking on a deeper process of reenvisioning the relationship between France and its empire. The process began in 1944, when delegates from metropolitan France and the colonies gathered in Brazzaville, the capital of AEF, to address questions of political participation and social welfare in the empire.[5] The discussions undertaken at Brazzaville culminated in 1946 when the Assemblée nationale constituante (National Constituent Assembly) approved the creation of the French Union, a reimagined French empire that would allow for the political participation of all overseas territories on a footing equal to that of the inhabitants of metropolitan France. According to the provisions of the Lamine Guèye law, all Africans in the French empire would, for the first time, enjoy the same rights of citizenship as their metropolitan counterparts.[6] Health was an important component of these reforms, and French officials explicitly linked the improvement of preventative health services to their broad political, social, and economic goals for the empire.

Delegates to the Brazzaville Conference and the Assemblée nationale constituante had high hopes about the power of progressive colonial policy to cement the relationship between France and its empire in the postwar period. The implementation of these policies, however, often fell short in practice.[7] Ongoing failures to realize an effective and efficient public health system revealed the limits of colonial reform—and of France's *mission civilisatrice* more broadly—in two important ways. First, despite far-reaching plans for health care reform, years of fighting resulted in significant shortages of personnel and supplies that drastically limited the government's ability to maintain even the most basic of health services for its colonial populations. Second, as African subjects were reimagined—and reimagined themselves—as citizens of the French Union, health took on new—and sometimes unintended—political meanings. While French doctors and colonial officials envisioned public health programs as a way to shape a new kind of "sanitary citizen" of the French Union, Africans themselves sometimes used their new citizenship status to reject public health provisions that they saw as coercive. This growing divide between best-laid plans and the realities of postwar colonial rule would ultimately expose the French government to passionate critiques at the UN and would create an opportunity for new global health organizations to compete with existing structures of colonial public health.

Reenvisioning Colonial Health in Wartime Africa

By the beginning of the twentieth century, European empires stretched across the globe from the Caribbean to Africa, Asia, the Middle East, and the Pacific. Colonial ventures faced a range of obstacles—environmental and human—in the territories they conquered. Public health programs allowed colonial administrations to address both the practical and ideological constraints on their imperial ambitions. Hospitals and clinics, for example, played an important role in helping European colonizers survive biologically "hostile" physical environments in their newly established empires.[8] More importantly, though, health services for colonial subjects provided an ideological justification for colonial rule, as an essential component of the "civilization" that colonizers claimed to be bringing to their overseas territories.[9] Medical services also ensured a healthy and fertile population that could serve as a source of labor for the extraction of raw materials, as well as a market for colonial products.[10] From a scientific standpoint, the colonies and their populations helped experts generate specialized knowledge in the emerging field of tropical medicine, and colonial subjects provided a pool of test subjects for medical experiments that could have raised ethical questions in the metropole.[11]

The first health services and medical research facilities in French Africa—aimed primarily at Europeans—were constructed in urban areas in the late nineteenth century. These included hospitals in Dakar, Senegal; Kayes, Mali; and Antananarivo, Madagascar, as well as a bacteriological institute, the Institut Marchoux, in Saint-Louis, Senegal. Health services for Africans expanded after the appointment of Ernest Roume to the position of governor-general of AOF in 1902. As Alice Conklin has argued, Roume's governorship marked a watershed in colonial policy—moving from a short-term strategy of conquest to an approach that focused on improving quality of life and colonial productivity over the longer term. This policy of *mise en valeur* was geared toward the optimization of resource use—including human resources—in order to promote the long-term prosperity and viability of France's overseas empire. It also implied an important role for the colonial state in directing the use of these resources. This shift mirrored the growing role that the French state and new sociomedical "experts" would play in the rational management of social problems in the metropole.[12]

To achieve his goal of improving health for Africans, Roume created the Assistance médicale indigène (Indigenous Medical Assistance Program; AMI), which provided health services free of charge.[13] Conklin argues that by setting up the AMI, Roume aimed to dramatically change the way Africans lived. Although he was not the first colonial governor to embrace the idea of the civilizing mission, she argues that Roume was the first with the financial and bureaucratic capacity to truly embark on such a mission.[14] One of the primary goals of the AMI was "the numerical growth and physiological amelioration of the indigenous races," a goal that reflected similar concerns about the quantity and quality of the population in metropolitan France.[15] France had faced a declining birthrate since the mid-nineteenth century and, as a result, government officials, demographers, and doctors were haunted for decades by fears of depopulation and biological degeneration. The demographic catastrophe of the First World War exacerbated these fears and provoked a wave of pronatalist measures, including improved infant and maternal health care facilities, special loans and credits for young married couples, and prizes and honors for mothers of large families. These aimed to increase the birthrate and to improve the overall health of children in order to generate a sizeable population of robust workers and soldiers. In the interwar years, colonial administrators and doctors transplanted this project to France's overseas colonies, where they hoped to increase the population by tackling high rates of infant mortality due to umbilical tetanus, pneumonia, malnutrition, malaria, and poor hygiene.[16]

Despite the concerted efforts of French doctors and colonial administrators, early medical programs in sub-Saharan Africa were slow to produce visible results. Given the limited resources available, health services for Europeans and Africans living in big cities were often prioritized over services for rural Africans, which were expensive to run. The few doctors that were stationed in the colonies were often forced to work out of poorly provisioned clinics.[17] In 1910, anthropologist Abel Lahille wrote, "Is the division of objects necessary for the functioning of the [health] service done in a methodical manner? Not at all. One product that is lacking from one dispensary can be found in another in an excessive and unusable quantity." He continued with two examples: "Timbuktu once received, in 1907, six kilograms of ipecac! At Kayes, the clinic was stocked with more than 100 kilograms of potassium iodide! By contrast, at the beginning of the winter of 1908, not even a gram of quinine remained."[18] Beyond the practical problems of funding, supplies, and personnel, the AMI also faced several cultural obstacles that arose from colonial racism and the limited understanding of African culture on the part of Europeans. One doctor, for example, claimed, "The indigenous people of Bobo-Dioulasso are of a distressing stupidity . . . deciding only with reluctance to submit themselves to [the care of] European doctors."[19] Colonial doctors and cultural observers thus portrayed Africans as superstitious and intellectually incapable of accessing modern scientific and medical knowledge.

Despite these obstacles, colonial administrators pushed forward with health care reform in AOF, and Roume's successors worked to expand the system he put in place. In particular, Governor-General Jules Carde—despite working in a time of global economic hardship during the 1930s—remained ideologically committed to the idea that human resources could and should be rationally managed. Carde's plan especially emphasized nutrition and the reduction of infant mortality through proper infant and maternal health care provisions.[20] Carde claimed that in spite of its shortcomings, the creation of an effective and efficient system of colonial public health was not outside the scope of French medicine or France's colonial administration. He wrote, "I persuaded myself that I had neither dreamed too grandly, nor that French doctors were incapable of adapting to this milieu a social sanitary organization aimed at protecting the well-being of our indigenous populations." Improvements should have been especially easy, Carde argued, at a time "when the applications . . . of Pasteur's teaching have rendered the fight against contagious diseases all the more simple."[21] If there was ever a time when reform should succeed in AOF, Carde believed, it was this moment, when scientific, social, political, and financial circumstances favored the development of services to protect France's colonial populations.

The next important moment for public health reform in France's African colonies came during the Second World War, as colonial officials worked to lay out changes that could be implemented after the war's conclusion. Planning for postwar medical reform was part of a broader empire-wide project that involved both metropolitan France and France's overseas territories. During the war the Comité médical de la résistance (Medical Committee of the Resistance; CMR), led by pediatrician Robert Debré, argued that previous administrations had not committed enough energy or resources to combating France's declining birthrate, nor had they worked hard enough to develop infant and maternal health care, a key arena of intervention for a country so intensely consumed by its ongoing demographic crisis. The CMR also condemned the Third Republic's leadership for its failure to promote medical and scientific research. One CMR report bemoaned the sad state of French laboratories and, echoing fears of general French decline in the interwar years, lamented that

"[France's] sanitary system was not at a level worthy of the culture and civilization of [the French] nation."[22]

During the war, the Vichy government made some important advances in the field of health, most notably the creation of France's first national public health institute, the Institut national d'hygiène (National Institute of Hygiene). Most of the reforms under consideration in the 1930s, however, were tabled until the end of the war. Debré admitted that despite years of negotiations surrounding the reform of medical education, "little has come of the interminable discussions that we have begun." Imploring his colleagues in the CMR to continue with the reforms envisioned in the previous decades, Debré called for clinic and hospital access for all and for the creation of special diagnostic and treatment centers. He also advocated for a renewed emphasis on preventative medicine and for a closer relationship between hospitals and universities.[23] Using the Third Republic as a model of what *not* to do, the CMR laid out a concrete plan for a new structure that would allow the government to address the health concerns facing the nation in the wake of the war. The new Ministry of Public Health and Population would have a much wider scope than the ministries it was intended to replace. It would focus on two primary goals: population growth and the improvement of overall national health, with a new orientation toward preventive care. Questions of population, birthrate, immigration, hygiene, preventative and curative medicine, and social insurance would all fall under its purview. It would create modern hospitals but would also establish primary care centers that would minimize the need for hospital admittance. The goal of the new ministry was to "empty the hospitals and fill the cradles" and, as Debré wrote, "to establish the equality of all French people in the face of sickness and suffering."[24]

Plans for the complete overhaul of France's public health establishment did not stop at the borders of the Hexagon, and colonial health reforms were quickly connected to efforts in the metropole. Extending France's medical and scientific grandeur to its overseas territories would serve as proof of just how modern—and modernizing—French medicine could be. According to its most enthusiastic proponents, an efficient and effective medical system in the empire would demonstrate the real benefits that colonial rule could bring. For colonial administrators in French Africa, the development of health services went hand in hand with—and sometimes even preceded—

general social and economic progress. Colonial officials insisted on rebuilding heath infrastructure from scratch in order to create a system that would be worthy of France's overseas empire.[25]

Dakar was to be the heart of the project. As Médecin-Général Ricou outlined in his 1941 "Proposal for the Reorganization of Health Services in French Africa": "All hope of renovating existing establishments should be abandoned in favor of a new resolve to build an entirely new *Centre hospitalier,* a modern establishment that responds to the goals we have set out to achieve and that, realized at the level of the Capital of our African Empire, will contribute to the aesthetic and—in some ways—intellectual embellishment of our Imperial Capital, and will reaffirm the quality of its sanitary facilities." Infant, child, and maternal health services would figure prominently in the new formulation. Reformers also called for the construction of suitable housing for European medical students and the creation of new libraries and an African medical journal (*Bulletin médical de l'Afrique Occidentale Française*). Ricou hoped that Dakar could become the intellectual capital of Africa, much like Paris was for Europe.[26]

Ricou's proposal outlined a series of wide-reaching changes designed to bring all health services in AOF under one centralized administration and to reorient colonial health services toward preventative social medicine. Although Ricou's plan highlighted the long history of French accomplishments in the field of colonial health, he noted that these were primarily individual and curative in nature. He further noted that, except on paper, few provisions existed for preventative public health care in most African locales. The plan that Ricou set forth in his proposal would thus herald a new era of "Social and Preventative Medicine" in AOF. Health services would no longer operate primarily on the level of individuals but rather for the benefit of the collective; they would focus not on specific cases but on the endemic and epidemic diseases that dominated the African continent. Ricou suggested that the two preventative disease services that existed in AOF before the Second World War—the Service général autonome de la maladie du sommeil (General Autonomous Service for Sleeping Sickness Control) and the Service central de la lèpre (Central Leprosy Service)—could be used as general models for the reorientation of health services in Africa toward a more preventative and collective model that would serve the "essential goal" of protecting the African race.[27]

The 1941 reform plan proposed to create a unified health system that would operate under the umbrella of the Direction générale de la santé publique (General Direction of Public Health; DGSP).[28] The DGSP would comprise two institutions: the Center for Hospitalization, Instruction, and Research and the Institute of Social Hygiene for French Africa.[29] Just as the medical profession in metropolitan France was struggling to unite teaching, healing, and research, so too were doctors in Africa working to unite these three strands of medicine in one system. While many of these institutions existed in some form in Dakar in 1941, reformers in AOF hoped to bring them together in a more coherent way while instilling in their personnel, policies, and services the importance of public health and preventative care.

The first element of the new DGSP was the Center for Hospitalization, Instruction, and Research.[30] While hospital facilities already existed in Dakar, Ricou explained that these lacked unity and cohesion and that many of the buildings had fallen into serious disrepair. The new hospital would remedy these problems. It would be divided into two facilities—one for Europeans and one for Africans—though both sections would share a common block with surgical, radiology, and laboratory facilities.[31] They would be named the Hôpital principal de Dakar (Principal Hospital of Dakar) and the Hôpital central indigène de Dakar (Central Indigenous Hospital of Dakar; HCI), respectively. Specialists would move back and forth between the two sections. Each section of the hospital would be equipped with a pediatric wing, which created a unique space within the hospital that could be devoted exclusively to the care of children, allowing interns to specialize in the field of child health. The pediatric wing would also facilitate cooperation between the hospital and sociomedical charities and organizations such as the Red Cross and the Berceau africain (African Cradle).[32] In order to ensure the proper functioning of its new hospital system, the DGSP would also have a centralized pharmacy for the federation. Ricou hoped to create a better-stocked storeroom and a standardized set of medications and technical equipment. Clearly reacting to the experience of shortages during the war, Ricou wanted to generate reserves of supplies in order to make certain that no medical post would ever find itself without the necessary equipment or medications.[33]

Although the hospital was to remain primarily an institution devoted to healing, wartime reform plans aimed to reorient colonial health services toward public health and social medicine. To this end, Ricou and his colleagues proposed another institution—the Institute of Social Hygiene—to work side by side with clinics and hospitals. The institute would be staffed by hygienists and epidemiologists and would unite all the preventative branches of colonial health in AOF under one umbrella organization that could oversee three divisions. First, it would include a section for the major epidemic and endemic diseases, which covered smallpox, plague, yellow fever, malaria, sleeping sickness, and leprosy, as well as social diseases such as syphilis and tuberculosis. Second, it would include a section for social problems, which included the protection of childhood, demography, urbanism, and nutrition, as well as a subsection for school medical inspection. The third section dealt with issues of hygiene—municipal clinics, urban sanitation, prostitution, and the maritime sanitary police. Even though the institute would be located in Dakar, its resources would be at the disposal of all of the colonies of AOF and would thus draw the majority of its funding from the federal budget.[34] Ricou hoped that the Institute of Social Hygiene would bring renewed respect to French science, and would quickly become "a pole of attraction ensuring for the Federal Capital an intellectual renown truly worthy of a Capital of Empire."[35]

In addition to a growing commitment to care and preventative health services—both for Europeans and for Africans—another important component of Dakar's new hospital system was better integration with medical education. Reflecting reforms in metropolitan France, the new hospital system in AOF intended to combine teaching with laboratory work and clinical experience, both for European doctors working in Africa and for Africans themselves.[36] The hospital in AOF was also given a special mission of acclimatizing Europeans to work in Africa and adapting African medical personnel to European standards of hygiene, which they could in turn spread throughout the African population. Ricou recommended equipping the medical school with a dormitory for students, where they would live in "conditions of habitability that conform to the norms of hygiene that we try to inculcate in our own students over the course of their studies." According to Ricou, this would allow African medical students in turn to be "our interpreters and our disciples in the brush," where they would be able to "bring their new habits and taste for hygiene and diffuse, by their own example and advice, our principles of moral and physical education." In addition to training African doctors to think and act more like Europeans, medical education in Dakar would also facilitate the adaptation of European doctors and nurses to the realities of African life, allowing metropolitan France and France's African empire to work more harmoniously as two parts of a synthetic whole, where personnel, scientific knowledge, technology, and medical products could be more easily exchanged.[37]

Feats and Failures of Wartime Public Health Reform

Despite Ricou's far-reaching plan to reimagine France's colonial health system, the onset of hostilities in Europe made the extension of health services for Africans difficult to accomplish.[38] On one hand, colonial health services in Africa did achieve some notable successes during the war. More women were taking advantage of the growing availability of prenatal and infant health consultations, for example, and the number of yellow fever vaccines administered per year was rising rapidly. On the other hand, while the colonial health services network was indeed expanding, it was not growing fast enough for French colonial officials to claim they were making good on their promise to bring "civilization" to France's African colonies. For the short term, colonial health officials reported a crisis of degeneration, depopulation, disease, and ignorance. In the longer term, the failure to provide sufficient services (or to convert Africans to these services) would call into question France's civilizing mission and, more broadly, French sovereignty on the African continent. While these difficulties had plagued the colonial administration in AOF long before 1939, the extreme circumstances of war further exacerbated the tension between promise and reality.

In certain respects, the reach and mandate of the colonial health services in AOF expanded a great deal during the war. Four times as many people were vaccinated against yellow fever, for example, in 1941 as in 1940 (372,632 in 1940 versus 1,544,689 in 1941).[39] By 1944, 11.5 million people, or two-thirds of the population of AOF, had been vaccinated.[40] The anti–yellow fever campaign was supported by increased production of vaccine serum by the Dakar Pasteur Institute, and in 1941 the campaign was further facilitated by a government decree that made yellow fever vaccination mandatory.[41] In certain colonies, the percentage of the total budget spent on health services was rising, indicating a more serious commitment to providing health care for Africans.

Figure 1.1. Postcard of the Pasteur Institute in Dakar, Senegal, AOF. Edition Maurice Viale, Dakar. Reproduction from author's collection.

In Côte d'Ivoire, for example, in 1940 and 1941 more than 20 percent of the colony's total budget was used for health, in contrast to 13 percent in 1939.[42] The number of infant and maternal health clinics expanded from 132 to 193, with the number of beds rising from 1,233 in 1940 to 2,644 in 1945.[43]

Despite Ricou's high hopes, however, most of the components of his ambitious reform program remained tabled until the end of the war. Funds and personnel were lacking, and a general breakdown in communications with the metropole made such an ambitious plan virtually impossible to implement in wartime conditions. Not only did the war delay plans for future reform, but it also shut down several reform plans in individual colonies that had been in the works since the mid-1930s. Doctors in Dahomey and French Sudan, for example, were in the process of establishing mobile hygiene units, but plans stalled after the war broke out.[44] The 1941 annual medical report from French Sudan complained that in order to establish mobile hygiene units and clinics in rural areas, both personnel and materials were needed, neither of which could be spared in wartime conditions. Reformers were often forced to pick and choose among their many projects. In French Sudan, priority was given to the creation of a new centralized pharmacy in 1941, while projects such as the expansion of Bamako's main hospital and the construction of new maternity clinics were tabled for a later date.[45]

Beyond this inability to implement reform, wartime conditions made it difficult to maintain even pre-1939 standards of care. Before the war, for example, the number of women attending maternal health consultations at clinics such as Dakar's Polyclinique Roume was increasing rapidly. The onset of hostilities, however, created a lack of available transportation and many women simply lived too far to come for regular checkups.[46] Fuel shortages also severely hindered mobile medical services such as the Service général autonome de la maladie du sommeil, which was in charge of eradicating sleeping sickness in AOF.[47]

Medical research in the empire suffered greatly as a result of the war. Ties between the Pasteur Institute of Dakar and its Parisian counterpart were severed for the duration of the conflict, resulting in shortages of laboratory equipment. As a result, the institute was unable to perform its normal volume of diagnostic tests and it was forced instead to outsource many of its analyses to military and other hospitals in the region. In order to continue with its practical work, the Pasteur Institute temporarily abandoned many of its research projects, vowing to revive them after the cessation of hostilities.[48] In addition to shortages of supplies, the high turnover of European personnel in hospitals, clinics, and laboratories made the normal functioning of health services difficult to maintain across the federation.[49] And while the effects of the war had left the production of certain vaccines—such as that for yellow fever—unhampered, the production of others—such as BCG serum at the Pasteur Institute of Kindia, Guinea—was shut down completely.[50]

By 1943 the situation had become sufficiently dire to warrant calling on American suppliers to supplement or cover orders for medical supplies such as smallpox vaccine serum, sleeping sickness medication, rat poison, and insulin.[51] In addition to shortages of vaccines and other pharmaceuticals, medical implements such as microscopes, x-ray film, and optical glass were becoming increasingly hard to come by. Health officials bemoaned the difficulties of maintaining a certain standard of care while awaiting "better days" and "more secure tomorrows." The 1943 annual report from the DGSP in AOF reported that its primary goal was to maintain the pre-1939 standard of health, "in spite of severe and paralyzing circumstances, in spite of the reduction of technical personnel, the dwindling of supply stocks, [and] the lack of transportation. . . . In a word, in spite of all manner of difficulties."[52]

The war also highlighted other perceived problems in France's African empire: "degeneration" and depopulation.[53] Existing fears about *dénatalité*, or low birthrate, were only further exacerbated by France's defeat in 1940. Just as in metropolitan France, health officials in the colonies associated a low population growth rate with a weak military, a meager workforce, and a generalized impuissance vis-à-vis other nations and empires. A 1941 medical report from Côte d'Ivoire reported that the colony was "faced with a grave workforce shortage . . . linked to the demographic crisis and the problem of indigenous childhood."[54] Because infant mortality in France had significantly diminished in the first four decades of the twentieth century, doctors and reformers promoted a solution to the population problem that revolved around encouraging families to have more children. In Africa, by contrast, the solution to the demographic problem centered on the concept of "faire du noir," or making the most of the African population as a resource. This meant promoting good health for mothers, protecting infant health, and campaigning against epidemic diseases. As one colonial health official wrote, "'Faire du noir,' for us, means extending our medical action; and above all resolutely orienting it toward the fight against the Great African Endemic Diseases . . . [and] against social diseases, which lead to weakness and degeneration, strike down the child, destroy the egg, sterilize the adult." This amounted to a new manifesto for colonial health services, embodying an important shift from a system that provided basic health services to Africans to a more all-encompassing system aimed to protect an entire population under the banner of preventative social medicine. The same official went as far as to state that the "principal task [of colonial health services] is the Protection of the Race and its harmonious development."[55] In the 1941 medical report from the West African colony of Dahomey, Médecin-Colonel Marquand, the chief of health services, wrote, "In what concerns population, what matters is to conserve those individuals who are already living, or who are about to be born."[56] At the heart of Africa's population problem was not the lack of babies born but the low survival rates for those that were.

Although the war had "paralyzed" Ricou's plan, reform-minded doctors in the empire were hopeful about the possibility of recommencing their work after the war was over. As one health official wrote, "We have already laid the first milestones that will mark our route; and we have already designed the foundation for the edifice we one day hope to construct. . . . We continue to march along, and if this term expresses an idea of laborious slowness, it expresses also and above all the idea of a sustained and perseverant progression toward the goals we have set out for ourselves."[57] As the war came to an end, however, French officials in the empire would need to reckon not only with the demographic crisis inflicted by years of fighting but also with groundbreaking political changes that resulted from the war. Health programs in postwar Africa would no longer be a "civilizing" service offered to colonial subjects. Now, instead, they would be a social good provided for new citizens of the French Union.

The Sanitary Citizen in Postwar French Africa

Medical reforms in postwar French Africa were in part about making a new place: a sanitary empire that would perfectly complement a reinvigorated postwar France. They also aimed, however, to create a new people—both literally and metaphorically—who would populate this new and modernized empire. The expansion of the colonial health care establishment was about more than physical bodies; it was also about political bodies. At the end of the war, the political status of France's overseas empire changed dramatically. Under the banner of the new French Union, "colonies" became "overseas territories," and for the first time the inhabitants of those territories possessed the same rights as people living in metropolitan France.[58] Citizenship involved more than just access to the ballot box, however. It also involved a sense of belonging, shared values, and common goals. In his opening remarks to the 1944 Brazzaville Conference, René Pleven exclaimed that "in the great colonial France, there are no peoples to emancipate nor any racial discrimination to abolish. There are only populations who feel themselves to be French and to whom France wants to give a growing role in democratic institutions and the French community."[59]

After 1946, health services provided colonial administrators with an important way of reenvisioning their subjects as citizens and imagining a new way for them to belong in a modern scientific and hygienic society. Citizenship, for the French administration, meant an increased obligation to participate in public health programs for the good of the collective. By contrast, many Africans—especially women—saw this new citizenship status as a framework for *rejecting* health provisions that did not fit with their values or with the realities of their daily lives. For them, French Union citizenship meant the right to more individual agency and more choices, even if those choices did not correspond with the kinds of health services used by French citizens in the metropole. Although postwar political reform was an important step toward resolving the inequalities inherent in the colonial system, the question of granting citizenship to Africans was a controversial one. Much of the debate centered on whether Africans were sufficiently "evolved" or "assimilated" enough to be good citizens. Likewise, failures of the colonial health system were often blamed not on the lack of investment by the French government but rather on the "backwardness" of Africans themselves, especially African women.[60]

Numerous health reports during the war lamented the failure of African mothers to properly clothe, feed, and care for their children. Health officials claimed that mothers' reluctance to cover babies and children led to mosquito bites and malaria and that their disinclination toward bathing facilitated the spread of disease.[61] They also complained that Africans worried little about sexually transmitted diseases and that rampant and unregulated prostitution only further endangered an already fragile demographic situation.[62] Yet mothers weren't the only ones at fault, according to medical officials. Just as wet nurses in the countryside bore the majority of the blame for infant deaths in France, so too did African *matrones* (midwives) fall prey to accusations of increasing infant mortality rates with their "superstitious" practices. In many ways this echoed the perception Parisian doctors had of French peasants' childbirth practices. While ignorance was cited as one of the primary causes of infant mortality generally speaking, the problem was seen as particularly acute in the countryside, farther from the reach of modern medical knowledge. Reformers were especially concerned with childbirth and childcare, which was handled primarily by midwives and other female healers.[63] According to a 1941 report from the HCI, instead of ensuring "proper" postnatal care for mother and child, *matrones* would sequester mothers and newborns in the home for eight days—doors and windows closed tightly—with the goal of protecting "the child from any evils spells that might be cast in its direction; because the blacks don't ignore 'tetanus' but like all their illnesses connect it to 'Curses.'"[64]

According to local health reports, these practices had little to do with religious observance but rather stemmed from women's ignorance about "modern" medical practices. The 1941 Dakar hospital report, for example, explained that—unconnected to any stipulations in the Koran—"indigenous women act only out of habit, ignorance, indifference, neglect, and fatalism." Colonial assumptions about the failures of African childcare were connected both to gender stereotypes and to ideas about the "backwardness" of the African race. The same report stated, "Old habits going back generations [and] ignorance of sterilization and disinfection and of simple cleanliness . . . are essential characteristics of the black race against which it is difficult for the European to fight."[65] One of the biggest killers of African infants, for example, was umbilical tetanus. Despite a campaign to provide *matrones* with clean tools and instruction in proper ligature techniques, the 1941 report complained that the rates of umbilical tetanus had not fallen and that the campaign would have to be renewed the following year.[66] According to these colonial health officials, mothers themselves were complicit in the deaths of their children, failing to call for help until after the child had already "fallen to the ground."[67]

If colonial doctors attributed infant mortality, low population growth rates, and poor general health conditions to the supposed backwardness of colonial subjects, health and medicine could also be a way of creating new, more modern citizens. In the postwar period these doctors took up the banner of "faire du noir" with renewed enthusiasm, with the goal of building a more coherent and efficient system of managing colonial populations. One of the most important steps undertaken in the immediate postwar era to manage population and bolster the family was the creation of an *enquête démographique,* AOF's rudimentary version of a census. Additionally, a 1946 law conferred on all mothers and infants in AOF the same legal protections enjoyed by their counterparts in metropolitan France.[68]

On the eve of the Second World War, a study confirmed that infant mortality and miscarriages were the primary causes of low population growth in French Africa. This conclusion led to a renewed interest in protecting the health of pregnant women, mothers, and infants through better-developed maternity clinics with provisions for extended bed rest, protection against malaria, and hygiene courses for new mothers. Just as in metropolitan France, motherhood was considered essential to the health of the nation, a vocation to be taken seriously by women and to be supported in turn by government-sponsored social services. To protect the children who did survive infancy, in 1942 the colonial administration created the Inspection médicale des écoles (School Medical Inspection Service; IME). In addition to reporting on sanitary deficiencies within the school system, the IME examined students at the beginning of each school year, verified and administered vaccines, and established a *fiche médicale*, a medical record for each student that would follow them through their entire school career. The goal of this service was not only to increase the health of African schoolchildren but also to impart a new hygienic awareness that young people could then bring back to their families.[69]

In some ways, these changes squared nicely with new international efforts to emphasize social medicine and preventative health care. According to the UN's Universal Declaration of Human Rights, drafted in 1948, "Everyone has the right to a standard of living adequate for the health and well-being of himself and of his family, including food, clothing, housing and medical care and necessary social services. . . . Motherhood and childhood are entitled to special care and assistance."[70] But despite this renewed commitment to expanding health provisions for mothers and children in the empire, the French colonial government did not conceive of health care as a right in the same way that new international institutions such as the UN did. Africans, moreover, engaged with the discourse about health and rights in unexpected ways that often did not align with colonial and global public health agendas. Looking back, we might expect to see Africans clamoring for health services based on their newly conceived universal right or, if not that, then at least based on their new French citizenship. In many cases, however, the opposite was true. While many Africans living in the French empire used the framework of citizenship to demand new rights in the domains of labor and family allowances, in the field of health they often used citizenship as a way of rejecting existing services rather than demanding new ones.[71] Instead of invoking their right for particular kinds of health care, many Africans—especially women—used their new citizenship to advocate for their right to return to more traditional childbirth and childcare practices.

Government statistics reveal that more and more Africans were using colonial health services in the French empire with each passing year up to the end of the Second World War. After 1946, when inhabitants of France's overseas empire were granted citizenship rights by the Lamine Guèye law, this trend came to an abrupt halt. Far from hurrying to the Ministry of Overseas France to demand better health care for themselves and their families, some Africans actually began to literally flee French medical teams, much to the chagrin of colonial health officials. One colonial health official from Côte d'Ivoire wrote that it was becoming increasingly clear that the "colonial medical service is encountering a number of clashes in the execution of its various tasks; clashes against inertia, ill-will, incomprehension, not to mention the hostility of the local population for which it has assumed the heavy responsibility of maintaining a good state of health."[72] Despite the early gains made before 1945 in drawing Africans to the clinic and in encouraging them to attend visits by mobile vaccination teams, in the postwar period the number of people using these services declined rapidly.[73]

The biggest drop occurred in infant and maternal health services, where attendance plummeted in 1946 and continued to drop through 1947.[74] Médecin-Colonel Urvois, the director of public health for Côte d'Ivoire, explained the causes of the diminishing responsiveness to infant and maternal health services, stating, "These can be summarized entirely by an erroneous interpretation of the stipulations of the law of 7 May 1946, awarding to indigenous populations certain public liberties." "The African woman," he continued, "provoked by a few agitators of bad faith, believes herself free from all constraints, even those rigorously imposed by the law for the protection of Public Health or other laws with the goal of ensuring the greater good of the race in view of eradicating all of the social diseases that threaten it."[75]

Many women claimed that as free citizens they were no longer under any obligation to submit to medical control by the French colonial government. Mobilizing the language of the French Republic, women in one Ivorian village told local authorities that they were "free—no more force—even 'for their own good.'" In another village, women told doctors that they had done just fine giving birth before the arrival of colonial doctors, and now that they were "free," they could return to practices that were more in line with their own cultural traditions and lifestyles. In a rare passage that gives voice to the feelings of African women toward the expansion of colonial health services, one health official in Grand-Lahou—a coastal town in Côte d'Ivoire—quoted a local woman's explanation of her reluctance to use the local *centre d'hébergement* (live-in pregnancy clinic): "I hear your sales pitch, I know our daughters will be well cared for, watched over, and fed, but do not forget that for a woman, to give birth is a bit like going to war for a man. Just as he wonders whether or not he will return, she asks herself the same thing, whether or not she will lose her own life in giving it to another." The woman continued, "In the face of the unknown, it is better for the birth to take place in her own home, where she is guaranteed the assistance of her family and her friends and the well wishes of her village."[76]

As African women rejoiced in their political rights, colonial officials increasingly found themselves unable to resort to their older—more coercive—methods of managing their colonial subjects. Perhaps the most important shift was the sudden inability of colonial officials to employ force as a tactic for filling the maternity wards, which were a key component in the plan to encourage a healthy and prolific African population. One medical inspector reported that in the clinic where he had once seen as many as 150 pregnant women assembled, all but 7 had deserted at the time of his last inspection. Another local health inspector in a neighboring village confirmed the political rationale behind this change in women's behavior: "The drop in the number of births taking place at maternity clinics can only be attributed to the evolution of contemporary politics, which are far from sympathetic to the regime of forced recruitment that we have employed until now."[77] Urvois explained that before 1946, women rarely availed themselves of colonial health services voluntarily, and as a result serious efforts were required in order to bring women to maternity clinics. According to one local public health director, visiting nurses sought pregnant women out and then notified local authorities, who would then order the women to attend regular prenatal consultations. After 1945, the women who had once reluctantly presented themselves for checkups and for stays at the *centres d'hébergement* for women with at-risk pregnancies now simply refused to comply with these coercive public health regimes.

Local authorities found themselves unable to force women to attend checkups and were left only with their powers of "persuasion." Urvois doubted that such efforts would be fruitful, given what he believed was the "ignorance of rural women about the benefits—and indeed, the necessity—of such consultations." He proposed using the *médecins-africains,* who were very involved in local political life, to influence their compatriots. He also proposed several reforms to the system, including shuttles that would bring women from more-remote areas to the clinics. Smaller posts could also be built in villages that were farther removed from the city centers. Additionally, Urvois advocated establishing "a less rudimentary level of comfort" at the clinics for women whose circumstances or condition forced them to stay for an extended period of time.[78]

While some colonial doctors saw women as the heart of the problem, others pointed to the patriarchal structure of some African societies as an important impediment to the advancement of infant and maternal health in France's African empire. The director of public health for the territory of Dahomey wrote in his 1948 report, "In this region men are opposed to sending their wives to prenatal consultations; the woman is required to work in the fields nonstop; the husband treats her as a slave and requires from her the maximum output." "Until 1946," he continued, "the local doctors were able to alleviate this problem by sending summons to pregnant women, requiring them to attend the consultations; the result was excellent and the women appreciated the care they received there." Once again, colonial doctors framed the problem in terms of a misinterpretation of new political rights. According to the health director in Dahomey, "Since the current political evolution African men have perceived these summons as an attack on their liberty and have once again forbidden their wives from presenting themselves at the consultations." The solution demanded by colonial health officials was further hygienic education for new citizens, with a special emphasis on general education for women. Colonial officials believed that if women had more political and economic power within the family, they would be able to overcome their husbands' resistance to modern French hygienic norms.[79]

Beyond the resistance to maternity services, colonial health officials also complained about wholesale rejection of all colonial health services in some locations. Some villages in Côte d'Ivoire, for example, refused en bloc to submit to vaccination campaigns. In certain villages, some residents even resorted to hiding in the fields to escape confrontation with colonial doctors. Local public health directors also reported resistance to rural and urban hygiene measures, prophylaxis of epidemic diseases, the segregation of people infected with leprosy, and health consultations in clinics.[80] Colonial officials insinuated that Africans believed that their new political rights gave them the liberty of passing on diseases to others, particularly when it came to "social diseases" such as syphilis and tuberculosis. According to Médecin-Lieutenant-Colonel P. Queinnec, who served as public health director of Upper Volta in 1948, venereal disease was "a problem of the highest importance." It resulted in "sterility [and] miscarriages" and, in the worst cases, "required entry into a medical facility." Prostitutes especially, explained Queinnec, had gravely misinterpreted their new status. He wrote, "Prostitutes—and they are numerous, both professional and amateur—have free rein. The laws which granted them citizenship also seem to have granted them the right of contamination."[81]

Ironically, despite health officials' attempts to cast African resistance as fundamentally un-French, the more that Africans began to opt out of health services in the name of their new status as citizens, the more their actions actually began to mirror those of French citizens living in the metropole. Indeed, many historians have noted the relative ease with which coercive public health measures were implemented in France's colonies, where the majority of the population fell under the heading of "subject," while citizens in France managed to escape the most restrictive public health policies. Debré—perhaps the most prominent French physician of the twentieth century—noted the frequency with which the French evaded public health measures in the name of their own personal liberty: "The French care very little about public health. For them, health is a personal affair. It has been said many times, the French do not submit themselves easily to collective disciplines." He continued, "Their individualism pushes them toward a certain egoism, the civic sense is not as developed as that in other nations. They seek to voluntarily escape official regulations, and do not consider it shameful to deceive the State. Legal disobedience is not looked down upon . . . and each man thinks that regulations are made for others."[82] In the postwar era, Africans would use the same framework of citizenship to reject health services as their counterparts in metropolitan France had done for more than a century.

Although colonial health officials in French sub-Saharan Africa wanted their constituents to understand that their new rights did not afford them the liberty of opting out of public health obligations, they also wanted to be able to administer these services to a willing population. They hoped that Africans would seek out public health services voluntarily, motivated by their recognition of the value of modern science, as well as by their desire to join the greater French cultural community. In a 1950 report, Médecin-Colonel Vernier, from the territory of French Sudan, wrote, "Our role is not to forcefully open their mouths to give for free a misunderstood and mysterious remedy, but instead to open their minds and educate them, with the goal that, someday, patients will voluntarily pay for medicines for which they completely understand the virtues."[83] The sanitary citizen, as envisioned by men like Vernier, would conform to modern "French" hygienic principles and demographic initiatives out of a fundamental understanding of how one's individual actions contributed to or detracted from the good of the collective.

In his 1947 report, Médecin-Colonel David, the local director for Toumodi, Côte d'Ivoire, wrote that "the maternity clinic and the dispensary—whose roles are to protect mothers and children and treat the sick—have nothing to do with politics."[84] But contrary to official attempts to pretend otherwise, the choice of African women to accept or reject these services was fundamentally a political one. While an examination of health and citizenship shows that medical care in postwar Africa was conceived of as a set of responsibilities as much as it was as a set of rights, this exploration also tells us something important about African understandings of citizenship. As Africans mobilized their newly gained citizenship to fight for labor rights, they simultaneously used it to reject health measures that they perceived as coercive. Africans in the French Union did not regard citizenship as something that should be bought wholesale, but instead viewed it as a collection of rights and responsibilities that they could tailor to their own lives, as well as to their own social, political, and personal aspirations.

~

When African resistance combined with the practical difficulties of implementing health care reform in the postwar period, the result was an uneven system that achieved varying degrees of success. Even as increasing numbers of women were opting out of colonial maternity services and more Africans were saying no to compulsory vaccination campaigns, the colonial administration was struggling to provide sufficient numbers of doctors to staff medical posts, fighting to obtain adequate quantities of vaccine serums, and battling to establish a school hygiene service that would protect young children from the ravages of endemic and epidemic diseases. In the wake of the war, thus, new rifts were emerging. There existed very real gaps between ambitious reform and on-the-ground realities, as well as between European and African visions of public health. These divisions would produce a crisis of colonial health that would have important repercussions as the French government attempted to defend its colonial project to a broad international audience in the era of decolonization.

If excellence in medicine and science had long been a cornerstone of *la civilisation française,* the fact that public health was foundering in the empire would provoke passionate criticism at the UN and raise serious questions about the French administration's ability to provide for its African constituents. This was especially problematic in an era when the WHO declared that "the enjoyment of the highest attainable standard of health is one of the fundamental rights of every human being."[85] As the UN began to expand its supervisory role in the imperial world after 1947, these failures in health reform would become a significant liability as anticolonial delegations at the UN linked shortcomings in health and education to broader inequalities of colonial rule in Africa. The crisis of French colonial medicine would also create an important window of opportunity for international health organizations such as the WHO to bring a new global perspective on public health to the African continent, one that would be based on a universal right to health rather than on legacies of colonial violence and inequality.

CHAPTER TWO

The United Nations and the Politics of Health

> Situated between two giants battling for global hegemony, neither France nor Britain can claim to be a first-rank power, even if the physical reaches of the Commonwealth place one nation slightly in front of the other. The United States has shown itself to be almost as hostile as the USSR to the colonial projects of the two European nations . . . and now, both nations find themselves to be simultaneously in a position of judge and defendant before the tribunal that is the United Nations, defending a project of which those participating know very little concerning the conditions and merits.
>
> —Report from the Government General of AOF, 1950

As colonial administrators and doctors in French Africa struggled to recover from the disruption of the war and Vichy rule and to reimagine their empire on the basis of the newly formed French Union, they also found themselves facing another set of challenges. In the immediate postwar period, they would also have to grapple with the creation of new international institutions—the UN, the WHO, and the United Nations Educational, Scientific, and Cultural Organization (UNESCO), among others—that would rapidly extend their reach throughout the world, including to territories still under colonial rule. These institutions would serve as arenas for the development of new global norms that emphasized the importance of political, social, and economic self-determination for all peoples. Despite their frequent claims that postwar colonial reform was intended to further the same goals of political and social development that the UN promoted, many colonial officials viewed the UN as a real threat to the future of their overseas empires. When France, Great Britain, and Belgium found themselves eclipsed by the United States and the Soviet Union at the UN, they feared that the anticolonialism of these two countries—along with pressure from a plethora of newly independent countries such as India and Indonesia—would ultimately come to dominate the UN.

By the early 1950s, French administrators and medical personnel would find themselves embroiled in an international conflict over the role that international health organizations would be allowed to play in the colonial world. But the drama that would ultimately play out at the WHO Regional Office for Africa in Brazzaville had its origins in debates that took place several years earlier: in San Francisco, where the UN Charter was drafted, and at Lake Success, New York, where anticolonial delegations to the UN General Assembly set in motion the process of establishing an unofficial system of international colonial oversight. Although the clash between French colonial doctors and international medical personnel advocating for independence would ultimately find its most important arena in the WHO Regional Office for Africa, the first battles over health, empire, and decolonization would take place in a different UN body: the UN Special Committee on Information from Non-self-governing Territories. This UN committee, established in the immediate postwar period—was a nod to delegations that had hoped to extend the regime of international trusteeship to all colonial territories. Unlike the UN Trusteeship Council, which could send visiting missions to and field petitions from the territories that fell under its purview, the special committee's limited mandate only included the review of annual reports about conditions in colonial territories. These reports—required by Article 73(e) of the UN Charter—focused solely on aspects of development: economic conditions, education, and social policy, including health. Explicit discussions of political conditions and human rights were not included, nor did the earliest iterations of the committee have much power to make substantive recommendations about how colonial empires should be run.

Yet despite the seemingly limited purview of the special committee, French colonial officials saw in these reports both an unprecedented threat to colonial sovereignty and an unparalleled opportunity to "sell" the newly repackaged French Union to a broad global audience. Having emerged from the war vanquished and reliant on financial support from the United States, the French government found itself in a precarious position vis-à-vis international public opinion. French officials staunchly denounced the emerging system of UN colonial oversight, but they also feared that opting out of this system might produce "violent" critiques of France's unwillingness to engage in cooperative endeavors and—more importantly—of the empire itself. Certain officials also saw these annual reports as a meaningful propaganda opportunity. They hoped that within the limited confines of discussions about social policy, education, and economic development—areas in which many administrators thought French rule had succeeded—they could convince the world once and for all of the fundamental benevolence of France's colonial project. Jean Chauvel, the French ambassador to the UN, made the bold claim that "The French Union belongs to the same historic movement as the United Nations Charter. It is connected by the same spirit and achieves in its own way the same goals of human dignity and liberation."[1] Public health, in particular, was a field in which many colonial administrators believed the French empire had genuinely done more good than harm.[2] But these reports were a double-edged sword: if they were capable of showing all that the French colonial public health system had achieved, they could also demonstrate where it had failed.[3]

The special committee played a crucial role in gathering data about life in Europe's colonial empires, and anticolonial delegations would use this information as evidence in their indictment of empire. These delegations reproached colonial governments for failing to guarantee a basic standard of living for their colonial subjects and for their inability to provide satisfactory infrastructure. They explicitly linked their broader critiques of empire to shortcomings in the field of health and social services, thus laying the foundation for the antagonistic relationship that would develop between the French government and the WHO. The battle for decolonization was not just about political will and military might; it was also about demonstrating to the inhabitants of colonial territories who was most capable of providing for their well-being.[4] While the special committee began simply as a means to process the reports required by the charter, the debates that took place there quickly evolved to encompass larger questions about the legitimacy of colonial rule. Conversations about health would no longer focus solely on the efficacy of vaccines or the need for mobile health teams in rural Africa. Now, they would also encompass discussions about how colonial governments had created conditions of structural inequality and had failed to provide for the needs of the people they were claiming to protect. As anticolonialism gained traction at the UN, discussions about health and social services were rapidly becoming debates about the fate of empire itself.[5]

The Origins of the Special Committee

In the spring of 1945, delegates from fifty countries gathered in San Francisco to sketch out the new postwar international organization that would replace the League of Nations. Of the participating delegates, all hoped that the new organization would provide a stable foundation for world peace. At the same time, however, those same delegates held vastly different views about the role that colonial empires would or would not play in that peace. For some delegations, particularly those from the Soviet Union, the Middle East, India, and Latin America, colonial empires represented the most tangible remnants of an outdated world order.[6] They believed that the only way to ensure a peaceful and equitable future was to eliminate those archaic systems of rule based on violence, racism, and deep-seated structural inequality. For other delegations—from France, Great Britain, Belgium, and the Netherlands—those same empires were the linchpins of global stability.[7] To destroy them would leave the European continent struggling to stay afloat in a political system now dominated by the United States and the USSR. The American delegation, for its part, was torn between the long tradition of American anticolonialism and the need to undergird European economic recovery.[8] With its own dark history of racism and violence, the US government was particularly sensitive to the way the American public might perceive its support for ongoing colonial rule. The African American press, in particular, tracked debates about the colonial question at the conference very closely.[9]

In the end, neither side was satisfied with the results that the conference produced. The delegations that had championed independence—or at least international trusteeship—for colonial empires felt that the organization founded in San Francisco could be characterized, at best, by its "timidity" and "ineffectiveness." Representatives from the colonial delegations worried that the loose system of accountability that the charter established ran the risk of encroaching on European sovereignty in their overseas empires.[10]

The UN Charter, approved by the conference delegates on 26 June 1945, contains three chapters that deal with the responsibilities that colonial powers had to their overseas territories. Chapters XII and XIII deal with trust territories and the system of international trusteeship, the successor to the League of Nations mandates system.[11] Chapter XI, the "Declaration regarding

Figure 2.1. The San Francisco Conference, 25 April–26 June 1945. Flags of the UN wave in the courtyard of San Francisco City Hall. UN Photo / Lundquist.

Non-self-governing Territories," deals with all other colonial territories. Because most of France's African territories were not trust territories—with the exception of Togo and Cameroon—here I consider only Chapter XI. Of the eight members of the UN that administered overseas territories, France was second only to the United Kingdom in the number of territories controlled. Of seventy-four non-self-governing territories, sixteen were controlled by France (AOF and AEF each counted as one territory), forty-four were under British control, seven belonged to the United States, three to the Netherlands, two to New Zealand, and one each to Australia, Belgium, and Denmark.

The most important article of Chapter XI was Article 73, which stated that the signatories of the charter who possessed overseas territories would recognize that "the interests of the inhabitants of these territories are paramount, and accept as a sacred trust the obligation to promote to the utmost, within the system of international peace and security established by the present Charter, the well-being of the inhabitants of these territories." They promised to promote social, economic, and political development and to ensure the just treatment of their colonial subjects and citizens, as well as to foster research that would directly benefit these populations. Last, they agreed to promote cooperation among themselves and with international organizations such as the UN.[12]

Perhaps the most seemingly harmless element of Chapter XI was Article 73(e), which stipulated that colonial governments would "transmit regularly to the Secretary-General for information purposes . . . statistical and other information of a technical nature relating to economic, social, and educational conditions in the territories for which they are respectively responsible."[13] It was this provision of the charter, however, that would elicit the most bitter controversy between colonial governments and those delegations championing independence—in particular representatives from Latin America, the Slavic states, the Arab states, the USSR, Liberia, India, Indonesia, and the United States.[14] The main disagreement over the reports stemmed from a confusion about the article's ultimate goal. While some representatives to the UN claimed that these reports were simply a means for the General Assembly to stay informed about conditions in dependent territories and to monitor their progress toward self-government, more-suspicious delegations accused the anticolonial representatives of attempting to create a system of oversight that would mirror what the Trusteeship Council provided for UN trust territories.[15]

Beyond their disagreement about the ultimate goal of this system of colonial "accountability," delegates to the UN General Assembly were also confused about the reports themselves. The requirement to provide "technical" information was vague at best, and the charter provided few details about how the process would work. It failed to specify who was responsible for collecting this information, which UN members were required to submit it, and on behalf of which territories.[16] Empire, after all, was not a one-size-fits-all model. Colonial representatives were determined to use these ambiguities—and the charter's lack of clarity—to their advantage. In the French case, for example, could the UN classify territories where inhabitants had gained full citizenship rights as "non-self-governing"? And how should the UN treat territories such as Guyana, Réunion, Martinique, and

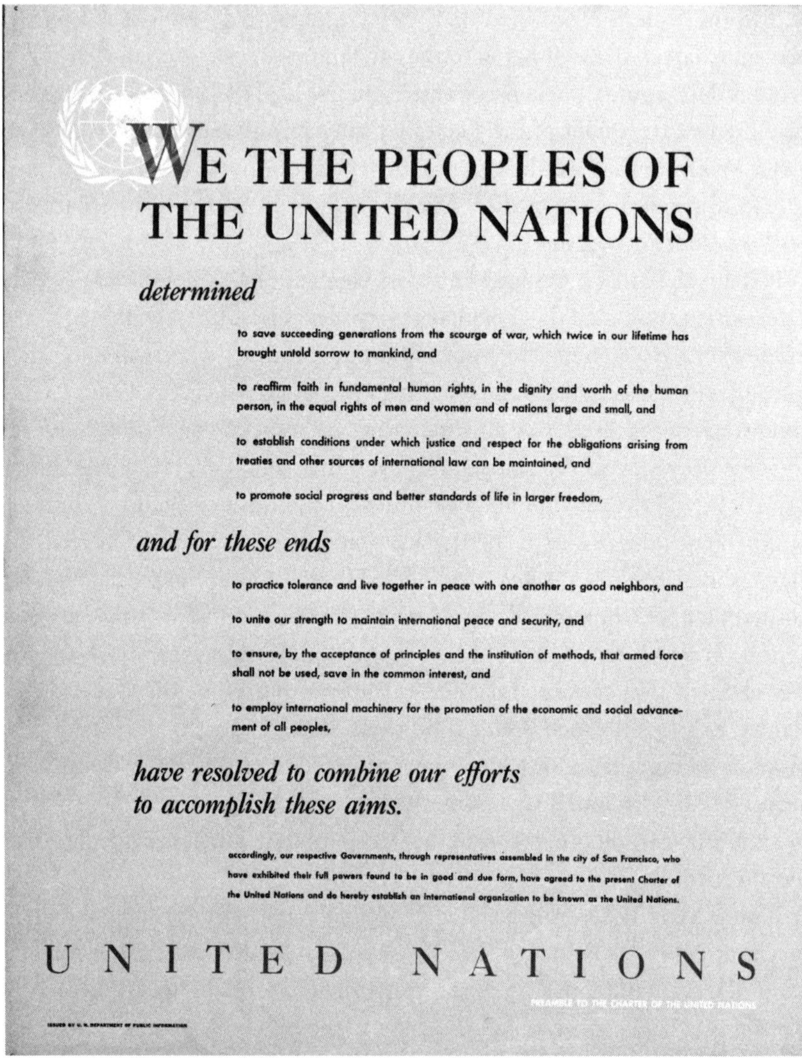

Figure 2.2. Preamble to the Charter of the UN, which was signed in San Francisco on 26 June 1945. UN Photo.

Guadeloupe, which had recently acceded to the status of French overseas departments?[17]

In order to facilitate the process of data collection, in 1946 the UN General Assembly created an ad hoc committee to work through some of the questions surrounding this system of international "accountability" for colonial governance.[18] Questions included, for instance, how could information be collected in a way that would allow comparisons to be made between colonies in different parts of the world and in different empires? What was the UN allowed to do with the information it collected? What kinds of recommendations would the UN be allowed to make? And how could this new international organization actually hold colonial governments accountable for the territories for which they were responsible?[19]

After months of debate, the General Assembly settled on a sixteen-member committee that would operate for a renewable three-year term. Half of the committee would be composed of member states with colonies, and the other half would be composed of members without. For each year of the three-year mandate, the committee would focus on one of three areas of inquiry: economic development, education, and social conditions—including public health. Although the committee was allowed to make general recommendations, it was not allowed to discuss political conditions or questions of human rights in colonial territories. The ban on political discussions notwithstanding, the atmosphere in the committee over the course of the late 1940s and early 1950s ranged from tense to explosive as the boundaries of the committee were pushed by "states hostile to all forms of dependence and in favor of the complete emancipation of all territories under the administration of another power," according to one French government official.[20]

In 1946 and 1947, the UN General Assembly invited member states responsible for non-self-governing territories to submit any data they wished pertaining to economic, educational, and social conditions. In 1947, an ad hoc committee replaced this system of voluntary submission with a standard form, which required the submission of detailed information on everything from the number of fisheries operating in a given territory to the number of cases of malaria reported per year.[21] The following year, some of the delegations to the special committee—in particular those from Egypt, India, and the Soviet Union—advocated for the inclusion of information about political participation, human rights, and race relations.[22] The French delegation

Table 2.1. Composition of the Special Committee, 1948–1951

	1948	1949	1950	1951
Members transmitting information	Australia Belgium Denmark France Netherlands New Zealand United Kingdom United States of America	Australia Belgium Denmark France Netherlands New Zealand United Kingdom United States of America	Australia Belgium Denmark France Netherlands New Zealand United Kingdom United States of America	Australia Belgium Denmark France Netherlands New Zealand United Kingdom United States of America
Elected committee members	China Colombia Cuba Egypt India Nicaragua Sweden Union of Soviet Socialist Republics	Brazil China Dominican Republic Egypt India Sweden Union of Soviet Socialist Republics Venezuela	Brazil Egypt India Mexico Philippines Sweden Union of Soviet Socialist Republics Venezuela	Brazil Cuba Egypt India Mexico Pakistan Philippines Union of Soviet Socialist Republics

Data Source: The 1948 data is from: United Nations, General Assembly, *Report of the Special Committee on Information Transmitted under Article 73e of the Charter,* Official Records: Third Session, Supplement 12 (A / 593) (New York, 1948), 1; the 1949 data is from: United Nations, General Assembly, *Report of the Special Committee on Information Transmitted under Article 73e of the Charter,* Official Records: Fourth Session, Supplement 14 (A / 923) (New York, 1949), 1; the 1950 data is from: United Nations, General Assembly, *Report of the Special Committee on Information Transmitted under Article 73e of the Charter,* Official Records: Fifth Session, Supplement 17 (A / 1303) (New York, 1950), 1; the 1951 data is from: United Nations, General Assembly, *Report of the Special Committee on Information Transmitted under Article 73e of the Charter,* Official Records: Sixth Session, Supplement 14 (A / 1836) (Geneva, 1951), 1.

feared that opening the discussion to include such matters would, "without a doubt, have the effect to further open this organism to all possible maneuvers of anti-colonial demagoguery."[23]

The Soviet delegation suggested giving the special committee powers similar to those of the Trusteeship Council, with the ability to accept petitions from colonial populations and to dispatch visiting missions to colonial territories. This, the Soviet delegation argued, would be the only way to guarantee that governments were in fact facilitating the transition from colonialism to self-government.[24] In the end, the committee ruled that while it could encourage the submission of information about political participation and other sensitive issues, it could not require it, nor would on-site visits or petitions be permitted. The impulse to evaluate the political transition toward independence was so strong, however, that even those limited discussions of fishing infrastructure and epidemic disease soon turned volatile, leading the French delegation to denounce the "inquisitorial nature" of the standard form.[25]

Debating Health, Critiquing Empire

As they amassed more data about colonial health systems, the members of the special committee found themselves in a position to make increasingly specific recommendations about what social services and public health infrastructure should look like in colonial territories. On the surface, many of these recommendations resembled what colonial governments were already trying to achieve in their overseas territories. The French administration, as we have seen, was already in the process of completely overhauling its public infrastructure in sub-Saharan Africa. Beyond these grand—and often overly ambitious—plans for health care reform, the French government had also created a special fund, the Investment Fund for Economic and Social Development (Fonds d'investissement pour le développement économique et social; FIDES), to promote the expansion of colonial infrastructure, including hospitals and clinics.[26] Within the special committee, however, discussions about health care infrastructure and social policy were intricately embedded in broader debates about structural inequality, colonial violence, and the various ways that colonial governments had failed to fulfill their commitments to the millions of inhabitants of their vast overseas empires. Discussions about health and social policy allowed anticolonial delegations to the UN to advance their political agendas surreptitiously without violating the ban on explicitly "political" discussions. Embedded in these discussions was a critique of colonial governance and its nefarious effects on the people that these governments were claiming to represent. Recommendations by anticolonial delegations to the committee pointed toward the goal of self-sufficiency in the realm of health and, eventually, the goal of independence.

The standard form required colonial governments to submit a wide range of data on public health in their colonial territories. It required them to report statistics on each territory's demographic situation, the general state of health and nutrition (including the incidence of epidemic disease), the principal causes of morbidity and mortality (including infant and maternal mortality), descriptions of the different medical services available, the number of staff working for each of the territories' health service branches, the qualifications required to practice medicine, the state of medical training facilities, and statistics on public health expenditure, including what percentage of a territory's total budget was spent on health and social welfare services. Colonial governments were also obligated to report on the existence (or lack thereof) of various public health provisions, including sanitation, clean water supply, infant and maternal health clinics, and disease control programs.[27]

While internal health reports from French territories in Africa tended to focus on health in a more strictly physical sense, many delegates to the special committee emphasized the connections between health, social welfare, and the future of society in dependent territories. This trend became more pronounced as the committee's mandate grew over the course of the 1950s. In the earliest meetings of the special committee, discussions about public health and social policy still remained largely separate. They focused primarily on medical conditions and the quality of life that the inhabitants of dependent territories experienced. Early discussions called for more accurate data, including more detailed statistics on infant and child mortality, information from hospitals about the implementation of preventative health programs, and statistics on diseases of malnutrition. Anticolonial delegations to the committee accused colonial governments of overemphasizing future plans in the reports rather than acknowledging the on-the-ground realities of colonial rule. They pointed to the shortcomings of colonial health systems in Africa as evidence of the broader failure of colonial governance. Low per capita expenditures, high rates of infant mortality, shortages of medical personnel, and insufficient hospital access, they claimed, were all indications that European governments were underinvesting in their territories overseas.[28]

As tensions mounted during the late 1940s, colonial delegations to the special committee contended that it was unfair to compare overseas territories to their more developed metropolitan counterparts.[29] They claimed instead that health conditions should be compared to those in independent territories at a similar stage of social and economic development. The Belgian delegation also pointed out that many of the shortcomings of the colonial public health administrations had less to do with their status as dependent territories than with the lack of financial resources that almost all countries were experiencing in the immediate postwar period. The British delegation added that shortages in medical personnel were common in many countries and that these deficiencies were not necessarily more acute in non-self-governing territories.[30] French delegates to the committee argued that the UN should give more recognition to colonial governments for the progress they had made, instead of making unrealistic comparisons between conditions in Africa and those in more-developed metropolitan territories. French health services in sub-Saharan Africa, for example, had made important progress in extending campaigns to fight malaria, yellow fever, and sleeping sickness.[31]

By the early 1950s, discussions in the special committee had shifted away from treating public health services and social welfare programs as separate entities. Anticolonial delegations lobbied for more-integrated health programs that would recognize the interrelatedness of economic and social problems and would better prepare indigenous populations for self-sufficiency and self-government.[32] In the same period, the WHO—as a specialized institution of the UN—offered a similar interpretation of the interconnectedness of health and social development, strongly grounding these in a framework of human rights: "Public health is the science and art of preventing disease, prolonging life and promoting mental and physical health through the organized community effort for the sanitation of environment, the control of communicable infections, the education of the individual in personal hygiene, the organization of medical and nursing services for the early diagnosis and preventive treatment of disease, and the development of social machinery to ensure for every individual a standard of living adequate for the maintenance of health, so organizing these benefits as to enable every citizen to realize his birthright of health and longevity."[33] For observers who saw social and medical problems as intimately connected, economic development could be a mixed blessing. On one hand, it made the financing of new social programs possible. On the other, economic development was also implicated in many of the problems facing dependent territories in the late

1940s and 1950s, such as the rise in cases of juvenile delinquency and the spread of epidemic disease in rapidly industrializing urban areas. With increasingly mobile populations, colonial officials claimed that it had become harder to track down families for routine medical examinations and follow-up vaccines.[34] According to critics of empire, ill-conceived economic development policies had resulted in a wide range of problems, many of which they connected to the social dislocation and "detribalization" that had been brought about by rapidly changing social structures.[35]

The final reports that emanated from the special committee only loosely papered over these tensions between the two sides. Disagreements over the root causes of ongoing health and social problems were often readily apparent in the texts. According to the report from its 1952 session, "much has been done to combat epidemic and endemic disease and to reduce infant mortality," but "the creation of a more healthy population, capable of increased production and better living, still remains the ultimate objective of all development policies and the essential condition for economic and social expansion."[36] In other instances, the reports were much more explicit in their critiques of colonial governance. The same 1952 report, for instance, highlighted the social disruption that colonialism had caused, and called for a "new foundation . . . on which the individual can build a new expression of his responsibility to his family and his community."[37] While colonialism may have brought hospitals and vaccines, it also brought a host of disruptions that would now need to be addressed by the incipient social services in these territories.

This shifting emphasis on social questions, however, did not eliminate concerns for basic health provisions. Rather, these became embedded in demands for greater self-sufficiency and well-being. Indeed, the social policy recommendations enumerated by the committee went hand in hand with recommendations to bring modern medicine to both urban and rural areas, to coordinate curative care and preventative public health measures, and to underpin these efforts with the "decentralization of operations and a mobilization of the people's interest." In one UN report on public health administration in dependent territories, the authors urged colonial administrators to consider the effects of health on economic development and to promote "the understanding of economic, social and psychological considerations by officers of the public health departments."[38] Medical and social concerns, the report argued, were intimately connected, and the expansion of these services should serve the ultimate goal of political independence. Concerns about the physical and social body had become, in the arena of the UN, inextricably linked to demands for political rights in the colonial world.

Since the cost of many of the recommended health and social programs exceeded the meager budgets of colonial governments, many of the special committee's recommendations focused on the ways that international institutions could support them through technical assistance programs.[39] The UN and its specialized agencies offered assistance in scientific research, social policy development, community organization, the rehabilitation of juvenile delinquents, and campaigns against malnutrition and epidemic disease.[40] Despite the breadth of these programs, however, little funding was actually available to support them on the local level. International aid thus usually took the form of international experts who acted as consultants. Colonial delegations contended that in reality, technical "assistance was available on a relatively modest scale" only. Moreover, since the UN had "emphasized the need of experts to be briefed on local conditions . . . this was where persons already serving in the Territories had advantage over international experts." Colonial officials were wary of allowing foreign personnel to work on the ground in the colonies and argued that international technical assistance was a poor substitute for financial support that could bolster programs that were already being offered by European governments in their colonial empires.[41]

On the whole, colonial officials viewed the expanding mandate of the UN Special Committee on Information from Non-self-governing Territories with extreme trepidation. Some French delegates to the UN saw the committee as a thinly veiled attempt to create an unofficial oversight apparatus for dependent territories that did not fall under the purview of the Trusteeship Council, an effort that they believed was in direct violation of the UN Charter.[42] Despite the ban on political discussions, the special committee regularly provided a forum for scathing critiques of colonial rule, especially from the Indian, Soviet, and Philippine delegations, which charged that alongside "economic exploitation" and "racial discrimination," the information provided by colonial governments pointed to "low standards of living and a lack of health and educational facilities."[43] In one meeting, the Soviet representative claimed that colonial governments "had condemned the indigenous populations of [dependent] Territories to an existence characterized by starvation and abject poverty under conditions of total lack of rights and ignorance."[44] Criticism at the special committee often provoked a flurry of anxious correspondence between officials at the French Ministry of Foreign Affairs and the Ministry of Overseas France, where officials worried about the negative publicity that those critiques could generate.[45]

Perhaps even more threatening to colonial sovereignty, however, were not the outright condemnations of the evils of colonial rule but rather the committee's orientation toward the principle of "indigenization," or the replacement of European personnel, values, languages, and social structures with indigenous ones.[46] By 1955, what had started out as a discussion about collecting data on health and social conditions had become a conversation about incorporating the political aspirations of local populations into social development schemes. The participation of native peoples was, according to the 1955 special committee report, necessary for any social policy "that aims at more than furnishing palliatives for immediate evils or perpetuating a paternalism that will prevent the development of local and territorial initiative." The goal of any social program should be to "study, alleviate and remedy the social problems which now face all communities, having particular regard to the problems arising from the contact of cultures and economic, political and social changes." At the UN, then, anticolonial delegations were now explicitly making the connection between poor living conditions and the political and economic changes that occurred as a result of colonial rule. The 1955 report argued that social development should be aimed at instilling in dependent populations the "moral and civic consciousness" necessary for them to participate in the evolution of their own society and "take an increasing share in the conduct of their own affairs."[47]

While both colonial governments and anticolonial delegations to the UN used the framework of "development" to talk about improving the lives of people living in dependent territories, each side meant something very different by their use of the term. The special committee's reports emphasized the need to build more sanitary housing for Africans, to provide more extensive health education, and, above all, to facilitate the participation of indigenous populations in every aspect of medical care and social services. For anticolonial delegations to the committee, these efforts were part and parcel of a broader effort to promote self-sufficiency and, ultimately, independence.

Figure 2.3. Fourth session of the Special Committee on Information from Non-self-governing Territories, 18 August 1953. At the rostrum (*left to right, front row*): Sergio Armando Frazão, of Brazil, Vice-Chairman; Victor Hoo, assistant secretary-general of the UN for the Department of Trusteeship and Information from Non-self-governing Territories; A. H. Loomes, of Australia, chairman; M. M. Wilfrid Benson and Arnold V. Kunst, respectively director and deputy director of the Division of Information from Non-self-governing Territories; and Lakshmi N. Menon, of India, Rapporteur. UN Photo / AF.

For colonial delegations, such as the French, they were an effort to make good on the unfulfilled promises of the civilizing mission, which threatened to undermine colonial sovereignty in an era of increasing international involvement. While the term *development* may have replaced that of the *mission civilisatrice*, for colonial officials the goals of these two projects remained closely connected.[48] For opponents of empire, on the other hand, development was not about reimagining the role that European governments could play in their overseas territories. Rather, it was a way to reenvision the role that local populations—with the help of international organizations—could play in shaping their own futures.

Marketing Colonial Health to an International Public

Given their growing disapproval of the role that the special committee had come to play as a forum for anticolonialism—in addition to the emerging consensus among colonial governments that the technical discussions that took place in the committee were unproductive—it is perhaps surprising that the French government continued to participate in the committee over the course of the 1950s.[49] Despite their frequent complaints that the committee was overstepping its mandate, French officials took its role as a forum for international public discussion extremely seriously. Their ongoing participation in the work of the committee was linked to French efforts to promote their repackaged vision of empire to a global audience, as well as to a desire to show France's commitment to changing norms of international cooperation in the postwar world.[50]

A 1948 publication entitled *What the United Nations Is Doing for Non-self-governing Territories* explained that part of the UN's mission was to "strike a harmonious balance between the aspirations of colonial peoples on one hand and the responsibilities of the colonial governments on the other."[51] While the UN had no ability to punish colonial governments for abuses in their overseas territories, as a forum for public discussion, the UN did have the power to shape colonial policy in indirect ways. By collecting information about the social and economic conditions in which millions of dependent people across the globe lived, the special committee had the ability to open up the inner workings of colonial governance to a broad international public. As Jozef Winiewicz, a Polish delegate to the UN General Assembly, explained during a 1949 session, "Chapter XI of the Charter has lifted the veil that hid from the rest of humanity the lives and destinies of the two hundred million inhabitants of non-autonomous territories . . . it is now up to the United Nations to see that the rights of indigenous peoples are respected."[52]

The data that the committee collected allowed critics of empire to draw comparisons between dependent territories, their metropolitan counterparts, and independent territories across the globe. They also allowed colonialism's detractors to offer critiques and to make substantive recommendations about best practices.[53] According to French legal scholar André Mathiot, the ability to shape "the force of public opinion" was one of the most effective means of action available to the UN. Indeed, given its inability to impose sanctions on its members for bad behavior in their colonies, the ability to openly criticize empire in an international public forum was one of the most important tools the special committee possessed. Any kind of monitoring or control by the committee could only emanate from the *droit de regard* (right of visibility) that Article 73 afforded the UN. Mathiot argued that in many ways this right of visibility was a much greater danger to colonial regimes in the postwar period than any kind of punishment the UN could impose for noncompliance.[54]

Refusing to participate in the work of the special committee, according to high-ranking French officials, would send the wrong message about the French government's willingness to participate in new international forums and, more importantly, to be held accountable for its policies in France's overseas territories. According to a memo from the French Ministry of Foreign Affairs, the French government had agreed to participate in the committee in order to avoid a "troublesome situation, given the liberal principles we profess to espouse, vis-à-vis opponents of the 'colonial system.' Such a situation would shed doubt and general mistrust about French intentions to uphold the engagements they had committed to in signing the Charter." Participating in the committee, moreover, would send the world an affirmative message about France's commitment to "international solidarity," which, this text argued, was one of the foundations of the French political system.[55]

Similar fears about the empire's international reputation shaped the way local French officials in Africa reported data to the UN. In a speech to the Grand Council of AOF in March 1950, Minister of Overseas France Jean Le-Tourneau stated, "It is necessary that everywhere in the world, every man understands that it is with more and more integration, complete and absolute, that France will pursue its efforts in Africa."[56] Despite the wide-reaching structural changes that made Africans citizens of the French Union, however, French officials were hesitant to make the case to the UN that its African territories were fully self-governing, or that the policies and structures that governed those territories were entirely an expression of African interests.[57] As colonial conflicts roiled in other parts of the globe—in Indonesia, Algeria, and Madagascar, for example—it became increasingly important to show that France's civilizing mission in sub-Saharan African had not been a mere smokescreen for economic exploitation, cultural imperialism, and violent conquest. It was critical to demonstrate the contributions that French rule had brought to the realms of public health, economics, social policy, education, and agriculture.

While the technical discussions in the special committee served as an important forum for anticolonialism, these conversations were also an arena where colonial officials could demonstrate their commitment to the principles of progress and development, showcasing their accomplishments in the fields of public health and social policy. Although the French government systematically rejected what it perceived as incremental encroachments by the UN on its sovereignty and autonomy in Africa, in practice many colonial administrators adopted a much more ambiguous position vis-à-vis the obligations set forth in Article 73(e).[58] French officials were acutely aware of the importance of transmitting information to the UN and of the effects—positive and negative—that that information could have on international public opinion.[59] While some French officials rejected the premise of the special committee—calling it a "grandstand for rabble-rousing that produced incitements to revolt and disorder"—the reports themselves were a different story.[60] While he was serving on the French delegation to the Trusteeship Council, Henri Laurentie explained in an interview with United Nations Radio in December 1949 that "an obligation is an obligation."[61] Put even more bluntly by Léon Blum in a *Le Populaire* article from the same month, any resistance to the UN's expanding role in overseeing colonialism would inevitably provoke the questions, "What's going on *chez vous* and what do you have to hide?"[62]

The biggest fear surrounding the transmission of the 73(e) reports was the critiques they could elicit from opponents of empire at the UN. In a 1949 telegram, the director general of political, administrative, and social affairs for AOF reminded public health officials in France's West African territories that any delay in transmitting data to the UN could "produce a dangerous effect and open up our administration to easy criticism."[63] In addition to the timeliness of the reports, head administrators also emphasized the importance of correct and consistent statistics and noted that any mistakes or discrepancies could run the risk of provoking empire's detractors.[64] In a letter to the high commissioner of AOF, the director of political affairs for the Ministry of Overseas France wrote that administrators should take the utmost care with the wording of the reports and should avoid any mention of terms that would evoke the "former colonial system"—such as the word *colony.* He advised them also to avoid any mention of racial discrimination and warned against overemphasizing future projects, which created an opportunity for criticism when reality fell short of best-laid plans.[65]

While part of the approach to submitting data to the UN was to avoid criticism at all costs, many colonial officials also saw these reports as an important propaganda opportunity for the French Union. When soliciting information from the different branches of the colonial administration in Africa, high-ranking officials in Paris and Dakar emphasized the need to focus on progress. A letter from Paul Le Layec, the director general of the interior for AOF, admonished colonial officials for emphasizing the difficulties encountered by their services and reminded them that "the reports that you are required to submit have for their destination an international organization of the highest order and should be composed in a way to present our action in the most favorable light possible." These reports, he noted, had the ultimate goal of "enlightening public opinion on France's work in her overseas territories." Le Layec stressed the importance of emphasizing the advances made as a result of financial cooperation between the metropolitan government and the administrations of overseas territories. Administrators were also asked to highlight the participation of the indigenous population of their territories at all levels of health and social services.[66]

Local officials within the public health services in AOF and AEF appear to have heeded these warnings when composing their reports to the UN. Taken in their entirety, internal colonial health reports from these territories—destined for the Ministry of Overseas France on Rue Oudinot in Paris—paint a picture of an entirely piecemeal system, plagued by administrative ambivalence, an almost constant lack of supplies and personnel, and frequent clashes between colonial officials and African families. Reports that were sent to the UN, however, conjure up an entirely different image of the French colonial health system in Africa. While admitting certain shortcomings, colonial officials suggested a coherent and conscientious system that put the well-being of Africans above other concerns. The introduction to a 1952 report on the protection of children and families, for example, stated that "the French administration in AOF has always considered it its essential duty to protect, to educate the population, and to improve their living conditions. The picture painted by the present report marks an important step in the success of a plan of social policy and action conceived solely of French initiative, long before the establishment of any international recommendations."[67]

The reports highlighted the achievements of the French in the field of public health, such as the conquest of yellow fever and the creation of a medical school in Dakar to train African doctors. By contrast, the reports' authors downplayed the myriad shortcomings of the colonial public health system, blaming problems on the effects of the war and the growing political resistance of Africans—especially women—to European medicine. In places where particular diseases—such as smallpox—still ravaged local populations, reports attributed failures in the medical system to individuals who, "by opposition or negligence, escaped vaccination." Nonexistent services, such as those to treat cancer, were described as "not yet formed."[68] Local officials also tried to put a positive spin on statistics that could elicit criticism from other members of the special committee. The rapidly rising numbers of patients hospitalized per year, for example, were a result of the "growing confidence among the indigenous populations in our medical action," rather than a product of the administration's failure to stop the spread of epidemic disease.[69]

Colonial officials performed a similar sleight of hand when it came to social programs. Struggling to fit the hodgepodge of social and medical services in AOF and AEF under the rubric of "social services," as it was laid out in the standard form, medical officials argued that since many medical services that were available to Africans were free of charge, this system did indeed constitute a kind of "social service." Papering over the very real voids, they claimed that "in fact, the organization of Public Health Services is conceived in such a way that we are dealing here with a gap that is more illusory than real." The same report stated, "The consultations and treatments given to indigenous populations in the dispensaries and maternity clinic are free, as are consultations and specialized treatments offered in hospitals. These no-cost services carry no restriction and do not discriminate based on one's social position or financial situation."[70] Colonial officials claimed that these piecemeal measures to combat infant mortality and epidemic disease formed a kind of de facto social service, whereas in reality only Côte d'Ivoire had actually created an official *service social*.[71]

While many French politicians and colonial officials seem to have genuinely believed that public health was one domain in which French imperialism had done more good than harm, they were also acutely aware of the shortcomings of the French medical establishment in Africa. Despite attempts to blame the effects of the war, or the impact of new political rights, the reality was an uneven and disjointed public health system that was closely tied to colonial imperatives rather than to African needs. As conflicts grew in other parts of the colonial world—both French and non-French—the need to demonstrate French benevolence in sub-Saharan Africa became all the more essential. French officials used the reports they submitted to the UN—especially reports on health and social services—as a way to market the newly formed French Union to a broad international audience and to show that, contrary to Winiewicz's accusations in the UN General Assembly, they did not wish to, "in an age of unprecedented social change[,] . . . maintain the privileges of colonial exploitation, held over from the dark ages."[72]

~

Ultimately the results of this colonial propaganda campaign proved ambiguous. Despite their attempts to portray empire in the best light possible, colonial participation in the special committee inevitability opened up France's empire to the kinds of anticolonial attacks that they had feared all along. Notwithstanding the French government's best efforts to fend off criticism, there was no way to go back to a pre-1945 imperial invisibility. Faced with charges of causing land deterioration, propagating racial discrimination, and keeping their populations "in conditions of ignorance and semi-starvation," colonial governments faced a reality of the postwar period that they had not foreseen at the signing of the UN Charter—a force of public opinion so strong that it could make or break the increasingly tenuous ties between metropole and colony.[73] As Mathiot explained it, the shift in international public opinion in the wake of the war, and the creation of a forum to institutionalize that opinion, had created an environment in which colonial peoples "reclaim[ed] the right to pursue for themselves, with the world as judge, a policy of emancipation."[74]

While the UN could not operate as a colonial tribunal in the strictest sense of the term, every aspect of the UN system of collecting information from dependent territories became, in a sense, an opportunity to judge the political progression of colonial peoples toward self-sufficiency and, ultimately, toward self-government. Although this was never the intent of the colonial governments that participated in the drafting of the UN Charter, the slow evolution of these policies over the course of a decade in effect created a space where every aspect of colonial administration could be measured against these goals. Even discussions about health and social policy eventually tied back to debates about self-sufficiency and political independence. While it is less clear in precisely what ways debates about empire at the UN shaped the daily practices of governance in the French empire, the impact that these discussions would have on the relationships between the empire and global health organizations is undeniable.

CHAPTER THREE

Between Colonial Knowledge and International Expertise

> It would not take long for a [WHO] Africa Office to grow in size and to become a pole of attraction for all of our African "troublemakers," both political and medical. There they would find a ready audience and the only possible outcome would be a decline in our own authority to the benefit of this international organization, whose critique of our sanitary project would be facilitated by multiple contacts with our malcontents.
>
> —Note from Médecin-Général Ambroise Gourvil to the director of political affairs for the Ministry of Foreign Affairs, 1951

In the spring of 1946, doctors and diplomats from across the world assembled at the Palais d'Orsay in Paris to sketch out the parameters for a new international health organization. Representatives to the meetings hoped that through universal participation, this new organization could transcend the limitations of the now-defunct League of Nations Health Organization and achieve a truly global reach. Despite the emphasis on full inclusivity, however, the question of European empires was largely ignored in the discussions. Over the course of several weeks, delegates hemmed and hawed over possible locations for the headquarters, debated the merits of using *health* or *hygiene* in the organization's title, and considered the advantages and disadvantages of different organizational structures. The problems posed by the status of colonial territories, however, remained far from the top of the agenda.

Given the relative inattention to the colonial question at the conference, perhaps one of the most surprising outcomes of these meetings was the creation of an organization that would have the ability to interface with the colonial world in ways that were unavailable to the UN more broadly. While the ability to send visiting missions and field petitions was restricted to the UN Trusteeship Council and its set of charges, the WHO would regularly dispatch medical personnel to a wide range of colonial territories, where they would have the ability to observe conditions on the ground and engage with populations that had no official voice at the UN. Because anticolonial delegations to the UN were already framing their condemnations of empire in terms of social problems such as health, French administrators and doctors were deeply suspicious of any role that the WHO might come to play on the African continent. They feared that through UN technical agencies such as the WHO, opponents of empire at the UN might be able to bring their critiques to bear on the ground in Africa, fueling the existing rumblings of anticolonial nationalism on the continent.

French officials viewed the push for a WHO regional office with particular trepidation. A permanent branch of an international organization installed on African soil ran the risk of driving a wedge between France and its colonies. According to one French official, "Beginning with very minor technical questions, non-autonomous territories might, little by little, be encouraged to develop an identity entirely independent from that of the Metropole."[1] Four years later, in 1951, the health director for AEF, Médecin-Général Ambroise Gourvil, penned a note to the political division of the French Ministry of Foreign Affairs. In the letter, Gourvil made the direct link between questions of a sanitary nature and the broader problem of growing anticolonial sentiment. By opening the door to international medical personnel, the French government would be creating an unprecedented opportunity for foreigners to influence the sanitary *and* political lives of France's African constituents. Colonial doctors also perceived international organizations as a potential threat to the civilizing mission, a way to deny the value of the expertise and scientific know-how that they claimed were at the heart of France's imperial project. If colonial populations could benefit from international expertise and funding, the French Union ran the risk of obsolescence. As the WHO's universalizing impulse began to extend into the African continent in the late 1940s, colonial administrators worried that what was really at stake was nothing short of French sovereignty in the empire.

Faced with this threat, the French government in Paris and its colonial outposts in Dakar and Brazzaville became the most vocal opponents of the

WHO's extension into Africa. In 1947, Belgian, British, and French officials gathered in Paris to discuss the possibility of creating their own technical organization as a means of staving off unwanted international intervention in their African colonies. As the French delegation explained in a memo to the Ministry of Foreign Affairs, "If [regionalization] is imposed on us from the outside, nothing can guarantee that it will not be a means of promoting [international] interference in our affairs, more often than not for imperial aims rather than out of concern for the material and moral well being of dependent peoples. But if, by contrast . . . we can demonstrate through the creation of a viable [regional] organization our desire to satisfy the demands of global public opinion, we will find ourselves in the more advantageous position."[2] Shortly after the founding of the WHO in 1948, French officials, doctors, and technicians joined forces with their Belgian, British, and South African counterparts to launch another kind of cooperative endeavor: the CCTA.[3] French officials believed that interimperial technical cooperation under the aegis of the CCTA could offset the potential threat that UN agencies posed to colonial sovereignty in Africa. This would be a way of keeping Africa safe for empire while also keeping African families safe from epidemic diseases, malnutrition, and the social disruption that resulted from urbanization and industrialization.

Debates about health, development, and colonialism at the UN had the unintended effect of fostering new kinds of technical cooperation between empires, where administrators saw intercolonial cooperation as the only defense against international "interference" in their overseas territories. Ultimately, the doctors and technicians working for the CCTA were unable to prevent the creation of a WHO Regional Office for Africa, and the two organizations were forced into an uneasy coexistence. The ongoing battle between the WHO and the CCTA serves as a useful historical window into two starkly different visions of postwar Africa. The first placed France's African colonies in the broader context of a reimagined French empire, where the French government would renew its commitment to developing its overseas territories and where Africans would enjoy the same rights as their counterparts in metropolitan France. In the second, WHO-sponsored, vision, these territories would serve as blank slates for international development projects, projects that would ultimately place Africans on the path toward self-sufficiency and self-government.

Regionalizing Global Health

In many ways, the WHO was a radical departure from previous collaborative efforts in the fields of medicine and public health. The work that had begun in Paris at the First International Sanitary Conference in 1851 was slow to generate results. The institution that it ultimately produced, the OIHP, was extremely limited in its scope, providing only a system to monitor the global spread of disease.[4] While much further reaching, the League of Nations Health Organization was limited by the US decision to opt out of the league.[5] When negotiations began in 1946 to create a new kind of international health organization, doctors and government representatives hoped to move beyond the limits of these previous organizations to create an institution that would be truly universal in its scope. The new WHO would not only encompass all peoples of the world; it would also adopt a more holistic approach to thinking about health and well-being. According to the preamble of the WHO Constitution, health is not merely the "absence of disease or infirmity" but rather "a state of complete physical, mental and social well-being." Moreover, the constitution affirmed, the "enjoyment of the highest attainable standard of health is one of the fundamental rights of every human being without distinction of race, religion, political belief, economic or social condition."[6]

If universal access to health care was integral to the foundation of the WHO, its creators also acknowledged they could not provide it using a one-size-fits-all model.[7] To respond to the challenge of adapting its work to dramatically different cultures, geographies, and social systems across the world, the WHO Constitution included a provision for "decentralization."[8] By working through a network of regional committees and offices, the WHO could avoid creating an overextended and inefficient bureaucracy and could stay attuned to the widely varying health needs of its constituents. The regions that were delineated during the First World Health Assembly were not required to create a regional branch, but they could vote to do so. While the principle of regionalizing health cooperation was not new—it had been pioneered by the creators of the Pan American Sanitary Bureau at the turn of the century—it was the first time it would be applied on a global scale.[9]

Although each regional organization established by the WHO would be able to maintain a certain degree of autonomy, much of the institutional framework for the regional offices was predetermined by the WHO's constitution. Regional organizations would be composed of both a regional committee staffed by representatives from each member state and a regional office under the charge of a director who would be named by the WHO Executive Council and approved by the members of the regional committee. The purpose of the regional offices was to formulate policies to govern "matters of an exclusively regional character," to convene technical conferences related to health concerns of that region, and to make suggestions to the WHO about how to improve its work there. Despite attempts to steer the ongoing discussions of regionalization away from politics, French officials found themselves fighting an uphill battle. According to a 1951 memo that the French delegation to the WHO Executive Council sent to the Ministry of Foreign Affairs, regionalization was as much about politics as it was about sanitary imperatives: "If multiple States in a region are united, for example, by racial or religious ties, what a privileged terrain the Regional office offers for the defense of their common doctrine."[10]

Indeed, the division of the world into regions was in many ways just as radical as the establishment of a universal health organization. In some ways, it was even more controversial. If imperial boundaries had been the primary dividing lines of the world before 1945, the WHO was proposing to reimagine the globe as six separate regions united by common cultural, climatic, and—most importantly—epidemiological conditions. As delegations to the World Health Assembly assigned countries and territories to the regions of Africa, the Americas, the eastern Mediterranean, Europe, Southeast Asia, and the western Pacific, they were rethinking more than just how health programs would be implemented.[11] They were also providing a way for former colonial territories to reinvent their identities in a world where longstanding European empires were beginning to unravel.[12] The effect was particularly poignant on the African continent, where populations that had lived under colonial rule for decades were beginning to imagine new modes of belonging that could transcend the boundaries previously delineated by European colonizers.

According to a definition set by the First World Health Assembly, the African region was composed of "all Africa south of the 20 degree N. parallel of latitude of the western border to the Anglo-Egyptian Sudan, to its junction with the north border of Belgian Congo, thence eastwards along the northern borders of Uganda and Kenya; and thence southwards along the eastern border of Kenya to the Indian Ocean."[13] A regional office in Africa would thus include the entire African continent, with the exception of North Africa (Morocco, Algeria, Tunisia, Libya, and Egypt) and parts of eastern Africa (including Sudan, Ethiopia, and Somalia). The island territories off the southeastern coast of the continent would be included in the configuration. Included in this region would be several of France's overseas territories, including AOF, AEF, French Cameroon and Togo, Madagascar, and Réunion.[14]

A regional office, once created, would include all member states of the region, regardless of whether those states were independent or were part of a larger colonial entity. This meant that Liberia, France, South Africa and Belgium would all exist on equal footing with one another in a future Africa office of the WHO.[15] When it came to voting on whether to establish that office, however, not all member states had a say. In the decision to create a regional branch of the WHO, only member states whose seat of government was located in that region had the right to submit a formal request. This meant that while France would ultimately be a full member of a future office, only Liberia and South Africa could decide whether the WHO should extend its reach into the African continent.[16]

By 1949, the WHO had already established two regional offices—the Regional Office for Southeast Asia in 1948 and the Regional Office for the Eastern Mediterranean in 1949—and was in the process of establishing regional organizations for Europe and for the Americas.[17] Countries in these regions eagerly sought WHO assistance for a wide range of programs. In 1949, the Regional Office for the Eastern Mediterranean had begun antimalaria operations and the WHO and UNICEF were providing BCG vaccines for an antituberculosis campaign.[18] In the Southeast Asian region, WHO advisers were working with local governments to develop maternal and child health services and were conducting a cholera study in India, in addition to overseeing various malaria projects in the region.[19] In Europe, the WHO was extending many of the projects that had been launched by the United Nations Relief and Rehabilitation Administration at the end of the war, including efforts to increase penicillin production in Eastern Europe and to provide infant and maternal health services in war-devastated countries.[20] But while other WHO regions tested out new modes of cooperation and took advantage of new sources of funding for technical assistance programs,

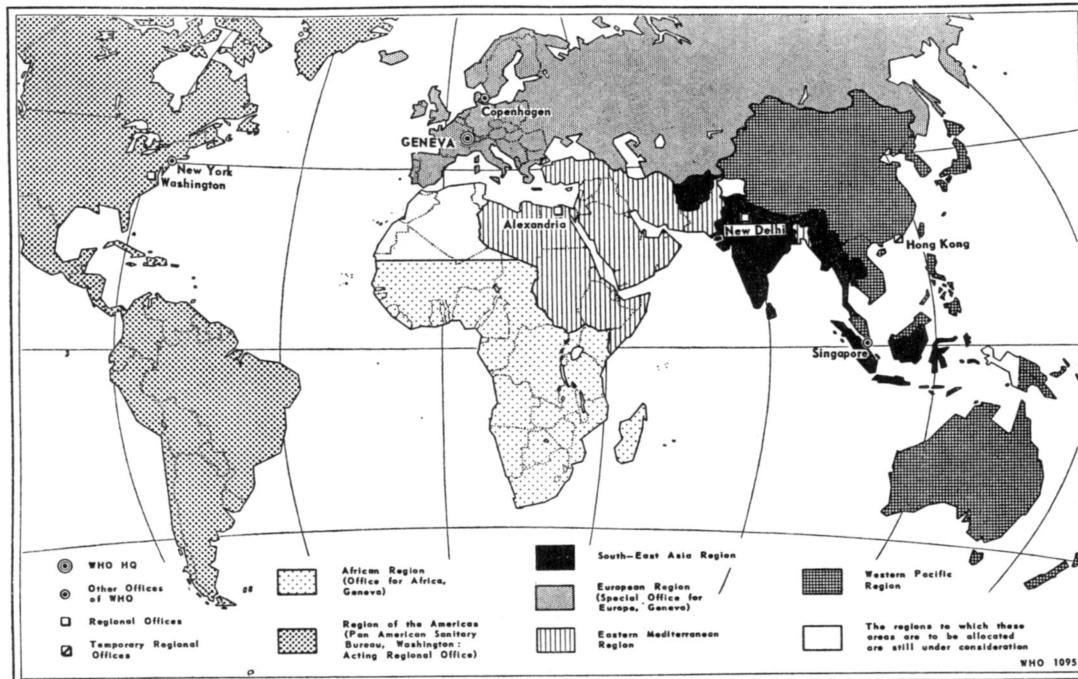

Figure 3.1. Map of WHO regions. Reprinted from *Work of the WHO: 1950, Annual Report of the Director General to the World Health Assembly and the United Nations,* Official Records of the World Health Organization 30 (Geneva: World Health Organization, 1951), 80.

many members of the African region remained reluctant to solicit WHO assistance.

Initially, some French officials were optimistic about the possibilities that the regional structure of the WHO could open up for French medicine. With its far-reaching overseas empire, the French government would technically be a member of each of the six regional offices of the WHO, with its overseas territories ranging from the Caribbean to the French establishments in India.[21] The French delegate to each of the regional committees could thus act as a sanitary attaché to each government in the region where they served. According to one memo, "The World Health Organization gives us access to *all* of the world's health administrations; it gives us considerable means of action over undeveloped countries who are in great need of assistance developing their health services." The regional offices would extend the reach of French medical expertise and would open new markets for French pharmaceuticals and medical technology. More importantly, however, they could bolster France's declining political influence across the globe: "It is necessary for us closely collaborate with the work of the WHO if we do not want to be ousted from the positions of privilege that we still hold in certain countries (ex. Afghanistan or Syria). We can no longer ensure a monopoly once these countries become members of specialized [UN] institutions."[22] In a period of rapid internationalization and shifting geopolitical boundaries, medical expertise could serve as an important bridge between France and the rest of the world.

But if the WHO regional offices were a potential instrument for the French to extend their influence in the postwar world, they were also a vehicle for newly independent states to agitate for the rights of peoples still living under colonial rule. French officials were particularly attuned to this conundrum when it came to negotiating opportunities for global health cooperation in France's African territories, where the path to realizing the goals of the French Union was often uncertain. The fact that only Liberia and South Africa had the ability to vote on the creation of a WHO Africa office made the situation particularly delicate. While French government officials were eager to take advantage of the possibilities for "cultural influence" and "commercial expansion" in other regions, the fact that the African region was primarily constituted by dependent territories under European rule made participation in a WHO Africa office a risky political move for French doctors working on the African continent.[23] As the WHO and other UN agencies advanced the process of regionalization, and as anticolonial voices at the UN grew more strident, French government officials turned instead to new modes of intercolonial diplomacy and technical cooperation in the hopes of staving off unwanted international involvement in their colonial affairs.

Regionalization and the Problem of Empire

In the aftermath of the Second World War, fears that anticolonial delegations to the UN would use international technical agencies to advance their agendas in Africa prompted a series of "colonial conversations" between French, British, and Belgian authorities. Throughout the late 1940s, authorities from these three empires met regularly to discuss the ways they could use intercolonial technical cooperation to respond to a situation of growing African nationalism, expanding US economic interests on the African continent, and the rising tide of anticolonial sentiment at the UN.[24] According to a memo from the French Ministry of Foreign Affairs, "No juridical artifice, no battle over the texts can save us from the interference or the critical eyes of the non-colonial powers. Their tradition of anti-imperialism easily allies itself with the general agitation of recently emancipated people of color to create an entirely new situation in which we need to acclimatize ourselves to living dangerously."[25] French officials posited that an autonomous intercolonial organization would be the best way both to keep international organizations from "interfering" in their African territories and to stave off internal critiques of imperial rule by anticolonial nationalists.[26] The goal of interimperial technical cooperation, as one French official put it, was to help the French create "a solid foundation that we can use to combat our detractors [at the UN] and that can stave off rabble-rousing and political attacks."[27]

In the immediate wake of the war, a series of bilateral initiatives between the British and French governments aimed to promote individual contacts between scientists, doctors, and technicians, culminating in a medical conference and a veterinary conference in 1946. The British government also launched exchanges with Belgian experts about measures to control epidemic diseases.[28] These early collaborative efforts aimed to help technical personnel improve their skills, exchange knowledge, and promote better living standards for colonial populations. As the possibilities for cooperation expanded and as tensions mounted at the UN, these exchanges began to take on an increasingly political orientation. If technical collaboration would help colonial governments fulfill their obligations to promote the social and economic development of their dependent territories, colonial officials also believed that cooperation could forestall direct UN involvement in their African territories.[29] Although French officials were uncertain whether any UN agency had the jurisdiction to send a visiting mission to an African territory without the consent of the administering government, they looked warily to other areas of the "developing world"—such as Haiti and the Amazon basin—where UNESCO and the FAO were sending teams to build "a synthetic approach to dealing with underdeveloped territories."[30]

In February 1947, René Massigli, France's ambassador to Great Britain, wrote in a letter to French Foreign Minister Georges Bidault that while cooperation between European empires in Africa "will not shut the mouths of the systematic adversaries of the colonial system," it would provide some support "for the defense that our representatives to the Assembly of the United Nations are called to present."[31] In April, Marius Moutet, the minister of overseas France, echoed these sentiments in a letter to Massigli: "On the international level, it will not be as a coalition of intimidated powers that we will succeed in halting the flood of just or unjust criticisms that have been made of our colonial project. The justification for our presence can only be found, in the eyes of the world, in our positive contribution of economic, social, and human value. Through their technical collaboration, the coordination of their research, and through the mutual enrichment of their methods, the governing powers can prove that they have substituted their outmoded concept of rivalrous imperialism for one of common responsibility."[32] Henri Laurentie, the director of political affairs for the French Ministry of Foreign Affairs, spearheaded the early discussions with the British Colonial Office. Laurentie, who had spent the bulk of his career in Cameroon, Chad, and then Brazzaville, was particularly attuned to both local economic and political imperatives, as well as to the growing interest that outside parties—particularly the United States and the UN—had in "developing" sub-Saharan Africa. As one of the primary architects of the 1944 Brazzaville Conference, Laurentie was also a firm believer in the capacity of the state to improve the lives of its citizens through concerted planning.[33]

In May 1947, delegates from France, Great Britain, and Belgium assembled under the gilded ceilings of the Salon de l'Horloge in the Ministry of Foreign Affairs. There to discuss the growing threat to their empires from the international community, they debated how they might respond to that threat with new approaches to imperial cooperation.[34] The discussions focused on a broad range of technical problems, including sleeping sickness and malaria control, vaccination campaigns, soil and forest preservation, irrigation, and transimperial communications.[35] While it is clear that the participants in the tripartite discussions saw some intrinsic value in developing technical cooperation between their respective governments, they frequently framed their work as a response to criticisms at the UN. In their discussions of a potential conference on the tsetse fly, for example, French delegate Robert Delavignette noted the importance of inviting both physicians and entomologists, "to give [the conference] the practical character that the Commission wants to show the United Nations."[36] Another delegate suggested inviting UN observers to a conference on medical and technical education in Africa, "to demonstrate that we are making an effort." According to Delavignette, such a conference would be a useful way of responding to criticism at the UN "that the Belgians, the French and the British train fewer doctors for the African territories than other countries." The conference, he argued, would be an opportunity to demonstrate "the great difficulties than arise in the training of indigenous personnel." Such a conference would also respond to African demands for broader access to the professions.[37]

Although the delegates from the three European colonial governments expressed a desire to respond to criticisms made at the UN, no Africans were included in the initial discussions of expanding interimperial cooperation, and delegates were wary of including them in future gatherings. According to the Belgian representative Pierre Ryckmans, former governor of the Belgian Congo, "It would be regrettable to invite Africans incapable of effectively participating in the work of a conference because they would realize they were merely being used as propaganda. As such, black Africans would have no place at a medical conference, but by contrast, if it was a question of livestock, the presence of local chiefs would be very useful." Moutet had a slightly more inclusive perspective, noting that Africans in France's overseas territories were beginning to enter the liberal professions. He warned, however, against creating a situation in which Africans could use the meetings for the purposes of "agitation."[38]

If the delegates were reluctant to include Africans from their own territories in future technical ventures, they also hesitated to include Liberia—the only sovereign state in the region—in their collaborative endeavors. One French memo noted that while Liberia's "geographic position makes its inclusion necessary in certain cases," the Liberian government often included American advisers in their delegations to technical meetings, and the memo explained that this might provide a back door for US interests into Europe's African territories. Questions of race also arose in debates about whether to include South Africa. Despite their own propensity to exclude African perspectives, French delegates openly condemned apartheid in South Africa, noting that to include them in upcoming gatherings would be "embarrassing."[39]

Over the course of three days, delegates discussed fields of possible collaboration and debated the nature of the UN threat and the most efficient ways to combat it. The French government believed that the surest way to preempt UN intervention in France's African colonies was not simply to sponsor a series of conferences in the fields of medicine, agriculture, and mass education, but rather to create permanent institutions to oversee this ongoing cooperation. According to a French memo on the May talks, "these institutions should be neither too specialized . . . nor too general so as to avoid confusion between them and real 'general commissions' like the Caribbean Commission," which might put French territories at risk of "foreign intrusions." The French envisioned separate offices to deal with different overarching questions, such as nutrition, malaria, or cocoa production.[40] After the three days of discussions, government officials from France, Great Britain, and Belgium quickly set plans in motion for future talks, and sketched out preliminary agendas for conferences on sleeping sickness, forest conservation, soil erosion, rural economy, and medical education.[41] Despite concerns about the political implications of involving the South African government, both Portugal and South Africa were invited to participate in the upcoming meetings, and delegates from Rhodesia soon joined them.[42]

Despite the wide range of fields in which French colonial officials sought to expand cooperation with other European empires in Africa, they were acutely aware of financial limitations on colonial development and of the growing criticism of colonial "underdevelopment" at the UN.[43] In April 1949, a meeting of high-level officials in the French Ministry of Foreign Affairs pointed to the dilemma of ongoing funding constraints and the need to invest in the empire at a moment in time when the structures of colonial governance were increasingly coming under fire at the UN.[44] Almost a decade later, on the eve of decolonization in French Africa, Jacques Kosciusko-Morizet, the French delegate to the Trusteeship Council, would give a speech lambasting the hypocrisies of UN debates about colonialism and development. According to Kosciusko-Morizet, the French deserved praise, not opprobrium, for their development efforts in Africa. Just a glance at the UN statistical yearbook, he noted, would show "by far that among the great evolved countries, France is the one that has made the greatest investments in favor of the underdeveloped world." The creation of FIDES, Kosciusko-Morizet explained, had been particularly instrumental in expanding medical, social, and economic infrastructure in the empire. But rather than lauding French achievements in the field of colonial development, he complained, "they depict our Africa as that of 1900" and "they compare underdeveloped dependent territories with the most developed countries and not with long-independent countries that are just as underdeveloped." Instead of drawing positive lessons from France's investment in its overseas territories in order to help out "their brothers in underdevelopment," Kosciusko-Morizet argued that anticolonial delegations to the UN had used the annual reports submitted by the French government to build their case against the French empire.[45]

These tensions between UN and French visions of postwar development, already palpable in the late 1940s, forced the founding members of the CCTA to frame their contributions in terms of their unrivaled expertise. Alexandre Parodi, one of the French representatives to the Trusteeship Council in 1949, explained, "In a world where, more and more, we can only defend our [colonial] project with technique, the quality of our practitioners is precious. Without financial resources all we have is our technical know-how." "The colonial question," he continued, "is one of the biggest concerns in French diplomacy. So we need to give overseas France the maximum support possible." Parodi echoed the belief that Laurentie—also present at the meeting—had expressed in earlier years that a unified intercolonial technical apparatus was the only way to put a stop to the "intrusion" of the UN into European colonial empires in Africa. While an office had been created, for example, to oversee cooperation related to sleeping sickness prevention, the failure to address other diseases left the door open to WHO involvement in other fields of health, such as nutrition and malaria. What was needed, according to Laurentie, was "a central office, of an administrative nature, responsible for negotiating with outside parties, and for investigating funding sources. It could be called: the African Institute for Technical Cooperation."[46]

Negotiating Intercolonial Cooperation

The name suggested by Laurentie didn't stick, but the idea of an umbrella organization to oversee the various cooperative projects did. Despite its waning interest in the project, the British government convened a meeting at the Colonial Office in London for September 1949 to finalize a plan for what this organization would look like.[47] Although the delegates from France, Great Britain, and Belgium had been open to including other governments in their conferences, the idea of founding a more permanent institution once again raised thorny questions about the possibility of associating themselves with the blatantly racist policies of South Africa—especially if the French chose to include Africans in the organization. Delavignette stated bluntly in an April 1949 meeting between representatives from the Ministry of Foreign Affairs and the Ministry of Overseas France, "If I wanted to torpedo the experiment, I would just invite the whole world to join." In the end, however, French hesitations over expanding membership lost out to British diplomatic concerns about excluding other anglophone territories in Africa.[48]

International developments in 1949 prompted French officials—especially Laurentie—to push for the strongest possible organization for technical cooperation in Africa. On the other side of the Atlantic, American interests were quickly turning to the problems of postwar international development. In his 1949 inaugural address, US president Harry Truman proposed "a bold new program for making the benefits of our scientific advances and industrial progress available for the improvement and growth of underdeveloped areas."[49] Later that year, using newly available American funds, the UN approved an "Expanded Program of Technical Assistance" to provide technical experts, training facilities, and materials to "underdeveloped countries."

Rather than focusing on industrial development, these programs aimed to improve social welfare conditions in these areas and to raise the standard of living for their inhabitants.[50]

These new funding sources, according to Laurentie, gave the United States and the UN renewed leverage in what French officials perceived as their unending quest to meddle in colonial affairs. UN technical assistance, Laurentie explained, would serve as a "clever smokescreen" for the Americans to take stock of the economic opportunities in sub-Saharan Africa. The French feared that the UN—out of gratitude for US funding—would then call on American technicians to work on the African continent. This infusion of cash from the United States would, moreover, allow UN agencies such as the FAO and the WHO to put their critiques of empire into action: "Their usual anti-colonialism . . . will lead them, naturally, in one form or another, to install themselves in our territories . . . thus far only the absence of funds has limited their indiscretion. Now they will be richer than ever and their fever is growing. To let them act as they please would be to impose on our experts and our technicians a *capitis diminutio,* to allow our authority overseas to suffer a serious blow, and to permit the United Nations to disseminate their deleterious propaganda within the confines of the French Union itself." The only way to prevent this, Laurentie believed, was to further strengthen the cooperative efforts of the "African powers" and to present a united front against international "intrusion."[51]

The French delegation arrived in London with competing instructions from the Ministry of Overseas France and the Ministry of Foreign Affairs, which—according to Laurentie—severely hampered their ability to put France's vision into action. He believed, however, that the meeting had put them well on the way to achieving their goal of formulating an institution that could "channel" UN technical assistance, as well as funds from Truman's Point Four Program.[52] Not everyone in the French administration, however, felt the same enthusiasm that Laurentie did for creating new venues for technical cooperation between colonial empires. Opposition from the Direction of Economic Affairs in the Ministry of Overseas France prompted Laurentie to pen a letter to Foreign Minister Robert Schuman, entreating him to support the project. He wrote that while France and its empire desperately needed international financial support, "the US has everything to win, and France is at risk of losing big." The French language was at risk of losing its position as the lingua franca of science and medicine, and, Laurentie explained, "any tendency on our parts towards mediocrity, physical or mental laziness, and anachronism will be rapidly and irremediably punished by the disappearance of French influence in technical domains, not just in the world but also in France and the French Union." Not only did Laurentie want the French government to support the creation of an official organization for intercolonial technical cooperation, but he also wanted his superiors to commit French scientific leadership to shaping its path in the long term.[53]

Growing anticolonial sentiment at the UN eventually led both ministries to agree to the general terms of the organization, but several important questions remained unanswered. Would the organization deal only with technical questions, or would it be asked to engage in economic matters as well? Would American observers be welcome to sit in on both technical conferences and regular sessions of the intergovernmental committee? In what capacity would Africans be encouraged to participate in the organization's work? And finally, should independent African states such as Liberia and Ethiopia be invited to join? In anticipation of the meeting between the (now) six governments that would form the new intercolonial organization, representatives from the French Ministry of Foreign Affairs and Ministry of Overseas France met in December 1949 to set out France's goals for the organization. According to the meeting's attendees, the most salient points were the construction of an organization that would be strong enough to offset any regional branches of the different UN agencies but weak enough to avoid encroaching on French sovereignty in France's African territories.[54] Acutely aware of the accusations being made against the European colonial administrations at the UN—especially by Indian delegate Benegal Shiva Rao—some attendees suggested the possibility of including Liberia and Ethiopia in order to give the organization a truly regional character and to "avoid the possibility that our overseas representatives perceive our cooperation as a reversion to the old model of colonialism at the expense of recent reforms."[55]

After several days of discussion in January 1950, the governments of France, Great Britain, Belgium, the South African Union, Portugal, and Rhodesia voted to establish the CCTA. Its scope, according to its charter, included "all domains affecting the wellbeing of populations in their territories in sub-Saharan Africa," with an emphasis on scientific and medical research that could jointly benefit those territories. Its primary functions would include convening scientific and medical conferences, assisting member governments in setting up new technical agencies, and making "recommendations to the Member Governments with a view to the formulation of joint requests for technical assistance from international organisations"—in other words, acting as an intermediary between colonial governments and UN agencies.[56] The Permanent Inter-African Bureau for Tsetse and Trypanosomiasis, the Inter-African Bureau of Epizootic Diseases, the Inter-African Labor Institute, and the Inter-African Bureau for Soils and Rural Economy would all fall under the umbrella of the CCTA.[57]

In certain regards, the creation of the CCTA was a revolutionary development. While intercolonial cooperation was certainly not unprecedented, never before had colonial governments in Africa signed on to such an extensive collaborative endeavor.[58] In other ways, however, this new organization had a fundamentally conservative aim and the men who ran the CCTA were extremely wary of overextending the organization's reach. One of the primary tasks of the organization's secretariat—which would be established in 1952—was to ensure "the best utilization of technical resources and scientific knowledge in the interest of progress in Africa, *without the creation of a new super-bureaucracy*."[59] Colonial officials contrasted this approach with that of the WHO, which they accused of creating an overstretched system with no real experience in the regions the organization purported to be helping. In Africa, colonial officials argued that the task of providing health services to Africans should be left to colonial doctors who had years of local experience.

Although they would ultimately be forced to develop a working relationship with the WHO Regional Office for Africa, the CCTA's members consistently suggested that the WHO was attempting to impose its own agenda in Africa, with little concern for the on-the-ground realities of life on the continent. The CCTA, for its part, claimed insider status as an institution "concerned primarily with Africa's needs, with developing mutual assistance between the territories of the region that were already almost all equipped with institutions adequate for pursuing their long term goals." The efforts of the CCTA, they contended, were not "subject to the ever-changing whims of interests external to the African continent." Member states believed that the purpose of the CCTA should be to respond to "African criteria, rather than global criteria that were all too often inapplicable."[60] By "African criteria," the CCTA's founders meant colonial criteria, seeking no input from Africans as they sketched out the parameters of their new organization.

In their publications, members of the CCTA were quick to assert the successes that colonial governments had achieved on their own, pointing out that projects overseen by individual governments could be even more effective than collaborative efforts. One CCTA publication stated that the adage "Sickness knows no bounds" was "one of the most banal clichés" and suggested that critics may have exaggerated the ongoing difficulties in the domain of African public health: "The truth is . . . the methods followed by the various governing powers in sub-Saharan Africa have often been very different and yet, there is no doubt that over the course of the past fifty years, Africa had ceased to be a particularly insalubrious continent." CCTA officials and technicians emphasized the pragmatic nature of cooperation between colonial governments on the African continent, framing it as a basis for sharing scientific and technical expertise rather than an attempt to supplant existing colonial health programs.[61]

As the earliest official inter-African organization for technical cooperation, the CCTA was setting an important precedent for what kinds of cooperation would be acceptable to colonial governments in the postwar era. While it appeared that the earlier, more isolated approaches of individual empires were being abandoned in favor of more cooperative efforts, these programs took care not to step on the toes of colonial administrations. They focused on sharing expertise and technical information rather than on coordinating programs and policies on the ground. But if the ultimate goal of establishing new modes of intercolonial cooperation was to keep the UN and UN agencies such as the WHO out of Africa, their efforts proved to be insufficient. As officials from the six founding members were working to establish the CCTA, South Africa and Liberia were also setting in motion the establishment of the very organization that the colonial governments had hoped to forestall: the WHO Regional Office for Africa.

The WHO's Threat to Imperial Autonomy

Because South Africa was a member of the CCTA (Liberia was not), South African officials had to carefully weigh the diplomatic costs against the benefits of requesting an African regional office of the WHO. In a memo to the other CCTA member states, the South African delegation outlined the advantages and disadvantages of setting the process in motion, focusing on the importance of international public opinion and the need to obtain international funding for African health programs. The memo stated that by creating a WHO Regional Office for Africa, the different administrations in Africa would be able to "demonstrate to the world the desire of the States concerned in Africa to improve the health of African peoples; and conversely not to deny to Africa the benefits of modern medicine and health." The South African government also expressed a desire to "fit into the accepted principle of regionalization being rapidly applied by the rest of the world" and to "obtain a pro-rata share of WHO advantages, possibly in rivalry with other Regions."[62]

The issue of whether a regional organization needed to be established in order for member states of that region to receive WHO funding was hotly debated in meetings between the African member states. Both Britain and the Union of South Africa argued that a regional organization was needed in order to benefit from the WHO's technical assistance programs. A close reading of the WHO Constitution by the French delegation later showed this to be incorrect.[63] While the French were reluctant to agree that rejecting a WHO Africa office would be akin to depriving their African territories of an important vehicle for progress, the South Africans made the explicit link between the involvement of the WHO in Africa and the future of the continent. According to the South African government, "Since the development of Africa is a direct function of the control of African maladies and menaces to public health . . . we would be wrong to dismiss the crucial importance of a Regional Organization for Africa."[64]

Explaining that the process of regionalization had already been successfully set in motion in other areas of the world, the South African government contended that the creation of a regional office in Africa would give the WHO an opportunity to make a positive contribution to African development. According to their memo, "If the Regional Office for Africa of the WHO is created, and when it is, it will be called on to become a technical element of fundamental importance in all matters concerning development in Africa. Public Health being the essential factor in all plans for Africa (in matters relating to policy, society, industry, agriculture, science, military and communications), this means that the Regional Office will exercise a considerable influence, directly or indirectly."[65] Conversely, South African officials feared that the refusal to create a regional WHO office in Africa would open up the African states to criticism from the international community, especially because it "may well be argued that no continent has greater need for health and medical progress than Africa." Such a reaction from other members of the WHO thus had the potential to create "an embarrassing situation." In an effort to quell the fears of their colonial colleagues, members of the South African delegation reminded the other member states of the CCTA that "a WHO African Regional Organization is limited to African Member States and would offer no direct right for extra-African powers to interfere in African affairs."[66] The problem of potential interference, however, was one that would haunt the relationship between the French colonial administration and the WHO until the independence of France's sub-Saharan African territories in 1958 and 1960.

On 18 February 1949, South African prime minister Daniel François Malan submitted a proposal to the WHO to establish a regional organization for Africa.[67] Despite South African reassurances that a WHO office in Africa would pose no threat to colonial sovereignty, the proposal set off a wave of frantic communication between the French Ministry of Foreign Affairs, the Ministry of Overseas France, and the French delegation to the WHO. While there was little that could be done to stop the proposal from being approved, the French delegation to the WHO noted in a memo to the health division of the Ministry of Overseas France that it planned to do everything in its power to delay the founding of an Africa office, since its creation would establish an important precedent for the involvement of other UN agencies in French Africa, including the UN Economic and Social Council itself. Having already reached out to the other colonial delegations via the French embassies in London, Lisbon, and Brussels, the authors of the note warned of the danger of allowing the WHO to "interfere directly and in a permanent fashion in the administration of non-autonomous territories in Africa" and of the financial burden it would create for its member states.[68] According to the French delegation, delaying the creation of a regional organization would allow more time to develop cooperative efforts within the framework of the CCTA. This, they argued, would be crucial for offsetting the potential influence of a WHO office for Africa.[69]

The Ministry of Overseas France, for its part, was more optimistic about the potential for using the CCTA as a counterbalance to the WHO Africa office, which, ministry officials argued, was bound to succeed "sooner or later." In a letter to the Ministry of Foreign Affairs, D. G. Pirie, representing the Ministry of Overseas France, pointed out that members of the CCTA would hold a majority in a future regional organization, and although they were unable to either propose or reject the creation of a WHO Regional Office for Africa, once one was created, they would enjoy equal participation with the two sovereign states of Liberia and South Africa. Pirie suggested that the governments of the CCTA hold a separate preliminary session before each meeting of a future regional organization in order to strategize as a group and coordinate a joint stance on the various issues that would be discussed at the annual meeting. But while Pirie was more optimistic about the future of a WHO regional office, ultimately his position fell in line with that of the Foreign Ministry, supporting their attempts to delay the WHO's work in Africa.[70]

Despite the best diplomatic efforts of the French government, however, the delegations from the other colonial governments ultimately decided that impeding the installation of a WHO office in Africa would do more harm than good. The Portuguese delegation responded that in spite of its opposition to the WHO office in Africa—which it believed would incur significant expenses for the Portuguese administration in Africa—it was too late to take action.[71] Massigli reported similar sentiments in Britain, where government officials believed any attempt to delay the creation of the office might be politically dangerous for Great Britain, especially given the enthusiasm that both Liberia and South Africa had shown for the proposal.[72]

Faced with this lack of support, French officials decided it would be politically unwise to pursue their opposition: "It goes without saying that if the majority found themselves in favor of the creation of a regional office for Africa, the [French] delegation would not, despite the various disadvantages attached to the creation of such an organism, be able to retreat in systematic opposition, which would—besides being totally ineffective—risk exposing us to anti-French propaganda, in our territories and in international public opinion." Once the office was created, it would be necessary to seek out a means to "avoid too accentuated an intrusion on the part of the WHO in our administration in order to conserve for the latter absolute control over any and all operations the WHO may be called to undertake in our territories."[73] After failing to stop the creation of a WHO regional office, French officials could only hope to stem the tide of international involvement into the political and social affairs of France's African territories.

~

For French officials—both in Paris and on the ground in Africa—the installation of a WHO Regional Office for Africa represented a very real threat to colonial sovereignty. At a time when the WHO and other UN agencies were extending their universalizing approach to development throughout the world, European colonial governments were launching their own campaign to stop international "intrusion" in their overseas empires. Although the CCTA, at times, reflected a good-faith effort to improve social welfare conditions in Africa through new modes of interimperial technical cooperation, a lack of funding and political will limited the organization's ability to undertake the kinds of large-scale projects that the WHO was sponsoring in other areas. The French government was ultimately unsuccessful in using the CCTA to block the establishment of the WHO Regional Office for Africa, and the tensions between the two organizations lingered through almost a decade of coexistence. This relationship would become even more fraught when representatives selected Brazzaville, the capital of AEF, to become the site for the WHO's African headquarters, giving international actors an unprecedented opportunity to shape the landscape of French colonial rule on the African continent.

CHAPTER FOUR

The World Health Organization Comes to Brazzaville

> We would like to note that all of our fears about the installation of the WHO in Africa have now been confirmed and to express that we were in fact correct not to cede to the argument of the South Africans, supported by the British, that "the committee will not be dangerous." . . . It is clear now that this view was entirely incorrect.
>
> —French memo on the regional policies of the WHO, 1949

ONCE PLANS TO ESTABLISH a regional office were under way, delegates to the WHO Regional Committee for Africa worked to set an agenda, develop a budget, and select a location for the office's headquarters. While colonial territories were not barred from throwing their hats in the ring as contenders for the site of the future headquarters, the chosen city did need to demonstrate a commitment to the same progressive ideals that inspired the work of the UN and the WHO. This included, most importantly, a commitment to racial equality and equal access to social goods and services. The chosen city also needed to possess adequate urban infrastructure to logistically house a regional branch of a global organization and be well connected to the rest of the world via an effective and efficient transportation system. After much debate, delegates to the WHO Regional Committee for Africa landed on the city of Brazzaville, the capital of AEF, as the location for its regional office.

The decision to invite the WHO to install its headquarters in a French territory was a crucial test of French colonial reforms, a test that Brazzaville would come dangerously close to failing. In spite of the far-reaching structural changes that replaced the French empire with the French Union, equality on paper did not always mean equality in practice, and living conditions in Brazzaville remained those of an unevenly developed colonial city. By inviting a progressive international organization like the WHO to install its African headquarters in one of the two capitals of France's sub-Saharan African empire, the French government was taking a significant risk. Although the 1946 constitution had indeed brought meaningful changes to the lives of Africans living in France's overseas territories, the legacies of colonial violence, inequality, and underdevelopment nonetheless proved hard to shake. When French officials proposed Brazzaville as a potential site for the WHO's African headquarters, they were confident that AEF's capital could serve as an example of France's modernizing efforts. They hoped that this would be an opportunity to show the broader global community that independence from a metropolitan government was not the only path to decolonization and that equality could be achieved within the structure of a new kind of political, social, and cultural union. Within a matter of mere months after the office's installation, however, the city of Brazzaville became the object of passionate international criticism. Top WHO officials, having had the chance to observe conditions on the ground, questioned the suitability of this colonial city to house the WHO Regional Office for Africa. The French administration soon found itself in what many high-ranking officials considered to be a colonial public relations crisis of global proportions.

The conflict surrounding the creation of the WHO regional office in Brazzaville illuminates the collision between French and international visions of African development. In the immediate postwar era, other regions of the world were working with the WHO to build (or rebuild) their health systems, to develop campaigns to fight malnutrition and epidemic disease, and to expand existing research networks to study those diseases. Discussions at the WHO regional headquarters in Brazzaville, by contrast, were dominated by quarrels over the cost of living in AEF's capital and disputes about the organization's right to engage directly with Africans through WHO propaganda. What is most notable about these clashes is that they rarely involved questions of public health, focusing instead on issues such as the unreliable postal service, the limited availability of European-style accommodations, and the lack of local entertainment options. These seemingly petty squabbles over Brazzaville's shortcomings, however, masked deeper tensions about the relationship between internationalism and imperialism and about the ability of an imperial capital to serve as the headquarters of a global organization like the WHO.

If Brazzaville in the early 1950s remained strongly anchored to traditions of colonial inequality and violence, it was also—according to the most vehement critics of French imperialism—an example of the ways that the French colonial government had underdeveloped the territories it claimed to be promoting. Colonial officials had been hopeful that public health was the one aspect of colonial rule in which the French could demonstrate an uninterrupted record of real commitment to development. But the arrival of an international health organization on French African soil would expose the empire to an unprecedented level of international scrutiny and criticism whose force—once unleashed—would be impossible to contain. Although French officials ultimately managed to quell concerns about Brazzaville's shortcomings, tensions between the French administration and the international personnel who came to work there would severely constrain the potential for global health programs in sub-Saharan Africa in the first decade and a half following the war, leaving a significant mark on the landscape of African public health.

An International Organization in an Imperial City

At a preliminary meeting of the WHO Regional Committee for Africa in 1951, the choice of location for the organization's African headquarters proved to be a particularly thorny issue, one that was intimately bound up in the broader global politics of decolonization. Whatever city the delegates chose—whether located in an independent country or in a colonial territory—had to uphold a certain standard of living for *all* of its inhabitants. It also needed to demonstrate a commitment to human rights and equal political participation. On top of this, the headquarters needed to be located in a city with modern infrastructure that could support a global institution like the WHO. These "civilized amenities"—as the South African delegate termed them—included a reliable postal service, sufficient working space for employees, ample hotel accommodations for hosting conferences, and an efficient local and international transportation network. Representatives to the regional committee also needed to consider factors such as climate, the geographic placement of the city within the African region, the cost of living and availability of housing for WHO employees, and, finally, the quality of educational and medical facilities, including those geared toward medical research and laboratory testing. Among the major cities in sub-Saharan Africa, this left few viable options.

The absence of racial discrimination was particularly important to the Liberian delegate, Dr. Joseph Togba, whom the Liberian president described as "purposeful, dynamic, thorough going and relentless."[1] Hailing from the only WHO member state in the African region never to have been colonized by a European power, Liberian doctors and government officials were especially sensitive to conditions in colonial territories in Africa. Togba frequently challenged the member states that participated in the CCTA, which Liberia had not been allowed to join. The Liberian perspective thus served as an important counterweight to the different colonial agendas within the regional committee. In one of the debates regarding the placement of the future WHO African headquarters, Togba noted, "There were still regions in Africa where Africans were not granted equal treatment with Europeans or other races. The Board should therefore instruct the Director-General that the headquarters of an Office for Africa—if established—should be located where Africans would be treated on an equal basis with other races."[2] Of the representatives present at the 1951 regional committee meeting, Togba was the only delegate to speak on behalf of African interests. The fact that the meeting was held in Geneva, thousands of miles away from the populations the regional organization was aiming to help, is a testament to how closely the delegates hewed to European and colonial agendas.

Debates about the location of the future headquarters dominated the meeting, and much of the discussion focused on how the office could accommodate the lifestyles and needs of the Europeans who would work there, rather than how the office could best serve African needs. Delegates proposed several locations, each with its own challenges. The South African delegation suggested Kampala, a proposal that both Britain and Rhodesia supported. Togba worried, however, that racial discrimination in Uganda would limit the ability of black Africans to participate in the work of the office, citing his own experience of having been banned from a conference hotel in Kampala because of the color of his skin.[3] For the Liberian delegation, Monrovia was the clear choice. It was in one of two independent states

Figure 4.1. Dr. Joseph N. Togba, director general of National Health Services, Liberia, and president of the Seventh World Health Assembly, sitting between Dr. Marcolino G. Candau (*left*), director general of the WHO, and Dr. Pierre Dorolle (*right*), deputy director general (1954). © World Health Organization, 1954.

in the African region. It was accessible from both Europe and the rest of Africa, and according to Togba, it had the best track record for human rights among the options put forward. Moreover, since the administration was on site, there would be no need to consult a faraway government, which would allow the regional office to save valuable time.[4] The third choice put forward was Brazzaville. Knowing that the WHO would never accept Léopoldville as a headquarters for the WHO in Africa, the Belgian delegation proposed Brazzaville, the administrative capital of AEF. Since Brazzaville was just a ferry ride away, the Belgian administration in the Congo hoped that it would be able to draw certain benefits from the close proximity of the office to their own colonial capital. The French and Portuguese delegations supported the Belgian proposal.[5]

In some ways, Brazzaville was a logical choice. Stretched along the banks of the Congo River, the capital of AEF was situated in a central location.

French construction there dated back to the 1880s, when Savorgnan de Brazza negotiated a treaty with the Makoko people, giving the French access to vast tracts of land in the Congo River region.[6] For decades, development there lagged behind other parts of the French empire. Brazzaville and the surrounding areas had little to offer in terms of natural resources, with only some smaller-scale rubber extraction, mining, and forestry.[7] Its central location and its connection to the port of Pointe-Noire, however, made Brazzaville an ideal location from which to coordinate the exportation of raw materials from the whole of AEF. By the 1950s, agricultural production in French Congo was on the rise, and farmers there were producing tobacco, palm oil, and coffee.[8]

Once a sleepy colonial town, Brazzaville exploded in the immediate postwar period, with urban development projects turning the city into "an immense construction site." Promotional travel materials touted public and private investments in Brazzaville's urban infrastructure, portraying the city as a paragon of colonial modernity. By the early 1950s, Brazzaville was equipped with modern apartment buildings that were "outfitted with every imaginable comfort."[9] French colonial rule also ensured relatively well-developed transportation and communication networks between Brazzaville and Europe, an important factor for an international organization based in Geneva. The first commercial passenger flight landed in 1936 in Brazzaville, one of five African cities to be served by a direct air route to Paris. Ongoing expansion of this network throughout the late 1930s and 1940s reduced the time that a traveler would spend en route to less than a day, opening up new possibilities for more extensive travel between Europe and Africa, as well as throughout the continent. As a 1950 Air France bulletin boasted, "Now linked to the Metropole by daily flights, black Africa is becoming a vast and open field for mechanical exploitation and at the same time a destination for exotic tourism."[10] The Maya-Maya Airport was, according to the *Air France Revue,* one of the "most beautiful in Africa," and the accompanying photograph depicted Europeans and Africans lounging in the shade of the "Relais aérien" veranda, smoking cigarettes and sipping espresso. Within the city itself, efficient transportation was provided by "spacious and comfortable" buses that "put Brazzaville in the avant-garde of the capitals of the French Union."[11] French rule in Brazzaville had also brought European-style medical facilities—including a Pasteur Institute—

to the city, making it an appealing choice for an international health organization.[12] According to its most avid promoters, after "70 years of struggle, work, perseverance, and patient and humane civilizing," Brazzaville could serve as the ultimate testament to "French presence and vitality" on the African continent.[13]

Beyond its rapidly expanding urban and medical infrastructure, Brazzaville also played an important role as the headquarters for the French Resistance during the war, which gave the city a symbolic importance within the empire. Shortly after the defeat of France in 1940, Charles de Gaulle launched his own army from the territories of AEF and Cameroon, turning them into what historian Eric Jennings has called "the first hotbed of French resistance." Despite our frequent association of the Resistance with de Gaulle's time in London, Jennings argues that it was in fact a quintessentially African phenomenon. AEF provided crucial raw materials, as well as a place from which to coordinate a massive military operation. Most importantly, though, these territories provided manpower. Indeed, especially in the early years of the war, the majority of French Resistance fighters were in fact black Africans who rallied to de Gaulle and Félix Eboué, the Guyanese governor of Chad. It was in equatorial Africa that de Gaulle reestablished the sovereignty of the French Republic, and it was there, in 1944, that French administrators from across the empire would gather to map out a more equitable postwar union.[14] The Conférence africaine française took place in Brazzaville in January and February 1944. Now regarded by historians as an inadequate attempt to promote equality in the empire, at the time the conference was hailed by many colonial commentators as a truly revolutionary step toward the foundation of a new postwar union of France and its colonies.[15] Brazzaville's reputation as a bastion of French republicanism and symbol of colonial reform appealed strongly to members of the WHO regional committee as they pondered potential candidates for the organization's African headquarters.

But if Brazzaville offered certain advantages in terms of infrastructure and history, it remained a quintessentially colonial city, built on decades of colonial inequality and violence. As Deborah Neill shows, local officials in Brazzaville cited political and sanitary justifications for the segregation of the city into European and African neighborhoods. In the first decade of the twentieth century, the layout of the city underwent a major reorganization, with African settlements relocated outside the European-dominated center. Health officials applauded the new city structure, depicting African dwellings as dens of disease and exemplars of poor sanitation. The new organization, they argued, would protect Europeans from contagious African illnesses but would also promote African health through its more modern layout.[16] The vast political restructuring of the empire in 1946 did little to bridge these divisions between African and European residents of AEF's capital. As late as 1958, the *Guide bleu* for Brazzaville, Léopoldville, and Pointe-Noire described Brazzaville's neighborhoods as highly segregated, with European residents living primarily in the *quartier européen* and Africans in the neighborhoods of Poto-Poto and Bacongo. Brazzaville, according to the guide's author, was a city that had been built in a piecemeal fashion, with very little thought given to the needs of its residents.[17] In his 1955 book *Sociologie des Brazzavilles noires,* French sociologist Georges Balandier explored the dynamism of Brazzaville's "villes africaines," while not overlooking the significant obstacles faced by their inhabitants—most notably high rates of unemployment, uneven urban infrastructure, and an unpredictable food supply.[18]

While Brazzaville fit many of the WHO's criteria for a regional office headquarters, Togba worried about the short distance between Brazzaville and Léopoldville in the Belgian Congo. He feared that WHO employees might seek housing or entertainment across the river, where discrimination was even more prevalent. This, he believed, would be a problematic situation for black employees working for the office.[19] Its proximity to Léopoldville notwithstanding, Brazzaville's well-developed communications network and favorable placement within the region made it an attractive option for the regional headquarters.[20] In response to concerns that the cost of living in Brazzaville was prohibitively high, the French delegation stated that the French government would be willing to provide four furnished apartments to house WHO employees. Dr. François Daubenton, the director of the regional committee, lauded the French government for its generous offer, noting that no employee would ever be able to afford acceptable housing in Brazzaville on a WHO salary. A memorandum from the French Foreign Ministry about living conditions in Brazzaville assured the delegations that the construction of more affordable housing was under way. The memo also touted the various scientific facilities that would be available to the new office, including the Pasteur Institute, a new hospital, and a new facility for AEF's mobile health services.[21]

The committee's ultimate decision was the result of political maneuverings by the different delegates, each trading favors to ensure that at least some of their propositions for the future of the committee would be passed. Liberia, for example, offered to support Brazzaville for the headquarters—if Monrovia failed—in exchange for the French delegation's vote in support of Togba for the position of committee president and of Monrovia as the next site for the regional committee's annual meeting. The French won Daubenton over to the Brazzaville camp in return for a promise to support his renewal as regional director. When the issue of the headquarters location was finally put to a vote, there were three votes for Brazzaville (France, Belgium, and Portugal), two for Monrovia (Liberia and Spain), and two for Kampala (Great Britain and South Africa). A second round eliminated Monrovia, and the final vote went to Brazzaville, with all delegations but the British and the South Africans voting in support of AEF's capital.[22]

Although members of the French delegation had managed to convince the majority of their colleagues in the regional committee that Brazzaville would be a suitable location for the WHO's African headquarters, many doctors and government officials in Paris and throughout the empire remained unconvinced. Some of them questioned the wisdom of inviting an international health organization to set up shop in one of France's African territories. The debate quickly escalated between officials in the Ministry of Overseas France and the Ministry of Foreign Affairs. When discussing the possibility of proposing a French territory as the seat of the new organization, certain members of the French administration expressed the belief that it was best to keep your friends close and your enemies closer. The WHO, moreover, could provide important financial support as the French government continued to invest in its African colonies. Dr. Georges Garcin, head of the French delegation to the regional committee, argued that France had a "major interest in the seat of the bureau being established in one of its territories, [since] this organism will be called to take on a considerable importance in Africa where Public Health is one of the most essential factors in all matters relating to development."[23] The Ministry of Foreign Affairs supported Garcin's view and, before the first annual meeting, sent instructions to the French delegations reminding them that "from the time of your arrival in Geneva, you should rally the other members of the regional committee to our cause . . . emphasizing the central location and rapid development of this city, as well as the exceptional communications network and lack of racial discrimination."[24]

Other members of the French administration in Africa were less than thrilled, however, by the idea of inviting an international organization to establish its regional headquarters in a French territory. Médecin-Général Ambroise Gourvil, from the Direction of Health Services in AEF, explained that the regional office would have the potential to become an important forum for opponents of France's colonial regime and would set a dangerous precedent for international interference in the empire. By allowing a WHO regional office to install its headquarters in Brazzaville, he wrote, "we are effectively giving the right of extraterritoriality to numerous persons whose comings and goings will be beyond our control, who are not necessarily our friends, and who will have the ability to create, *sur place,* a political climate unfavorable to French rule." The result of these complications, according to Gourvil, would be "serious difficulties" for the French administration, "especially for the proper functioning of our Public Health Services in Africa, whose action depends on a climate of confidence in order to be effective." Gourvil recommended that rather than inviting the regional office to install itself in Brazzaville, the French should instead ensure its installation "as far as possible from any of our territories."[25]

Ultimately, the French government concluded that the potential benefits of being able to closely monitor the WHO's activities outweighed the potential complications that the office posed, and it extended an official offer to house the regional office in Brazzaville. The WHO Executive Council accepted, and on 23 July 1952, the agreement was signed by Brock Chisholm, director general of the WHO, and by Maurice Schuman, the French minister of foreign affairs. Construction of the regional office was slated to begin shortly after. But while the accord between the WHO and the French government was achieved with relatively little friction, and the installation of the regional office was soon under way, the French administration's troubles with the WHO Africa office had only just begun. Indeed, the drama surrounding the choice of headquarters foreshadowed a decade of conflict between international and colonial forces on the African continent, a conflict in which Brazzaville—and the French colonial administration more broadly—would become inextricably implicated.[26]

WHO Propaganda and the Problem of Colonial Sovereignty

For the French colonial administration, international personnel working in the empire posed two interconnected threats. First, they were uniquely positioned to observe conditions on the ground in the colonies, providing fuel for anticolonial critiques at the UN. Second—and perhaps more dangerous for the French administration in Africa—they had the ability to converse directly with Africans. Thus the first goal of the French government vis-à-vis this new international institution was to keep careful tabs on its work and, more importantly, on the comings and goings of international personnel who came to Brazzaville to work for the WHO. In a memo to the high commissioner for the republic in AEF, the minister of overseas France asked to be kept apprised of any and all developments at the regional office. This, he explained, was the only way to prevent any activity that might run counter to French interests. He wrote, "Given the breadth of financial means at the WHO's disposal, the [Regional] Office has the possibility of playing a significant role in our African territories. It may equally, given the Organization's ways of seeing and acting, attempt to play a role that does not conform to our interests or views. This is why I am asking you to follow, with very particular attention, all of the Office's activities, projects, and accomplishments."[27]

French fears that WHO employees might act as agents of anticolonial propaganda reached a climax after a series of explosive debates surrounding the staffing of the regional office. As preparations for the Brazzaville headquarters progressed, French officials strategized about how to keep the office relatively small and autonomous. Limiting the size of the office's staff, they argued, would allow colonial governments to continue to direct health policy in their respective territories without too much interference from Geneva.[28] Belgian and British delegations supported this view and voted in 1951 to limit the staff of the office to four or five people. This, they believed, would provide enough personnel to establish a working relationship with the different African health administrations without running the risk of overshadowing them.[29] In opposition to the colonial delegations, Daubenton, the regional director, proposed a staff of ten to eleven people. Among the positions that Daubenton proposed, one would provoke intense controversy among the colonial members of the committee: a WHO public information officer.[30]

Figure 4.2. Dr. Francisco J. C. Cambournac and an African clerk photographed in front of the WHO building in Brazzaville. Dr. Cambournac was the director of the WHO's Regional Office for Africa, Brazzaville, from 1954 to 1964. © World Health Organization / Paul Almasy, 1954.

At the first meeting of the regional committee in 1951, Daubenton invited Field Horine, the acting director of public information for the WHO, to speak about the different functions of the public information officer within the WHO regional offices.[31] Horine remarked on the importance that the WHO's constitution attributed to "enlightened public opinion," explaining that it was "important that the public be kept informed about the activities of the WHO (without resorting to 'advertising,' per se) if we wish to win their support for the activities of the organization." While Horine explained that it would be difficult to ascribe a specific role to the information officer in the regional office at such an early stage, he suggested the principal task would be to keep the local populations "informed about the activities of the United Nations in the domain of health, by means of contact with local health administrations, by radio addresses, and by newspapers, magazines and illustrated pamphlets." Dr. Pierre Dorolle, the deputy director of the WHO, added that it was not enough to "do well, we also need to teach."[32] According to Daubenton, the public information officer would serve several important functions for the regional office, staying up to date on all matters that could potentially affect public health conditions. This staff member would track epidemic disease outbreaks, social and political disturbances, and natural catastrophes. They would also be responsible for keeping Africans informed about the goals of the WHO and educating them about its programs and activities.[33]

Despite the ostensibly benign nature of this position, French delegates to the committee categorically opposed allocating funds for a public information officer in the regional budget. When discussing the matter with their colleagues during the 1952 regional committee meetings, the French delegation cited the more pressing needs of the region, particularly the need to expand disease control programs. In their internal correspondence, however, French officials focused on the ways that the WHO threatened France's colonial agenda, rather than on a consideration of African needs. According to one French memo, "The point of departure was a minor one—to recruit or not to recruit—for the regional office, an information officer. The real reason, however, for our profound opposition to the recruitment of an information officer is that we do not trust agents of propaganda—and that is indeed what we are dealing with here—of the World Health Organization. The entire task consists, in effect, of convincing the world that any action in the field of health started the day that the WHO touched down on this abandoned continent."[34] French officials and doctors accused the WHO of letting the medical achievements of colonial governments and the CCTA "slip by in silence" in their reports and radio programs and they reproached anticolonial representatives to the WHO for maintaining a willful ignorance about existing health programs in Africa.[35] The French delegation to the regional committee repeatedly insisted that it would rather put the funds that had been allocated for a public information officer to another use, pointing out that the goal of "informing local populations about what is being accomplished for them . . . could be achieved more easily with actions than with words."[36] Although one could write these complaints off as colonial paranoia, fears that UN agencies might serve as a vehicle for anticolonial propaganda were not entirely unfounded in the early 1950s. Indeed, similar debates were taking place in the UN Special Committee for Non-self-governing Territories, where the delegation from the Philippines was pursuing a resolution that would require colonial schools to teach students both about human rights and about the work that the UN was doing in favor of dependent populations around the world.[37]

The other colonial delegations to the regional committee unanimously supported the French motion to strike the position of information officer from the budget, but Chisholm rejected the French proposal out of hand. When the French delegation approached him to address the issue, he responded that as director general it was his prerogative to allocate funds within the WHO's budget—"in accordance with the norms decided in Geneva." The position of public information officer was, he contended, "indispensable for the proper functioning of the Office."[38] Chisholm was, according to the French delegation, "an Anglo-Saxon Puritan, severe, reserved, cold, anticolonialist by principle, contemptuous of France, impregnated with the mentality of a missionary and proselytizer . . . who ruled over the regional committee in an almost tyrannical fashion."[39] One French memo accused him of ruling the WHO "the same way his Scottish ancestors, in the seventeenth century, would have ruled their clan."[40] The French delegation to the regional committee wrote to the Ministry of Foreign Affairs that Chisholm's presence at the meeting, coupled with that of other WHO and UN observers—including a representative from the Division of Non-autonomous Territories—had caused trouble for the French on more than one occasion.[41] The Liberian delegation supported Chisholm's position, and Togba—one of the only non-Europeans on the committee—made it known that he would oppose any measure that could potentially render the WHO Africa office a "poor relation" of the other regional branches, whose staffs all included a public relations position.[42]

In the face of Chisholm and Togba's opposition, French delegates remained intransigent, demanding both that the position of information officer be stricken from the 1953 and 1954 budgets and that the Executive Council of the WHO be forced to take into consideration requests from the regional committee on budgetary matters. Garcin, the head of the French delegation, pointed out that no one could possibly understand the conditions on the ground in Africa better than the governments of the member states themselves and even went as far as to suggest an amendment to the WHO Constitution that would allow regional offices to determine their own budgets. After all, Garcin argued, at stake was not only the public image of France's empire but the very preservation of French sovereignty on the African continent.[43] In a letter to the French delegation to the WHO Executive Council, Garcin pointed out that the powers of the member states within their regions were in fact quite limited and that "important regional decisions fell to the Director General and the World Assembly, in which members having little or no interest on the African continent comprised the overwhelming majority."[44]

What is most striking about these discussions is how infrequently they referenced medical matters. Indeed, much of the tension within the Africa office was couched in political terms and was framed as a battle between colonial and anticolonial elements of the WHO, with little or no reference to questions of health. In its report to the Ministry of Foreign Affairs, the French delegation noted the irony of a statement that Togba had made in which he congratulated the participants of the meetings for confronting the issues as "doctors and not as politicians." The French report condemned the Liberian delegation for being the first to "politicize the debates" by attacking the European delegations.[45] When Togba reproached his colleagues for banding together as a colonial faction, the French rejoined that this was a misleading accusation. Since all decisions made by the regional committee were subjected to general approval by the entire organization, the French argued that they were in fact a small minority pitted against an overwhelming anticolonial majority at the WHO. Because the other European delegations were content to remain silent during the proceedings of the regional sessions, the French had stepped into the role as "the heads of a colonial coalition having as its primary goal the reduction of scope of the Regional Office."[46]

After these tense exchanges during the 1952 regional committee meeting, the French delegation advised both the Ministry of Foreign Affairs and the Ministry of Overseas France to proceed with extreme caution in all dealings with the WHO. They noted that the colonial governments could not longer consider themselves to be "at home" in the region. Despite their "immediate knowledge" of regional affairs, their colonial agendas would now always be subordinated to "an incompetent extra-African majority." As such, the French delegation recommended "close surveillance" of all WHO activities in the region, with the goal of "blocking its extension, within the constraints of our limited means." They also recommended the expansion of cooperation in the domain of health within the framework of the CCTA in order to offset the activities of the WHO.[47]

Some members of the French delegation expressed regret at having already conceded so much of France's colonial sovereignty in Africa to an international organization. The French administration in Africa, they believed, would be increasingly unable to defend the last shreds of imperial autonomy as the WHO expanded its involvement on the continent. In their report they noted that even if the colonial governments were able to regain control over the regional budget and stop the creation of a public relations role in the office, "the delegation should not allow itself to be deceived. It would only be a pyrrhic victory."[48] For the French, the relationship with the WHO was an important one, because, as the first specialized UN institution to be established in France's African territories, "its approaches can be considered a kind of test that will tell us what will happen in the case that any other international institution should do the same." The French delegation suggested that while there was potentially still time to "profit from the advantages offered by the WHO," this could only come at the expense of careful monitoring and "a concerted action undertaken in cooperation with the other administering powers of the region."[49]

Brazzaville's Public Relations Crisis

The friction at the 1952 meeting gave French doctors and officials a reason to worry about the possible havoc that international organizations might cause in France's African empire. But it was only a taste of the drama to come. The following year, Daubenton would launch his own attack on France's colonial administration in Africa, focusing on the shortcomings of its equatorial capital. The French delegation to the WHO had avidly supported Daubenton's candidacy for the position of regional director, even voting to approve his renewal past the mandated retirement age. By the third meeting of the regional committee in 1953, however, relations between the French and Daubenton had more than soured. French officials worried that they were seeing their worst fears coming true in the Dutch physician's disparagements of France's African capital. This criticism, they worried, risked exposing the French government to even more intense vilification at the UN. The anticolonial nightmare that the French had dreaded since negotiations began for the creation of a WHO office in Africa was, in their minds, rapidly becoming a reality.

Daubenton, born in 1888 in Rotterdam, had served as the director general of medical services for the Dutch army for several years before his appointment to the WHO. Before the Second World War he spent twenty years in Africa, overseeing health services for Africans in the mining region of Witwatersrand in South Africa.[50] After the war he was working as a technical expert in public hygiene for the WHO Regional Office for the Eastern Mediterranean in Alexandria when Pierre Dorolle nominated him for the post of regional director for Africa on 24 October 1950.[51] Although most delegations to the African region received Daubenton favorably, some—particularly the Belgian delegation—opposed his manner of conduct as "too personal" and accused him of colluding with Togba.[52] Despite this criticism, however, the majority of the delegations—including the French delegation—voted in favor of reappointing Daubenton as regional director for 1952 and again for 1953.[53]

In 1953, however, the proceedings in Kampala were disrupted by what French delegate Garcin called the "Daubenton Bomb," a unrelenting assault on Brazzaville based on what Daubenton believed to be its fundamental unsuitability to serve as the site for the WHO's African headquarters. His reproaches focused on the failure to recruit employees to the Brazzaville office due to the high cost of living and the lack of appropriate housing for European personnel. Daubenton noted, for example, that the French government had only guaranteed four furnished apartments, and given that more than sixty families of French bureaucrats were waiting for housing in Brazzaville, it seemed that there would be a very long wait before acceptable housing would be available for other WHO employees. He also remarked that several employees of the regional office had already fallen ill as a result of climatic and environmental conditions, and he doubted that any employee would be able to last for longer than a two-year stint there. Daubenton grumbled about the lack of affordable and accessible transportation for employees to be able to take recuperative vacations in the area, stating definitively that these conditions were impeding both the maintenance of the existing staff and the recruitment of new employees.[54]

Beyond the primary issue of staff housing, Daubenton pointed to other difficulties for the functioning of an international organization: slow inter-African communication, postal delays, and high electricity costs. He also enumerated other aspects of life in AEF's capital that would be bothersome to European employees: "Entertainment is rare, clothing is expensive, with little or no choices, and what is available deteriorates quickly as a result of primitive washing methods." He noted other difficulties that hindered the proper functioning of the office, including the lack of supplies (paper and so on), and he remarked that the absence of a local travel agency made it difficult for employees to coordinate their travel plans. This, he argued, was particularly problematic for an international organization, whose staff needed easy access to quick and efficient transportation. Questioning the logic of maintaining a regional headquarters in "the most expensive city in Africa, if not in the world," Daubenton mused whether it did not behoove him, as regional director, to signal to the WHO that their funds could be used more efficiently elsewhere, enabling them "to extend the reach of its program without sacrificing the interests of its personnel."[55]

In his report to the French government, Garcin responded to Daubenton's complaints by explaining that the difficulties were in some cases the product of the WHO's own internal regulations. In other cases, he rationalized, the problems were a result of the normal obstacles that emerged when establishing a new branch of a major global organization. Last, he noted, many of the complications that Daubenton had claimed were unique to Brazzaville were in fact difficulties that would have been encountered in whatever African city might have been chosen as the headquarters for the office. Only the failure to recruit employees, he noted, was unique to the Brazzaville office. This he attributed to Daubenton's own anti-Brazzaville campaign, which Garcin thought was discouraging potential candidates. The problem was compounded by the unwillingness of the French administration in Africa to address the situation, a reluctance that was potentially linked to France's anti-WHO and anti-UN prejudice.[56]

There was a general consensus among the members of the regional committee that Daubenton's attack was grounded in his own personal disappointment. This would be his last professional endeavor before retiring, and the difficulties he encountered in setting up the office were indeed numerous. As the French delegation's report put it, "Of course, he is elderly, more concerned with detail than with the essentials . . . but we cannot ignore the fact that for many years he had desired to have an important impact on sanitary services in Africa. He had but a year and a half to get the Regional Office off the ground, and to get it through the inevitable difficulties of installation. Perhaps, feeling the impending onset of retirement, he was too quick to criticize."[57] Another report from Garcin noted that Daubenton's age, personality, and "aversion to this French territory" made him unwilling or unable to overcome the obstacles that could have been expected in the installation of the office.[58] Garcin's report stated, however, that whatever the implications for France might be, Daubenton would himself be leaving the organization as "le grand vaincu" (the great defeated one), having failed to achieve his objective of getting the Brazzaville office on its feet.[59]

Personal or not, Daubenton's complaints had launched an international public relations nightmare for France's administration in Africa. Knowing the political danger that any criticism of France's overseas project posed in the broader context of the UN, French officials took the regional director's grievances very seriously. In a memo to the minister of overseas France on 30 October 1952, the minister of foreign affairs wrote, "I am sure that, like me, you will find it indispensable to urgently take all measures necessary to assure the installation of employees for the Regional Office in the most favorable conditions possible. It is a question of national prestige. Any prolongation of the current situation will, in effect, generate a serious prejudice against us in the international sphere, and will lead the WHO to transfer to another city those offices that had been established in Brazzaville."[60] The withdrawal of the WHO from France's empire, according to the minister of foreign affairs, would mean a "loss of face" for France. It would "be considered by the powers hostile to us as a total failure of our system . . . and would set a precedent for the departure of other international organizations from French soil." If French officials ever had doubts about installing the headquarters in Brazzaville in the first place, the danger posed by international criticism had become even more real in the wake of Daubenton's threats to transfer the headquarters to another African city. One report noted that the removal of the WHO regional office from Brazzaville would "say to the world that the second capital of l'Afrique Noire Française is incapable of hosting a small regional office of an international organization."[61] Losing the regional office would also mean giving up the hope of being able to use "the *milieu français* to influence the Members of the Regional Office and orient their spirit in a direction favorable of our desires and views."[62]

Rejecting outright the possibility of moving the seat of the regional office, the French Ministry of Foreign Affairs and the Ministry of Overseas France embarked on a public relations campaign to address Daubenton's critiques and to rally diplomatic support from the other delegations in order to save the Brazzaville office. While little could be done to address the high cost of living in Brazzaville, the French delegation proposed that the problems of salary, housing, and vacation time could be ameliorated if it could convince the French government to agree to provide more affordable housing and the WHO to agree to revisit its own remuneration system. Under the existing arrangement, only four of the fifteen employees of the regional office benefited from subsidized housing, but Masselot, the head of the French delegation, thought that if the French government could provide housing for all of the office's employees, this would adequately address Daubenton's most pressing concern. Masselot contended that while the housing shortage was most severe in the city center, the Cité du Djoué—a complex built seven kilometers outside Brazzaville by the Société d'énergie électrique de l'AEF—could provide a potential solution. He suggested that the funds to purchase the apartments could come from FIDES, which would allow employees of the Brazzaville office to rent them for a nominal fee.[63]

Another member of the French delegation pointed out that the problem was less about "Africa adapting itself to the WHO than the WHO adapting itself to Africa." The French delegation had long recommended instituting a system similar to what employees enjoyed in France's own colonial administration, which gave French employees in Africa longer vacation times and special bonuses to compensate for the inconveniences associated with unfamiliar and "unsanitary" working conditions.[64] Some delegates—Togba in particular—took offense at the suggestion that Europeans be given special consideration when working in Africa, arguing that the committee should instead be focused on Africanizing the regional office, not making special accommodations for foreigners.[65] Despite the reservations of certain dele-

Figure 4.3. Postage stamp commemorating the tenth anniversary of the WHO, designed and engraved by Albert Decaris, 1958. © 2017 ADAGP, Paris / ARS, New York. Reproduction from author's collection.

gates, however, it was finally decided that there was a certain amount of flexibility in the system to allow regional offices to account for differences in the cost of living from region to region. Ultimately, the committee recommended that the salaries of the employees in the Brazzaville office be reconsidered in light of working conditions in central Africa.[66]

Although the French delegation worked hard to control the damage done by Daubenton's report, its members felt ill-equipped to control the "feverish" judgment of the other delegations. As Garcin explained in his report, the other European delegations had already decided that "if Brazzaville was indeed the hell that Médecin-Général Daubenton described, it made sense to transfer the headquarters to another city." In response to the regional director's criticisms, the committee voted to assemble an ad hoc committee to decide the future of the regional office headquarters at Brazzaville.[67] The committee—composed of delegates from France, Belgium, Liberia, and Great Britain—was tasked with studying the means of improving the situation on the ground in Brazzaville. A British representative from Kenya, however, suggested that the time would be better spent in an effort to research conditions in other African cities, with hopes of finding a more suitable location for the regional office's headquarters. The French delegation rejoined that this move was premature and would prejudice the outcome of the committee's work in favor of a transfer.[68]

French representatives warned that if the British delegation continued to push for a transfer, they would be forced to treat the creation of the ad hoc committee as an act of aggression by the other member states. The committee agreed, then, that for the time being, it was best to restrict its work to improving the situation in Brazzaville, only turning to the possibility of moving the headquarters if no suitable solution could be found.[69] With the exception of the British and Liberian delegations, most of the ad hoc committee's participants agreed that if Brazzaville's shortcomings could be ameliorated, there would be no need to relocate the headquarters. The French delegation attributed this general goodwill to the French government's guarantee that it would provide more affordable accommodations for WHO employees. Masselot and Garcin noted in their report that the responsibility now rested in the hands of the French administrations in Paris and Brazzaville to ensure the successful construction of new housing. They feared that if French officials failed to fulfill that promise, the WHO would be likely to leave Brazzaville definitively.[70]

In his report on the third annual meeting of the WHO Regional Committee for Africa, Garcin offered the French Ministry of Foreign Affairs a comprehensive plan for addressing the Brazzaville crisis and the damage wrought by the "Daubenton Bomb" during the session. He reminded ministry officials that the regional office in Brazzaville was "dangerously threatened," and he recommended an internal investigation to determine "the exaggeration or the inexactitude of Dr. Daubenton's allegations."[71] Garcin advised reaching out to other member states—especially Liberia and Great Britain—to remind them how important it was for the French administration for the regional office to stay in Brazzaville, and to explain the lengths to which they were willing to go to ensure that it did.[72]

Garcin's plan emphasized the need to convince authorities in AEF to work on improving living conditions in the capital and to commit to finding a solution to Brazzaville's housing crisis. He noted that any help that the colonial administration in Brazzaville could provide would obviously be constrained by budgetary limitations. He suggested that France's other territories—as well as the metropolitan government—share the financial burden of the project, since what was at stake were not just "the interests of AEF, but French interests in general." In the context of the ad hoc committee, he recommended steering the conversation away from an exclusive focus on the cost of living and the housing shortage and reminding the other delegates of the various other criteria necessary for a regional office: a convenient geographical position, ease of communication, and a relative lack of racial discrimination. He suggested that bringing these topics to the forefront would be a way to remind the other delegations of the reasons that the committee had chosen Brazzaville as the headquarters in the first place.[73]

Although Garcin's plan emphasized the need to take whatever steps necessary to retain the WHO regional office in Brazzaville, he also warned against taking an overly conciliatory stance, which might lead the French "too far on the path of having to make concessions and in turn according too much power to the WHO." Garcin suggested that another approach to the Brazzaville crisis was possible if the Ministry of Foreign Affairs decided not to pursue the diplomatically oriented strategy outlined in his report: "We can make it known to the WHO that we place a great value on maintaining the seat of the Regional organization in Brazzaville" but that "in the case that the headquarters were transferred from this location we would completely withdraw from the regional organization and all of its activities in Africa." He suggested that this strong-handed approach might discourage the organization from attempting to take any radical action vis-à-vis the Brazzaville office but that it might in fact be unwilling to compromise. While not ideal, that situation would "at least have the advantage of releasing us from its grasp in Africa," finally satisfying those colonial officials and doctors who had hoped to keep the WHO out of Africa all along.[74]

~

Ultimately French authorities chose the more diplomatic path, saving the Brazzaville office and, more importantly, saving face for the French empire. The ad hoc committee that had been created to study means of improving conditions in Brazzaville was able to devise a solution to the employee housing shortage. Indeed, the WHO Regional Office for Africa remains in Brazzaville to this day, outlasting the French empire by several decades.[75] Although, in the end, French officials and doctors managed to mitigate the threats they believed the WHO posed, the international public relations crisis that had erupted over the location of the WHO's African headquarters had revealed the delicate line that French colonial authorities in Africa had to walk between preserving French sovereignty within the empire and adapting to new international norms of cooperation after the Second World War. The task, moreover, of maintaining a favorable international perception of France's imperial project after 1945 proved to be difficult.[76] The installation of the WHO regional headquarters in Brazzaville served as a test both of French colonial reforms *and* of postwar internationalism. While Brazzaville's most enthusiastic publicists depicted the city as the zenith of colonial modernity, in reality, AEF's capital remained strongly anchored to the darker side of its colonial past. By inviting an international organization to establish itself within the city limits, French officials and doctors risked exposing ongoing inequality and underdevelopment to some of the empire's most ardent critics.

The WHO, for its part, was forced to adapt its progressive ideas about equal access to health care to a location where conditions were decidedly less than equal. On a regional committee dominated by European personalities, African perspectives—such as that of Liberian physician Togba—were often silenced. The committee quickly became an unexpected battleground in the struggles for and against decolonization. Indeed, rather than dedicating their time to discussing the latest approaches to eliminating malaria or new technologies to screen for tuberculosis, the doctors and government officials who formed part of the WHO Regional Committee for Africa allowed their deliberations to be dominated by seemingly petty disputes about issues having little to do with health and everything to do with the European perception that the WHO posed a significant threat to colonial sovereignty on the continent. These quarrels did little to forestall the process of political decolonization that would ultimately unfold in the late 1950s and early 1960s, but they did succeed in severely constraining the WHO's ability to do its work. Before exploring the challenges of building public health programs in Africa within the political constraints of a decolonizing world, we first turn to a third organization that played an important role in shaping the landscape of public health in postwar Africa: the CIE.

CHAPTER FIVE

Family Health, France, and the Future of Africa

> How numerous are the French physicians who were great pioneers, bringing mankind fresh grounds for hope! The founding of an institute devoted to the various problems of childhood and to giving the best guidance to those who, in their turn, will guide others, is something which does honour to the French government. Once more French science is in the forefront of progress.
>
> —Dr. W. Bonne, WHO representative to the inaugural ceremony of the CIE, 1950

As the WHO was launching its Regional Office for Africa in 1952, another organization—the CIE—was also making African medical history in Brazzaville. That December, the CIE sponsored the first major children's health conference in postwar Africa, entitled "The Problems of Childhood in the Tropical Countries of Africa." Over the course of five days, delegates assembled in AEF's capital to discuss malnutrition, infant mortality, epidemic disease, sanitation, child psychology, and the rising rates of juvenile delinquency in Africa's industrializing cities. For a symposium on child health in Africa, however, Africans were notably absent from the gathering. And although the conference coincided with the inauguration of the new WHO Africa office in the same city, only three WHO representatives attended the meeting. At a moment when health was undergoing a process of unprecedented globalization, the conference in Brazzaville promoted first and foremost the work of *colonial* physicians and scientists, with a particular emphasis on the legacy of French medicine and science. While the primary goal of the conference was to promote the sharing of technical information, more important for many of the attendees was the crucial opportunity that the meeting provided for French doctors to stake a claim in the emerging field of social pediatrics.[1]

At the CIE's inaugural ceremony, two years earlier, many of the speakers pointed to this international organization's fundamentally French mission. Dr. W. Bonne, the WHO's representative to the ceremony, described the CIE's founding as a turning point in the history of French medicine. Going forward, French experts would be once again on the cutting edge of science and medicine. But Bonne's optimistic exclamation also gestured to a painful truth for French doctors and scientists in the twentieth century: the almost complete displacement of the French in the medical and scientific world by American and German experts.[2] If the need to safeguard colonial sovereignty topped the agendas of many French officials and doctors working in sub-Saharan Africa, for many, the desire to restore France's long-lost prestige in the field of medicine came in a close second.

When pediatrician Robert Debré founded the CIE in 1950, one of his primary aims was to carve out a new global sphere of influence for French medicine in the postwar world and to establish French doctors and scientists as experts in social pediatrics. Debré had close ties to the French political world, was a member of the Academy of Medicine, and had served as the leader of the CMR during the war.[3] A strong believer in the singularity of France's medical and scientific history, Debré also put a great deal of stock in the notion of the *mission civilisatrice,* which to him entailed shaping both the people and the environments of what he called the *les pays déshérités* (the disinherited lands). It was this belief in France's civilizing mission that would inspire his work abroad. Just as Charles de Gaulle had promoted "a certain idea of France" through his political engagements, Debré would actively cultivate a unique identity for France through his approach to medicine. For both men, France's illustrious past was inextricably tied to its future as a great power.[4]

In terms of its approach to health, the work of the CIE was solidly grounded in the practices of social medicine, which connected health outcomes to broader social and economic processes and approached the problem of community well-being from a holistic perspective.[5] Pediatrics and family health services were central to this mission. Indeed, by the postwar period, children's health had become a cornerstone of public health programs across the globe, and colonial territories were no exception. In Debré's estimation, there was no better place to launch the CIE's international work in social pediatrics than on the African continent, where he would be able to draw from a vast pool of French medical and social experts. By working in France's African empire, the CIE would also be able to help the French colonial administration demonstrate its commitment to child welfare through collaborative research and through its innovative approach to teaching.[6] Debré's choice to focus on African childhood and its discontents thus allowed him to straddle the moral problem of how to "save the children"—a widely acknowledged global imperative after 1945—and the political problem of saving France's empire.[7]

Yet while both colonial and international health initiatives embraced children as the future of Africa, visions of what that future should look like varied greatly.[8] For French doctors and researchers working for the CIE, the future of African childhood was decidedly French. Over the course of the 1950s, the CIE sponsored courses on social pediatrics in Africa and oversaw extensive research projects that transcended the borders of individual territories. Central to this work was the contention that colonial expertise still mattered in the age of globalization and—perhaps even more importantly—in the era of decolonization. Through the CIE, Debré hoped to promote the idea that French doctors and researchers could offer a unique perspective on the problems of child health in the "developing world," a perspective gleaned from decades of experience in the field of colonial health. Indeed, the choice of Brazzaville for the CIE's inaugural event in Africa was no coincidence. Beyond serving as the headquarters for the WHO in Africa, Brazzaville was also just a ferry ride away from one of the most important centers of innovation in infant, maternal, and child health in sub-Saharan Africa. As Nancy Rose Hunt has shown, "the Belgian Congo had the most extensive medical infrastructure in postwar Africa," with the highest rates of medically supervised births and a rapidly expanding network of family health and welfare facilities.[9] By launching the CIE's African ventures in Brazzaville, French doctors were not only staking a claim in one of the most important emerging fields in medicine, but they were doing it in a region of Africa where they could easily demonstrate French medical prowess to the most accomplished leaders in the field of African child health.

Here we will look at the history of the CIE, from its origins in Paris to its first forays into child health on the African continent. Through its work in social pediatrics in Africa, the CIE provided a crucial venue for French doctors to reestablish their role as international leaders in science and medicine. It also provided them with an important opportunity to reassert the relevance of colonial knowledge at a historical moment when key regions of the world were proclaiming their political independence and relying on international experts to help them build independent health systems. The CIE provided a space for physicians in the empire to engage in global conversations about child health, while still protecting their work from the fierce criticism that they often faced at the UN and the WHO. By depicting the crisis of African childhood as the unlucky but unavoidable result of economic development, the CIE contributed to a narrative wherein modernization and industrialization were the real culprits of the crisis of child health, rather than colonial rule itself. By repackaging colonial medical expertise as a body of knowledge about health in the tropics, French scientists, physicians, and social experts hoped to extend their own influence in the field of international health, making their contributions more palatable to a global audience that was becoming increasingly hostile to colonial rule on the African continent.

The Rise and Fall of French Medicine

For centuries, Paris had been a hub for the study of medicine and science, drawing students from across the globe to study the human body and its maladies. In 1896, American physician L. Harrison Mettler visited Paris and subsequently published an enthusiastic review of the world's medical capital for the *Journal of the American Medical Association.* He commended the French for equipping their capital with "the most modern scientific and sanitary improvements" and praised the extensive reach of the Parisian hospital system. Mettler wrote, "To see Paris is to have seen the world; few are the tourists, however, that ever see Paris. A room in a hotel near the Opera and a few buildings viewed from an open barouche is not Paris. . . . Ah! No, be not deceived; medical Paris cannot be seen in a three-days' sojourn, with an occasional call at the Pasteur Institute or the Hotel Dieu Hospital." Invoking the Paris of the past, Mettler noted that while the rest of Europe was struggling under the weight of the Dark Ages, Paris shone as a beacon of enlightenment. Medicine, according to Mettler, was one of the most "flourishing departments" of the University of Paris, founded in 1253 by Robert Sorbonne. There was no question for Mettler that medicine and science were at the very heart of French civilization.[10]

In 1909, another American physician, William Osler—one of the four founding professors of the Johns Hopkins Medical School—published his own impressions of France's capital. According to Osler, in Paris, the glory of French science and medicine were inextricably linked to the experience of daily life. He wrote, "The history of science is writ large in the city; in monuments, in buildings dedicated to the illustrious dead and in streets called by their names. There are more statues to medical men in Paris than in Great Britain and the United States put together."[11] In his own 1974 memoir, *L'honneur de vivre,* Debré evoked a similar image of French medicine's impressive legacy. He recalled, for example, the importance that institutions like the Pasteur Institute had for him and other young doctors at the time: "Since my childhood and until my old age, the Pasteur Institute has played a role in my life. The success of Pasteur's discoveries, and the admiration that developed among young French people for their genius—a symbol of beneficent science and national heroism—are among my first memories."[12]

Yet despite these accolades, the seeds of France's demise as the medical capital of the world had already been sown by the second half of the nineteenth century. One of the primary problems with French medical education, critics claimed, was that—unlike in Germany and the United States—it had never been successfully integrated with medical research. Although French laboratories had achieved several important breakthroughs in the nineteenth and twentieth centuries, laboratory scientists did not provide instruction to medical students.[13] While most French experts at the time agreed that science and medicine should be united in medical education, no wide-scale reform was achieved before the Second World War.[14] Perhaps the harshest critique of French medical education came from American medical reformer Abraham Flexner in two reports he authored for the Carnegie Foundation for the Advancement of Teaching. He published *Medical Education in the United States and Canada* in 1910, and his second report, *Medical Education in Europe,* was released two years later.[15] Both documents reflected changing currents in the field of medical education: medical education, Flexner argued, needed to take place within both the hospital and the research laboratory, with a strong preparation in the sciences that would begin in the classroom.

Flexner's report on medical education in Europe was a far cry from the praises sung by Mettler just fifteen years earlier.[16] The 1912 report demonstrated that in Flexner's trilogy of healing-teaching-research, the French system fell decidedly short on the last component.[17] Successful medical education required the integration of laboratory and clinic; anything short of this would inevitably compromise productivity and scientific progress. Flexner wrote, "The fact that the clinician . . . having once secured a post, commonly ceases to produce must be ascribed largely to the fact that he has thenceforth nothing to gain—though something to lose—through scientific productivity." If the natural evolution of medical education was toward a system that integrated laboratory and clinic, Flexner argued, then "it is clear that a consistent, organized and motivated university school of medicine does not exist in Great Britain or France to-day."[18] After the First World War, the Rockefeller Foundation (RF) launched what would ultimately prove to be an abortive attempt to reform French medical education from without. Working through the RF's Division of Medical Education, American physicians Richard Pearce and Alan Gregg conducted surveys of public health and other medical institutions in Belgium, Great Britain, and France and offered recommendations about how to align these health systems with the principles that Flexner had set forward. French institutions—with their close ties to the state and strong roots in the past—proved resistant to these changes. Within the Hexagon, international efforts to reform medical education were slow to produce results.[19]

Despite these obstacles, Debré remained confident throughout the early interwar period that French medicine was on its way to recuperating the international prestige it had lost over the course of the previous decades. He traveled extensively during this time, spending a year in England in addition to an extended stay in Morocco, observing firsthand what health conditions looked like on the ground in Africa. He participated in several international health initiatives and traveled to Poland, Austria, and Hungary to observe their medical systems as part of a League of Nations Health Organization medical exchange program. He also made trips to the United States, Italy, Germany, Great Britain, the Netherlands, and South America to observe their pediatric facilities, as well as to promote French medical innovations, such as the BCG vaccine against tuberculosis.[20] These voyages instilled in Debré a new spirit of optimism about the role that French medicine could play in the world. He wrote: "The welcome we received over the course of our missions in Europe, in Latin American and in the United States justified our hopes, those of France's return to the path of grandeur. In Latin America and Sweden I had the feeling that the world was once again turning toward France, sensing the return of its influence."[21]

By the 1930s, however, it became clear to Debré that his confidence had been misplaced. In his memoir, he described the dark malaise that settled over the Hexagon, a fatal combination of social degeneration, political division, and demographic decline. "Beginning in the 1930s, all of the French could see that France was ill," he wrote. "Europe could not find its balance and America was passing it by. France was unable to recover from the terrible bloodletting it had undergone." France's political and social crisis, according to Debré, was intimately connected to its demographic crisis: a country unable to replenish human life could not regain its prestige in other fields. "Appearances were misleading," Debré continued, "but in reality the anemia was profound because, after a short period of fertility, the number of births each year failed to surpass the number of deaths, which in turn revealed the nation's lack of *élan vital*." In this atmosphere of stagnation, governments came and went, workers labored under terrible conditions, scientific progress stalled, and social questions went unresolved. The United States, by contrast, saw an explosion of economic growth beginning in the 1940s, coupled with an outpouring of scientific and technological creativity. France had, without question, been ousted from its position as the world leader in science and medicine.[22]

Rather than wallow in past failures, Debré embraced a proactive approach to rehabilitating French medicine in the postwar era. As he explained in his memoir, "We needed now to attack more vigorously, to present ourselves in countries where we were unknown, where our language was unknown, our past forgotten, our capabilities doubted. To recover an honorable place in the scientific world after defeat and disaster, we needed to work indefatigably to bring ourselves—in spite of our destitution—up to date with recent findings and new movements of thought, and to engage the latest discoveries."[23] In the aftermath of the war, it became clear to Debré that French doctors could not regain their position simply by invoking the past accomplishments of institutions like the Pasteur Institute. They needed instead to work to expand their operations on a global scale. The solution, according to Debré, was a two-pronged strategy: first, a complete overhaul of the French system of medical training and research—especially in the field of pediatrics—and second, the expansion of French medical intervention to all corners of the globe. It was from this second aspect of Debré's strategy that the idea for the CIE was born.[24]

International Children's Health *à la Française*

The CIE was the product of a most unusual arrangement between a national government and an international organization. While it would draw its funding both from the French government and from UNICEF, the CIE promised to offer something that UNICEF—in its initial incarnation—did not: permanence.[25] When UNICEF was created, it was intended to be a temporary organization, aimed at dealing with the medical and social fallout of the war. When Debré lobbied UNICEF's administrative council for a more permanent organization that could be tasked with solving longer-term problems such as the training of medical personnel, he was told that more immediate issues took precedence. Beyond creating an organization that could coordinate long-term international cooperation in the field of social pediatrics, the CIE also undertook to provide a particularly "French" take on solving the global crisis of child health. In the aftermath of the war, Debré had worked diligently to represent French interests and perspectives within both UNICEF and UNESCO, but he was unsatisfied with the possibilities for carving out a place for French experts in organizations dominated by Americans. From the outset of his participation in UNICEF, Debré dreamed of creating a permanent international children's organization that would be spearheaded by French doctors.[26] As Debré explained in his memoir, "I wished for my country an active role in accomplishing UNICEF's task, a role that would ensure a place for the French language, thought, and way of envisioning problems of cooperation. The creation of a similar institution would permit the resurgence of French influence in this domain and facilitate the renewal of its intellectual authority in the world."[27] The goal of this new children's organization was thus not only to promote child health on a worldwide scale but also to foster French medicine's global role.

Both the UN General Assembly and the US State Department were reluctant to accept a separate French international children's organization, but Debré fought relentlessly to push the CIE's creation through the necessary diplomatic channels.[28] He noted in particular the resistance he faced from his Anglo-Saxon colleagues but recounted the overwhelming support given to him from his Turkish, Yugoslav, Swedish, and Venezuelan peers, who he claimed had "the closest connections to French culture and medicine."[29] After much diplomatic maneuvering, Debré eventually succeeded in convincing his colleagues at the UN of the necessity of his proposition and secured the requisite funding from the French government and the UN. By early 1950, Debré was ready to launch his new organization.[30]

On 18 January 1950, doctors, politicians, and diplomats gathered in the resplendent Salon de l'Horloge at the French Ministry of Foreign Affairs to inaugurate the CIE. The mission of the CIE, according to its charter, was to "encourage the study throughout the world of problems relating to childhood, the dissemination of a knowledge of hygiene and puericulture, and the technical training of specialized personnel." The organization would pursue these goals by offering training courses in social pediatrics for physicians, nurses, social workers, public health officials, teachers, and government administrators. In training this new generation of medical personnel, the CIE's founders hope to promote social pediatrics on a global scale and to encourage collaboration between governments and international institutions dedicated to the study of childhood, health, and development.

While intensely committed to its global mission, the CIE's founders—led by Debré—were careful to emphasize the institution's fundamentally French character.[31] Seated beneath the glittering chandeliers of the Salon d'Horloge, the attendees of the inauguration listened to a series of speeches that reflected Debré's vision of France's essential role in global health. Pierre Schneiter, the French minister of public health and population, credited French doctors for recognizing that problems of childhood extended past the immediate circumstances of the postwar world. His government, he affirmed, would continue to honor French munificence and scientific prowess through its ongoing commitment to improving child health on a global scale. Yvonne Georges-Picot, the vice president of the municipal council of Paris, echoed these sentiments, stating that "the work to be accomplished calls for the efforts and the devotion of all. It is natural, therefore, that in Paris—this Paris which has always stood forth, as we well know, for its traditional spirit of humanism and universalism—it should be our concern to do everything in our power for the children of the entire world."[32] Both Schneiter and Georges-Picot emphasized the CIE's connections to France's long tradition of medical and humanitarian greatness, and both saw this new institution as a way to ensure a prestigious place for French doctors and social reformers in the future. Indeed, Schneiter had high hopes that the work of the CIE would draw medical professionals from across the globe to "this crossroads of ancient intellectual fame which is Paris" and, "in harmony with our oldest traditions, radiate afar our culture and disseminate the teaching of our men of science."[33]

While Schneiter and Georges-Picot lauded French medical and scientific achievements, they were careful to ground them within a broader framework of international health cooperation. The CIE, they explained, was meant not to compete with UNICEF but rather to complement this "emergency" organization by providing a permanent center for the study of child health problems around the world.[34] While the CIE was French in statute, Schneiter assured his audience that it was to be international in spirit. Indeed, he claimed that they had "tried to make of this French creation an institution as international in its legal status as its foundation under French law could possibly permit it to be." The organization would serve to foster collaboration among the world's best physicians and scientists, and its executive board was to be composed of experts from different national backgrounds. When the CIE was founded, doctors from France, Sweden, Great Britain, and Poland were represented on the board. Trainees and researchers affiliated with the center were also to be drawn from different locations across the globe.[35]

Debré's simultaneous insistence on the CIE's "Frenchness" and on its profoundly cooperative character was a politically astute approach for a country that—just half a decade earlier—had found itself on the wrong side of history. After five dark years of Franco-Nazi collaboration, cooperative initiatives like the CIE demonstrated that French medical leaders and government officials were capable of playing by the rules of postwar internationalism. By hosting an organization like the CIE in Paris, the French government was demonstrating not only its efforts to work within the framework of liberal global governance but also its intentions to help lead the march toward peace and prosperity in the postwar era. During an era when the French state had neither the military strength nor the political clout to retain its colonial possessions, it meant everything to convince the world that France still had a brand of civilization worth exporting, either through direct colonial control or through the more indirect channels of development and medical aid. The strategies of drawing on past prestige and of expanding French medicine into the developing world were mutually reinforcing tactics designed to strengthen France's position in the postwar era, and both were integrated into Debré's vision of the CIE.[36]

The speeches given on the day of the CIE's inauguration celebrated France's historic role in promoting internationalism and touted the universality of French values. According to Schneiter, researchers coming to Paris would find "an atmosphere of mutual understanding, the greatest documentary and reference facilities and a synthesis of knowledge and information concerning the child."[37] Participants who hailed from other countries were equally willing to indulge Debré's vision of France's past medical and scientific glory, as well as its legacy as the birthplace of the Declaration of the Rights of Man and Citizen. Professor Arvid Wallgren, the Swedish representative on the CIE Executive Board, lauded both the generosity of the French government and the important tradition of human rights in France. He exclaimed, "It is typical of the French spirit that this International Children's Centre should have come into being here in France. For you, 'Liberty, Equality, and Fraternity' are not just meaningless words, but realities, inherent qualities of the French nation. Moreover, you do not limit your passion for this ideal to your own people. 'La douce France' is not indifferent to other countries. Rather than a French Children's Centre, it is an International Centre which is here created today." In Wallgren's formulation, children played an especially important role in France's beneficence, as "the weakest of human beings, as well as the most precious."[38] At a time when scientists and physicians from other countries were making names for themselves as pioneers in the field of social pediatrics, the inauguration of the CIE was a crucial moment for French doctors to assert their own contributions to the field of child health and to have those contributions recognized—and celebrated—by the broader international medical community.

The CIE Comes to Africa

If the reassertion of French medical expertise on the global stage was central to the mission of the CIE, equally pivotal was the role that colonial expertise would play in that broader mission. Not long after its inauguration, the CIE's founders began the process of installing the organization's headquarters at the Château de Longchamp, nestled amid the lush greenery of Paris's Bois de Boulogne. Almost simultaneously, they also began planning their work in another French capital, more than six thousand kilometers away. The CIE's 1952 conference in Brazzaville would set the tone for its first decade of work on the African continent by celebrating colonial achievements and facilitating an in-depth exploration of the most pressing health problems facing children in postwar Africa. Over the course of the 1950s and 1960s, the CIE would work to develop scientific and educational initiatives in the field of child health both in Europe and in Africa, extending the reach of French scientific advancements and providing an institutional space to assert the ongoing relevance of French colonial expertise.

Almost immediately after its inauguration, the CIE launched both its teaching and its research initiatives, piloting its first courses in 1950 and 1951 and its research laboratory in 1952.[39] The CIE's courses were intended to be international in scope, and although they were based primarily in Europe, they drew participants from across the globe, including from colonial territories in Africa.[40] The first sessions, which took place in France, Italy, Switzerland, and Great Britain, focused on topics such as the rehabilitation of physically handicapped children, prenatal and neonatal care, nutrition, child psychology, demography, infectious childhood diseases, and vaccines. In 1952, the subject matter was expanded to include the study of antituberculosis campaigns, social services, and pediatric genetics.[41] For Debré, these classes were about more than the simple transmission of information from professor to student. They were intended to be an "exchange of views" and a "joining of experiences and techniques." All of the courses included a practicum component, such as a visit to a laboratory, medical facility, or social services center.[42] The theory behind each of the courses that the CIE offered—in particular the courses on social pediatrics—was that medical professionals should be able to put aside their "personal interests, beliefs, and ideologies" in favor of cooperative work on the "common problems" of childhood that transcended national boundaries. In addition to their work in the classroom and on-site, participants were encouraged to form bonds that would extend beyond their professional lives. In order to help foster these relationships, participants in CIE courses and colloquia were lodged in the same hotel or residence and shared their meals in a common cafeteria on the grounds of the Château de Longchamp.[43]

Despite this transnational approach, the CIE's founders recognized early on that geography, climate, and culture—as well as political and social structures—had a significant effect on the kinds of medical problems that children and families faced. Although the medical faculty who designed the CIE's social pediatrics courses intended for them to be universally applicable to all participants, in 1951 members of the CIE's administrative council acknowledged that physicians coming from tropical regions—especially Africa—faced a unique set of concerns. The European social pediatrics courses did not cover diseases like malaria or nutritional deficiencies like beriberi and kwashiorkor, despite the great importance of these issues to physicians working in sub-Saharan Africa. To respond to these growing concerns about the unique health and social conditions of the African continent, the CIE—in conjunction with the Ministry of Overseas France—sponsored a five-day conference in Brazzaville in December 1952, shortly after the WHO Regional Office for Africa began its own work in AEF's capital.[44]

Over the course of a week, participants engaged with a wide range of topics, from intestinal parasites to juvenile delinquency. As they moved through their discussions, these doctors, nurses, social workers, and government officials were careful to situate their proposals for collaboration within a cautiously circumscribed framework of international cooperation that aimed to complement, rather than to replace, colonial health programs.[45] While mindful not to step on the toes of European governments, they also acknowledged the long-standing international interest in problems of childhood in Africa, citing the example of the 1931 Conference on African Children, sponsored by Britain's Save the Children Fund.[46] The 1952 meeting would thus serve as another opportunity for doctors, experts, and administrators to evaluate the ongoing difficulties that medical services faced in the battle to improve the lives of babies, children, and adolescents living on the African continent.

Unlike the 1931 conference—which had been attended mostly by missionary doctors and representatives from humanitarian organizations—participants in the 1952 conference hailed primarily from colonial health services in Africa, along with three representatives from the WHO and two from UNICEF. Countries and territories represented at the conference included AEF, AOF, Belgium, Cameroon, France, Great Britain, Madagascar, Portugal, South Africa, Spain, and Togo. Colonial representatives in attendance came from all branches of European administrations in Africa. From the Belgian delegation, for example, delegate Moreau de Melan was in charge of penitentiary services in the Belgian Congo, while his colleagues Dr. Périn and J. Aerts came from health and indigenous education services, respectively. From AEF, representatives included Médecin-Général Alain Talec, the director general of health services; Médecin-Colonel J. Ceccaldi, the director of Brazzaville's Pasteur Institute; G. Sautter, a geographer for the Institut des études centrafricaines; and J. Gardair, the director of social services. The CIE representatives present included only French nationals, who were almost exclusively associated with the Ministry of Overseas France or French colonial health services.[47]

The predominance of colonial voices—coupled with the complete absence of African perspectives—shaped the discussions of health and social problems in powerful ways.[48] While just two months earlier colonial delegations had found themselves defending their overseas empires at the annual meeting of the UN Special Committee on Non-self-governing Territories, the 1952 Brazzaville conference on child health challenged neither the basic premise of colonial rule nor colonial governments' ability to provide essential services to inhabitants of their overseas territories. Instead, the discussions were focused on working through concrete problems that colonial health services faced, without calling into question the broader social and political frameworks that undergirded those services. Participants, moreover, presented existing health services in such a way as to showcase the successes that colonial governments had already achieved. The most enthusiastic endorsement of French colonial rule came from Jean Cédile, the secretary general for AEF. In his opening remarks, Cédile exclaimed, "Our Africa, in a decade, has accomplished unimaginable progress. . . . This Africa, in full evolution, and which has already surpassed the elementary stages of civilization, has begun to open itself even more to our work of brotherly humanity." He continued, "Our cities offer the spectacle of development and of a transformation that would have been inconceivable only a few years earlier."[49]

Brazzaville in particular, Cédile noted, held a special place within the French empire. The explosion of development projects in AEF's capital, coupled with the city's wider symbolism within the history of the French Union, made it a fitting choice of location for launching the CIE's work in Africa. Brazzaville had served as the capital of Free France during the war and was also the location for the 1944 Conférence africaine française, where important leaders from metropolitan France and the empire met to sketch the initial contours of what would ultimately become the French Union.[50] Present at the 1952 child health meeting were several alumni of the Brazzaville conference of 1944, including Médecin-Général Adolphe Sicé, high commissioner for AEF, and Médecin-Général Marcel Vaucel, who had served as the director general of health services in AEF in 1944.[51] According to Cédile, the spirit of 1944 was in the air at the 1952 child health conference not only because of the individuals present but also because questions of medicine and childhood had figured prominently in the vision of the French empire that emerged from the 1944 meeting.[52]

According to Cédile, Brazzaville's economic and social progress had several manifestations, including the expansion of social services and children's health facilities. Within the city—and across France's African empire more broadly—he noted, "You will see hospitals and dispensaries being built, schools for doctors and nurses being developed, in addition to the functioning of a number of institutions intended to save, care for, and raise babies, as well as a variety of services to advise and to guide mothers, both before and after the birth of their children." In addition to these fixed-location services for families, AEF also boasted a host of mobile services in rural areas. The most important of these services was the Service d'hygiène mobile et de prophylaxie (Mobile Hygiene and Prophylaxis Service), to which Cédile attributed a drastic drop in stillbirths and infant mortality as a result of its fight to conquer some of the "most devastating" epidemic diseases in French Africa. Social services in AEF complemented the federation's medical institutions: courses in childcare and housekeeping were available to women, and the territorial administration was building new schools to train African social workers. Cédile also recounted the different educational opportunities that existed for both European and African children, including—most importantly—an elite high school to train the future leaders of France's African empire. These investments in material and social progress, he argued, would serve as a useful model of "development" on which other conference participants could draw.[53]

Even more significant than advancement in these tangible realms, Cédile argued, was the progress he believed that the French had made in helping Africans reach their "full potential as human beings." He explained, "It is the development of man that is the ultimate goal that we are pursuing within the French Union." "In all of the territories in our charge," he claimed, "every individual, whatever his race, religion, or skin color, is assured the respect of his personality, and his dignity as a human being. His promotion toward the intellectual ideal and toward his material well-being is our primary concern." Cédile believed that this evolution would come in time through an increasingly close association with French civilization. Assimilation, he noted, was both the means and the end of the French project in Africa. Children would play a special role in this process, as "both the hope and the condition for the future."[54] The model that the CIE was advancing for health and social services in France's African territories, in other words, was not about putting Africans on the path toward self-sufficiency or independence, but rather was oriented toward making them more French.

Not all of the conference participants, however, were as uncritical as Cédile when it came to France's colonial record. In her own address to the conference, Eugénie Eboué-Tell drew participants' attention to the darker side of postwar development in equatorial Africa. Eboué-Tell was the widow of Félix Eboué—the hero of de Gaulle's African resistance—and was a political figure in her own right, attending the conference as a representative of the French Union. She was also one of the only people of color in attendance at the conference. As a former schoolteacher in Guyana, Eboué-Tell had a long-standing interest in questions of child health and well-being. Action in favor of African childhood, she contended, would need to take place on two levels. First, she explained, colonial doctors and officials in Africa would have to reckon with the immediate symptoms of the crisis of African childhood: infant mortality, epidemic disease, and juvenile delinquency. But they would also have to confront the underlying cause of these symptoms, which Eboué-Tell saw as the long-term crisis of social and economic development in Africa, development that she claimed was still "far from being realized."[55]

While the ultimate goal of family health and social programs was to remedy these ongoing inequalities, Eboué-Tell argued that immediate action was also needed to help the African child "integrate himself into a civilization that is not his own." The mixing of European and African societies, she claimed, had created a "psychological disequilibrium." Since it would be impossible to return to a precolonial Africa, government services would have to reckon with the social uprooting caused by the transformation of African society by European imperialism, "of which juvenile delinquency is only the final stage and most visible manifestation."[56] Colonial development schemes often ignored broader social and economic inequalities and paid little attention to the psychological well-being of African youth. "The errors committed in these domains," she claimed, "which resulted more often out of indifference than ill-will, add up to produce the 'evolved' African in the worst sense of the term: a being that has lost his traditional values without having acquired a profound knowledge of a foreign civilization."[57]

Beyond the psychological ruptures that were part and parcel of colonial rule, Eboué-Tell also pointed to the ongoing crisis of physical health among African children. She explained that in no other domain was the gap between the "evolved world" and the "insufficiently developed world" as stark as in the realm of child health. She cited the differences between the rates of stillbirth and infant mortality, as well as the differing life expectancies, in Africa and Europe. The causes of these divides, she argued, were medical, economic, and social. This "waste of human resources," she claimed, was intimately connected to the broader problem of colonial underdevelopment. Without actively addressing these ongoing inequalities, there would be no way to improve the quality of life for people living on the African continent.[58]

If Eboué-Tell's speech offered a more critical counterpoint to the perspectives given by Cédile and others, she was alone in her strident condemnations of the disappointments of colonial development. While the conference would touch on many of the same issues raised at the UN Special Committee just months earlier—including nutrition, social problems, health services, and education—it did so without questioning the fundamental legitimacy of the colonial system. If participants spoke outright about ongoing medical challenges in sub-Saharan Africa, they were much less forthcoming about the underlying causes. They blamed poor health outcomes on African cultural practices or attributed them to "industrialization," without linking them to the social, political, and cultural disruption brought by colonial rule or by the structural violence that accompanied it. For Cédile, this project of "making man" (*faire l'homme*) was a problem of governance constrained only by the financial resources available to colonial governments. By joining forces with other medical professionals under the aegis of the CIE, French doctors would be able to work more efficiently toward their "ideal of progress," paving the way for an African future that was more intimately bound up with its metropolitan counterpart.[59]

Teaching Social Pediatrics in Paris and Dakar

The discussions that had begun in 1952 in Brazzaville were continued in the CIE's social pediatrics courses in Paris and later in Dakar, as part of an effort to understand the ways that geography and climate—as well as social, political, and economic particularities—continued to shape the problems of child health in the "developing world." Implicit in the content and organization of these courses was the notion that—even in an era of rapid globalization—European medical personnel were still the most qualified experts in the field of African children's health. These courses, moreover, allowed colonial officials to respond to the UN's call for increased international cooperation in technical fields, while still permitting colonial doctors to shield their work from the criticism they often faced in international bodies such as the UN and the WHO. Unlike at the UN, where critics of colonialism often drew connections between poor health outcomes and the ongoing problems of imperial rule, the CIE's courses and colloquia provided an opportunity to celebrate the achievements of colonial medicine, as well as a venue to assert the ongoing relevance of colonial expertise.

In the fall of 1955, physicians and sociomedical personnel from across the globe gathered in Paris to study problems relating to child health in the tropics. They came from AEF, AOF (Côte d'Ivoire), North Africa (Morocco, Tunisia, and Algeria), South America, Asia (China, Cambodia, and Vietnam), and the Middle East (Israel, Lebanon, and Syria). Over the course of five weeks, they participated in the CIE's course on tropical pathology, which combined theoretical exposés, working groups, and visits to laboratories and hospital services. They also visited pharmacological production facilities that were pioneering new drugs to treat tropical diseases.[60] Throughout the course, participants and faculty explored the impact of both physical and social environments on child health and considered the medical repercussions of prolonged contact between European and African societies. Experts hailing from France's overseas empire played a key role in designing the structure of the course, and the on-site visits were clearly intended to foreground French contributions to science and medicine.[61] These visits included a trip to the Pasteur Institute, where participants were able to observe the plague, leprosy, and cholera laboratories firsthand, as well as the "consultation center for exotic diseases." Guided by Debré himself, they also visited the infant medical clinic at the Paris Children's Hospital, as well as the National Blood Transfusion Center, the Museum of Man, and the Museum of Overseas France. Far from fostering a critique of French colonial health—or of France's overseas project more broadly—these visits celebrated the role of France in the world.

In 1956 the CIE's program for social pediatrics in Africa was expanded and for the first time the courses were actually held on location, in Dakar, the political and medical capital of France's West African federation. As Debré stated in his opening remarks to the session, the ability to hold these courses on location in Africa represented a "new horizon" for the study of social pediatrics. According to Debré, there were obvious limitations to holding a course on tropical pediatrics in a European city, where the practical visits would take place in facilities very different from those operating in the tropical world. In Dakar, by contrast, course participants would be able to benefit from firsthand experience in Africa, which would allow them to appreciate "the vastness of the tasks to be accomplished there."[62]

The Dakar social pediatrics course allowed participants to explore their subject matter up close, from the perspective of the very institutions tasked with overseeing questions of child health in France's African colonies. Participants were required to complete a brief practicum in infant and maternal health at the Clinique médicale infantile at the Hôpital le Dantec, in the Plateau neighborhood of Dakar. In Dakar, conference organizers also scheduled on-site visits to the Pasteur Institute, Dakar's urban hygiene services, and the

Organisme de recherches sur l'alimentation et la nutrition africaine (Research Bureau for African Diet and Nutrition; ORANA). Dakar's central location also allowed participants to venture outside AOF's capital in order to explore the development of public health services in neighboring regions. On a trip to Thiès, a Senegalese city about sixty kilometers east of Dakar, course participants observed experiments in the joint WHO-UNICEF antimalaria campaign. In Bamako (French Sudan), they visited the Trachoma Institute, the Marchoux Institute for the study of leprosy, and the offices of the Mobile Hygiene and Prophylaxis Service.

By working on location in Africa, participants in the social pediatrics course were able to delve more deeply into the specificities of child health on the continent. A series of sessions on African nutrition, for example, considered family eating habits, traditional African diets, and the challenges of breastfeeding in the tropics. The course also provided an extensive exploration of innovative measures to prevent the spread of epidemic disease. Dr. Francisco J. C. Cambournac, a Portuguese physician who would later serve as regional director for the WHO in Africa, presented the newest methods for fighting the transmission of malaria in tropical regions, in addition to an exploration of the disease's broader social and economic impacts.[63] Even more than the previous year's sessions in Paris, the Dakar social pediatrics course paid close attention to the connections between physical bodies and the broader social contexts in which those bodies lived. Vaucel, for example, drew on his experience in the French colonial health service to explain the social impact of sleeping sickness in sub-Saharan Africa. Presentations by Gérard Dulphy—the director of social affairs at the Ministry of Overseas France—focused on the development of social services on the African continent and on the role of the child in industrializing African societies.[64]

Despite the incredibly diverse range of material covered by the course, all of the sessions were unified by their emphasis on the value of European—and specifically French—expertise and by their celebration of colonial achievements in the fields of science, medicine, and social work. Perhaps even more importantly, though, was the way that these courses framed medical and social problems in postwar Africa as natural outcomes of modernization, industrialization, and urbanization, rather than as the result of decades of colonial inequality and violence. By casting the crisis of child health as a more universal problem connected to climate, geography, and general patterns of global economic development, French experts were able to respond indirectly to some of the more vehement critiques of colonial rule that were emerging in the UN Trusteeship Council, the UN Special Committee on Non-self-governing Territories, and the WHO. It was in this same spirit that the CIE conducted its first multilocation study on social welfare, with a focus on juvenile delinquency in sub-Saharan Africa.

From Social Medicine to Social Work

In 1959, the CIE published its *Study on the Living Conditions of the Urban African Child and Their Influence on Juvenile Delinquency.* Drawing on three years of data collected in Cameroon, Côte d'Ivoire, and Madagascar, it considered the causes of the marked rise in youth crime in postwar French Africa. While the goal of this investigation was to provide the French government with data that it could use to support the development of social services in France's African territories, the subject of the study also squared nicely with demands by anticolonial delegations to the UN that colonial governments pay closer attention to the ways that urbanization and industrialization in their empires had negatively impacted local societies.[65] Just as the special committee had pointed to poor health outcomes as a potential indicator of colonial negligence, its members also focused on growing social unrest as a symptom of ongoing inequality and oppression. From the French perspective, the choice of locations for the study was no coincidence. Although there is no mention of it in the text itself, it was widely known that these three territories were significant sites of political and social unrest in the late 1940s and 1950s.[66] The ability to attribute social and political instability in these areas to forces outside the colonial system was crucial for the French delegates to the UN, who found themselves faced with growing opposition to French rule in Africa.

For the majority of the colonial period, the health administration in France's African territories had concerned itself primarily with fighting epidemic disease and establishing clinics, hospitals, and maternity wards. In the wake of the Second World War, however, the interests of the colonial administration turned increasingly to the social problems plaguing African society, with a particular focus on children and the family.[67] While these issues had certainly been on the radar of colonial administrators for decades, never before had questions of community welfare been of such paramount concern to institutions that had been preoccupied first and foremost with the health of physical bodies.

The impetus in the mid-1950s to create a network of social services in France's African colonies was not entirely a new one. Local administrators in AOF had envisioned such a service as early as 1938, but annual reports in this period lamented the fact that so little had been done to get the project off the ground. In Côte d'Ivoire, for example, health officials in the 1940s complained that no steps had been taken to launch a full-scale social service program. They also noted that social workers were few and far between, working only in the most populous areas, such as Abidjan and Bouaké.[68] In the late 1940s, health service directors in Senegal and Upper Volta made similar observations about the "embryonic" state of AOF's social services. In his annual report for 1949, Médecin-Colonel Mondain, the director of health services for Senegal, noted that only two social workers were active in the territory and that while very "devoted" to their positions, they did not always have the capacity to focus exclusively on the family. Instead, local doctors often asked them to fulfill the role of nurse or midwife in the face of ongoing personnel shortages. Mondain's report suggested that the experiment in social services might be reinvigorated by recruiting a few European social workers who could instruct African women in how to best perform that role.[69]

Some colonial officials—in Côte d'Ivoire in particular—were optimistic about the possibilities for expanding social services in their territories.[70] In 1950, Médecin-Colonel Xavier Sainz, the head of health services in Côte d'Ivoire, wrote that the creation of a social service branch in 1951 would be a "happy innovation" and would play a key role in France's quest to "improve the human condition and ensure the future of the [African] race." Although the goal of social services, according to Sainz, was to educate the masses, he cautioned against trying too hard to remake Africans in the image of Europeans. The efforts of social services, he wrote, should be directed primarily toward young people, working hand in hand with existing health services and educational institutions. Social services could, according to Sainz, help fulfill certain public health goals, such as teaching hygiene to school-age children and infant care to young girls. The school itself, Sainz explained, should be a "model house to serve as a real example" to students with regard to its cleanliness, lighting, and ventilation. Students, he advised, should be taken to visit hospitals, dispensaries, and water purification stations in order to teach them about the basics of sanitation and hygiene. Social services would also be charged with the protection of orphans and children in moral danger, with the goal of halting the rising rates of juvenile delinquency.[71]

Despite Sainz's optimism about the role that social services could play in Côte d'Ivoire and beyond, funding and personnel shortages continued to present seemingly insurmountable obstacles. Efforts to create a unified social service in AOF dragged on unsuccessfully until the mid-1950s. By 1955, some territories had successfully started small-scale programs, but a unified social services branch for AOF existed only as a pipe dream in the imaginations of the most optimistic colonial administrators.

While internal reports reflected the fragmented nature of the social services that did exist in France's African territories, reports destined for the UN and for the WHO told a different story. Although they acknowledged the social dislocation that postwar economic development had caused, these reports also portrayed a much more coherent approach to ameliorating the human condition in France's colonies than what actually existed. A 1952 report on the protection of family and childhood explained that the "traditional political, social and economic organization of AOF," far from guaranteeing social stability and security, had in fact created a long-standing sense of insecurity: "physical insecurity in the face of grand epidemics . . . economic insecurity as a result of land exploitation, and social insecurity as a result of the serious lacunae created by a collective social structure." While the actions of the French colonial administration had initially promoted the stabilization of African societies and economies, the report admitted that over time, "contact with European civilization and its constant attempts to raise the standard of living of the native populations ultimately broke this stability and created new social problems heretofore unseen in Black Africa."[72] Despite the sometimes nefarious effects of colonial efforts, the report claimed that the majority of African children found themselves in "an environment conducive to their development and their education" and had access to the "protection and the care necessary . . . to become adults." The lack of organized social services was, according to the report, more of an apparent gap than a real one, since various services of the colonial administration (health, work, and education) collectively filled many of the same functions.[73]

Critics of empire at the UN, however, weren't so easily fooled. They argued that many of the social problems that experts had identified in African societies were direct products of their dependent status. A 1952 UN Special Committee report on social conditions explained that "programmes of social advancement have not only to overcome problems of ill-health and poverty of a long-standing character, but also, and often at the same time, problems of social adjustment emerging with economic change. The opening of new channels of communication, the development of trade, urbanization, the change from a subsistence to a cash economy and economic progress in general have tended to disrupt established forms of social organization. New foundations are required on which the individual can build a new expression of his responsibility to his family and his community."[74] Juvenile delinquency, according to the anticolonial delegations at the UN and the UN Special Committee, was a particularly notable symptom of the social dislocation that could accompany colonial rule. The 1952 report noted, "The village, even in transition, is usually able to prevent or control juvenile delinquency. In the towns, with family ties loosened, a number of the more adventurous young people, capable of becoming good citizens, require the assistance and supervision of trained social workers."[75] The first step, however, was to conduct an in-depth study of the problem—both its causes and its manifestations—before colonial governments would be able to address the social fallout of their ill-conceived development plans.

Thus it was in response to both the shifting concerns of the French colonial administration and the demands of the UN that the CIE undertook its investigation into juvenile delinquency in sub-Saharan Africa in the mid-1950s. If keeping the UN and its agencies out of Africa was an important goal of postwar intercolonial cooperation, it was also essential for the French administration to demonstrate that it was taking international criticism seriously, especially if it was going to successfully make the case that the French Union represented a real break with France's colonial past.

According to the study's introduction, France's African territories had seen a rapid rise in the incidence of youth crime since 1945. Despite this fact, no systematic study of this phenomenon had been undertaken by the French colonial administration, which had to content itself with extrapolating from data on juvenile delinquency collected in metropolitan France. The CIE study began with an exploration of possible causes for the growth in juvenile delinquency, including detribalization, urbanization, the breakdown of the traditional African family structure, and the "the pernicious influence of the cinema and the bar."[76] What was so worrying about the rise of juvenile delinquency, according to Ika Paul-Pont—one of the principal investigators on the project—was not the crime itself but rather the fact that it was potentially a symptom of greater social upheaval. Economic development brought with it myriad social problems, and experts and government officials—perhaps motivated by growing international attention to these problems—were becoming increasingly aware that they had neither the tools to study them nor the means to address them.[77]

The CIE research teams conducted their study through a series of questionnaires, filled out by a social worker on behalf of a young person upon arrest or while on trial. Despite the shortcomings in their methodology, CIE researchers identified several patterns. They found that the majority of infractions in Tananarive, Douala, and Abidjan consisted of theft. Among delinquents, the rate of "abnormal" family situations was much higher than in the control group. In Douala, for example, 30 percent of delinquent youths came from families with divorced parents, compared to 18 percent in the control group. More delinquent youth lived with strangers or alone (19 percent versus 6 percent in the control group) and more were likely to be orphans. In all cases, young people who had been convicted of a crime were far more likely to be children of farmers living outside the city limits, and sometimes outside the territory itself, and were much more likely to express dissatisfaction with their work, their education, and their living situation. Juvenile delinquents were found to be less likely to spend time with family members and classmates than were their nondelinquent peers, and they were also found to be more likely to gamble and to frequent the cinema and bars. Other considerations, including ethnicity, religion, and geographic positioning within the cities, were found to have little or no correlation with the likelihood that a young person would commit a crime.[78]

Drawing on both their statistical findings and qualitative data from case studies, CIE researchers attempted to draw some general conclusions about the rise of juvenile delinquency in French Africa. Historian Sarah Fishman has shown in her work on juvenile delinquency in France that experts attributed the rise of youth crime during the Second World War to the sudden absence of fathers.[79] In France's overseas territories, the explanation for the rise of juvenile delinquency was a rather different one, but it was still connected to a breakdown of traditional family structures. CIE researchers blamed the rapid rise in youth crime not on the absence of fathers, per se, but rather on the increased mobility of children, who left home to find work or attend school in larger urban centers and were generally left to their own devices. Thus the concern was not about the absence of mothers or fathers specifically but rather about a general breakdown of family authority. This overhaul of traditional social structures, coupled with poverty and unemployment in African cities, led children and young people to turn to theft for survival.

Fishman shows that despite the attempt to blame the breakdown of paternal authority in the home, the real causes of the rise of juvenile delinquency in metropolitan France were economic. The same economic problems in Africa—brought about by industrialization and urbanization and compounded by the social and political inequalities that were part and parcel of colonial rule—had led to a similar increase in youth crime in France's African territories. Poverty that had been customarily mitigated by traditional social structures in rural areas was left unchecked in rapidly developing urban centers. Here is how one social worker described the New-Bell neighborhood of Douala in her report:

> Population density and the proximity of inhabitants is striking from the first glance. . . . It is among a sea of corrugated tin—the most common construction material that strikes you with its ugliness and filth—that men, women and children circulate. . . . Entrance into the New-Bell quarter is done without transition. Whether you enter from the neighboring quarter of Bali or Yabassi, the passage is brutal. . . . Everything is dense and squeezed together. . . . Darkness only brings rest late in the night. . . . Disorder, already striking in the city center, is made worse on the periphery by torrential downpours which lead to the accumulation of water during the rainy season.

Parents from rural regions of Cameroon would send their young boys to live with distant relatives in the city, with the hope that they would either attend school or learn a trade. As the territory continued to industrialize and a growing number of young people were living in nontraditional family situations, the rates of juvenile delinquency began to rise.[80]

In the conclusion of their report, CIE researchers recommended developing services to address the problem of children in moral danger. They emphasized the importance of using correctional institutions to rehabilitate juvenile delinquents, rather than to punish them. And finally, they advocated for the development of a postpenal regime to ensure the readaptation of young people into society as productive workers. While much of the report focused on developing solutions to help young people after release, its authors also encouraged the colonial government to expand programs to prevent juvenile delinquency, including summer camps and organized sports, in order to give children a more structured way to spend their free time. They also recommended the creation of more public schools, as well as professional training programs that would give young people better qualifications to work. The authors of the study expressed their hope that by determining the factors contributing to youth crime, a more proactively preventative regime could be instated and, for those who did enter the juvenile justice system, a more humane postincarceration regime could be established.

While the impetus to develop social services in France's African territories clearly predated the UN, there is no doubt that this renewed push to understand and confront social problems in the mid-1950s was also a response to criticisms at the UN that European colonial governments had condemned their dependent populations to lives of chaos and poverty. In their study of juvenile delinquency in Cameroon, Madagascar, and Côte d'Ivoire, CIE researchers were careful to situate the miseries of France's African territories within the broader context of global economic development, refuting the claim that these territories owed their economic trouble and social dislocation to their dependent status. While anticolonial parties at the UN continued to call for independence as the only road to full social and physical well-being for colonial populations, the CIE report proposed expanding social services and further integrating colonial practices with the French model of reeducation and social rehabilitation. Their recommendations echoed a sentiment that had been expressed in the 1952 report on the protection of family and childhood, which stated that what would bring a return to social peace and harmony was not political independence but rather the development of a French model of family services, a model that would be based on "respect for the individual" and would "assure total and effective protection for the family and the child."[81]

~

Although the CIE did not shy away from investigating the most pressing crises facing African families in the 1950s, the studies that it produced and the courses it offered often uncoupled those crises from the larger problems of colonial violence, economic and social inequality, and ongoing segregation. The CIE's courses on social pediatrics—along with its three-year, multilocation study of juvenile delinquency—portrayed poor health outcomes and social instability as unfortunate but natural products of industrialization, urbanization, and economic development. By neutralizing the role that colonization had played in creating the medical and social problems that often crippled African communities, the CIE was able to market the knowledge that colonial experts had generated within the empire to a broader community of scientists, physicians, and social workers within what they termed the "developing world." In doing so, the CIE provided a crucial venue for Debré and his colleagues to reclaim a place for French doctors, scientists, and social experts in the fields of medicine and public health.

As French doctors struggled to regain a degree of international prestige through their work with the CIE, the WHO was continuing its own battles against poor health conditions in Africa and against the staunch resistance it faced from colonial governments in Africa. An exploration of two of the most important WHO programs Africa in the 1950s—malaria eradication and supplemental nutrition campaigns—makes clear the far-reaching impact that the tensions of decolonization had on the relationship between colonial health institutions and postwar global health efforts.

CHAPTER SIX

Fighting Illness, Battling Decolonization

> It is current international terminology to speak of developed countries and underdeveloped countries, from the economic and social points of view. Like all classification, this one is too rigid and unsuitable for application to the African continent. . . . Belgium, France, Portugal, the United Kingdom and the Union of South Africa have all contributed, with untiring generosity and an unflagging desire for progress, their methods, their techniques, and their cultural and scientific resources, for the benefit of less developed people for whose administration these great countries have been responsible.
>
> —Dr. Pierre Dorolle, deputy director general of the WHO, "Opening Speech to the Malaria Conference in Equatorial Africa," November 1950

IN HIS INTRODUCTORY REMARKS to the 1950 malaria conference in Kampala, Uganda, Dr. Pierre Dorolle, the deputy director of the WHO, highlighted an important connection between colonial development and international development. Just as new UN development programs were proposing to bring international technical expertise to bear in "less developed" nations, so too, he argued, were colonial governments contributing their own scientific, medical, and technical expertise to the development of their overseas territories. If Dorolle's speech highlighted an important point of overlap between colonial and international development programs, however, his words also reveal a potential contradiction between two fundamentally incommensurate visions of postwar Africa. Indeed, remarking on the need to recognize the significant contributions that colonial governments had made to building public health infrastructure on the African continent, Dorolle concluded his comments with a warning: "It would be a serious blunder for an international organization such as the WHO to base its action on anything but the realities of the situation."[1] Far from pioneering their work on a blank slate, international personnel working for UN agencies would have to confront a wide range of colonial development programs already in place in Africa, programs that were often ill conceived, underfunded, and inextricably bound up in the broader imperatives of colonial rule.

We have seen the way that the fraught relationship between the French colonial government and the UN shaped French receptivity to UN agencies such as the WHO in Africa. The seemingly wide range of possibilities that had appeared to emerge in the domain of international cooperation after the war were in reality constrained by an equally broad set of colonial agendas, most notably the need to defend the very idea of empire to an increasingly hostile international public. The deep-seated tensions between postwar internationalism and postwar imperialism also profoundly influenced the shape that development programs would take on the African continent after 1945.

If international agencies such as the WHO presented a significant threat to empire, they also offered something that French administrators in Africa desperately needed: a way to fund the colonial development projects they had envisioned during the war and were still struggling to bring to fruition in the late 1940s and early 1950s. Faced with rising rates of infant and child mortality, French colonial officials were painfully aware of their inability to fund projects such as house-spraying campaigns and supplemental nutrition programs from colonial coffers.[2] Circumstances thus forced the French to turn to UN technical assistance programs in order to provide basic health care for their African constituents. As some delegations to the UN became increasingly critical of colonial failures in the domains of health and social welfare, the ability to fund the expansion of health care initiatives became more crucial than ever. So while colonial doctors and administrators were in part motivated by their desire to protect imperial sovereignty, they also saw UN technical assistance programs as an important source of funding to help them combat the most pressing health crises in their territories.

In order to assess the ways that the complex relationship between the UN and the French colonial administration shaped the way that health care was provided to Africans, we will look at two areas of health intervention: first, disease prevention and eradication, and second, nutrition research and supplemental feeding programs. These case studies are not meant to be exhaustive; rather, they serve as windows onto the complex web of health and social programs that emerged as a product of (often competing) national, colonial, and global agendas. The global health programs that were developed in French sub-Saharan Africa at this moment of profound imperial uncertainty were developed in a piecemeal fashion, enacted by a broad set of actors with vastly different budgets, with disparate perspectives on the underlying causes of illness, and—most importantly—with incommensurate political goals.

Perhaps even more significant than their disjointed nature, however, was the fact that, until the late 1950s, these programs remained shrouded in a cloak of profound uncertainty about the value—and the danger—that international development initiatives posed for colonial empires. Despite the French administration's pressing need for financial support, postwar global health programs remained deeply enmeshed in the broader conflict between empire and internationalism, which often resulted in serious limits to their reach. If we can attribute the French government's broader reluctance to cooperate with the WHO in Africa to fears about allowing a UN agency to get eyes on the ground in France's colonial empire, global health programs themselves also threatened colonial expertise. Although the language of the civilizing mission had all but fallen away by 1945, in some ways the notion that European administrations could offer unparalleled scientific and technical know-how to the citizens of their colonial empires held even more currency after 1945, at a time when UN delegations from newly independent nations were bringing the more coercive aspects of empire into the limelight.

The Quest to Eradicate Malaria

This battle to protect colonial expertise and imperial sovereignty profoundly shaped the implementation of global health programs in French Africa, and perhaps none more than the fight to eradicate malaria.[3] While a cash-strapped colonial administration in French Africa was forced to reach out to international sources of funding for antimalaria programs, the execution of these public health initiatives was often hampered by French suspicions about the role that international organizations would play in the empire. While colonial health services had to rely on the WHO and UNICEF for costly supplies such as DDT (dichloro-diphenyl-tricholoro-ethane), French officials feared that these organizations might undermine colonial expertise and normalize the presence of international personnel in the empire.

Historian Randall Packard has rightly insisted that we consider broader political and social contexts when we evaluate the failures of the WHO's Malaria Eradication Program (MEP). According to Packard, malaria eradication was part and parcel of larger economic development schemes in the era of decolonization, as well as an essential component in the global battle against communism. But his analysis overlooks one key element of this broader sociopolitical context: mounting anticolonial sentiment at the UN, the parent organization of the WHO. In this section I argue that if the MEP was unsuccessful in achieving its goal, we must consider this failure in light of the protracted attempt to preserve empire in Africa at a moment when anticolonial delegations to the UN were pressuring colonial administrations to relinquish control in their overseas territories.[4]

Since its inception in the early twentieth century, the French colonial health system in Africa placed a special emphasis on services aimed at infants and children. These services, however, focused primarily on improving general hygiene, building modern maternity clinics, and providing better training for nurses and midwives.[5] And while the French administration also mobilized resources to fight epidemic disease, until the Second World War, malaria was just one of many afflictions that concerned French health services in Africa. In the late 1940s and early 1950s, however, newly available data on infant and child mortality revealed an important correlation between infant and child death rates and the incidence of malaria. One French report on malaria in Dakar noted that the disease was the "number one enemy of the indigenous child," accounting for between 26 percent and 39 percent of childhood mortality.[6] While anticolonial delegations to the UN had often criticized the accuracy of colonial statistics, experts working in the field of global health had little doubt that malaria was responsible for a large percentage of morbidity and mortality in the newly termed "developing world."[7] In 1955, a UNICEF report on aid to Africa called malaria "the greatest menace to the well-being of humanity," and throughout the course of the 1950s, colonial health officials began to pay increasing attention to the role that this disease played in France's African empire.[8]

Malaria is an infection of the blood that is usually spread by the female anopheles mosquito, primarily in tropical regions of the world. The symptoms of the disease include fever and chills, and it can often result in death.[9] Despite malaria's prevalence in sub-Saharan Africa, medical and scientific research efforts until 1945 had been occupied primarily with the eradication of sleeping sickness, yellow fever, and smallpox. The lack of an effective and affordable malaria treatment that could be promulgated on a global scale meant that antimalaria efforts before the Second World War remained piecemeal at best.[10] But by the late 1940s and early 1950s, however, the focus of global health agendas began to turn toward malaria, and so too did the focus of colonial health officials in sub-Saharan Africa. Despite this shared agenda, the conflict between empire and internationalism in postwar Africa placed significant constraints on the WHO's ability to execute its antimalaria efforts in the region of the world that needed these programs the most.

Before the launch of the MEP, antimalaria efforts worldwide had focused primarily on controlling the spread of the disease and on treating infected patients. The far-reaching project of eradication reflected a strong sense of postwar optimism about the potential for global health organizations to coordinate large-scale public health efforts and for new technology—such as DDT—to overcome previously insurmountable obstacles to eradication.[11] Malaria took precedence over other diseases both because of its geographic reach and because of the sheer number of people affected. Malaria had, for some time, been one of the most significant killers of children and infants and one of the highest causes of adult morbidity. The disease touched an astounding number of people worldwide. In 1958, for example, the WHO estimated that there were at least three million deaths annually from malaria across the globe and that at least three hundred million cases existed.[12] Although malaria control programs had been operational for decades, these programs—which were based on the use of chemoprophylaxis and insecticides—were intended to limit the effects and the spread of malaria, not to eliminate it entirely.[13]

Two factors were necessary to launch a global program of malaria eradication in the mid-1950s: first, an approach to vector elimination that could be implemented on a global scale, and second, a universal organization to execute its implementation. DDT, a Swiss invention, was initially used by the US military during the Second World War, after which it was made available for general use. DDT rapidly became the star of antimalaria programs when it was discovered that a single application on the walls of a dwelling could kill mosquitos for six months to a year, thereby eliminating the vector responsible for transmitting malaria from person to person.[14] Once the results of initial tests of DDT spraying in Greece showed that the insecticide continued to prevent the spread of malaria, the scientific foundation had been established for a global program that could theoretically eliminate malaria worldwide.[15]

As Packard argues, much of the drive for malaria eradication was framed in economic terms.[16] While malaria was a direct killer of children—future workers—experts also cited malaria as a primary cause for low food production in tropical areas, which in turn created serious nutritional deficiencies, another important cause of infant and child mortality and morbidity. According to a 1948 WHO report on malaria,

> We must bear in mind that malaria is generally not a disease affecting just a number of individuals, as tuberculosis or V.D., but a disease of the *community* and a *rural* disease par excellence; that malaria is prevalent in tropical and sub-tropical areas where food production and agricultural resources are potentially very high, and that, by affecting the mass of rural workers, it decreases their vitality and reduces their working capacity and thus hampers the exploitations of the natural resources of the country. At a time when the world is poor, it seems that control of malaria should be the first aim to achieve in order to increase agricultural output.

The report went on to explain that "man is the principal 'natural resource' of the world" and that the failure to address one of the most aggressive endemic diseases was, in effect, condemning people living in tropical regions to a life of poverty and malnutrition.[17]

The WHO had been active in supporting malaria-control programs since the late 1940s and early 1950s, providing experts, equipment, and funds for insecticides. Then, at the 1955 World Health Assembly, it was announced that the WHO would "take initiative, provide technical advice, and encourage research and coordination of resources in the implementation of a programme having as its ultimate objective the world-wide eradication of malaria."[18] And thus the WHO, in conjunction with other UN agencies such as UNICEF, embarked on the largest-scale disease eradication campaign that had ever been seen in human history. Eradication, according to the WHO's definition, entailed "ending the transmission of malaria and the elimination of the reservoir of infected cases in a campaign limited in time and carried to such a degree of perfection that, when it comes to an end, there is no resumption of transmission."[19] The program was to be based on a series of national eradication programs that could be coordinated on a regional level, since it was easy for mosquitos to spread the disease across national borders. Each individual program would begin as a pilot program that would allow local experts to tailor the campaign to the specificities of that geographic zone. After, technicians and experts would be able to expand the campaign to encompass a wider geographic area.[20]

For the French colonial government, concerns about malaria were connected not only to colonial productivity but also to a desire to respond to critiques at the UN that colonial governments were underdeveloping their overseas territories.[21] Although a handful of malaria control programs were already under way in French Africa in the late 1940s, the first concerted effort to discuss the technical considerations of malaria eradication in Africa was the joint WHO-CCTA conference. Participants gathered in Kampala, Uganda, from 27 November to 9 December 1950 to discuss the possibilities for a coordinated antimalaria campaign in sub-Saharan Africa. Topics of discussion included the geographic distribution of the disease, the available methods of malaria eradication (insecticides versus chemoprophylaxis), malaria research on the African continent, and the need for international cooperation to support an expanded antimalaria campaign. While still recognizing the importance of responding to outbreaks with emergency measures—such as the use of antimalarial drugs—the conference recommendations emphasized the value of preventing malaria with the use of residual insecticides such as DDT.[22]

Colonial Money Troubles and the MEP's Threat to French Expertise

After the Kampala conference concluded, colonial governments in sub-Saharan Africa set out to launch a series of pilot programs with the aim of developing an antimalaria campaign that would be properly suited to the environmental, epidemiological, and social conditions of those territories. Using a combination of chemoprophylaxis and house spraying with DDT, health officials in French Africa piloted programs in Madagascar, Cap Vert, and four areas of AEF: Fort-Lamy, Libreville, Pointe-Noire, and Bangui.[23] The costs of these programs, however, quickly exceeded the capacity of the colonial budgets, even with supplemental funds from FIDES.[24] By the mid- to late 1950s, colonial health services in French Africa would be forced by financial constraints to turn to the UN, the WHO, and UNICEF for resources to expand these initial efforts.

The extension of these locally tailored antimalaria campaigns, however, quickly became tied up in the broader clash between colonial and global imperatives, provoking intense debate about the nature of UN development initiatives. Concerns about the dangers that UN technical assistance programs posed were closely connected to French fears about anticolonialism at the UN. While possibilities for international cooperation continued to expand in the 1950s, so too did the emerging regime of international colonial oversight. As the delegations to the UN Special Committee became increasingly critical of colonial rule, the French administrations in AOF and AEF became progressively more wary of cooperating with UN agencies. Opening the empire to the WHO, the FAO, and UNICEF would not only give the UN much-needed eyes on the ground in dependent territories, but it would also challenge the notion that decades of colonial rule had given the French unsurpassed scientific and medical knowledge about the African continent.[25]

According to French doctors and colonial officials, the problem with UN technical assistance programs was that while they did provide some funding, their primary task was to supply expertise to "developing" regions of the world. If a Swedish or Soviet technician was just as capable as a French expert of launching a malaria eradication program in AOF, then what aim did the ongoing French presence in Africa serve? At a time when sheer force was no longer a valid justification for the rule of one people by another, scientific and cultural capital became all the more important for legitimizing ongoing colonial rule, especially in an era when former subjects had become citizens. The French government made it clear that it would be extremely reluctant to seek out technical assistance, from the UN or from any of its specialized agencies.[26]

French officials, in their internal correspondence, spoke frankly about what they saw as the potential dangers posed by this new regime of international development. In 1950, for example, a letter from the Ministry of Foreign Affairs to the Ministry of Overseas France registered concern about the growing interest on the part of the UN in "underdeveloped territories" across the globe. The letter explained, "While we have thus far managed, to a certain extent, to put the brakes on any investigation into African problems by these organizations, these territories have come to interest them more and more." In order to determine the right attitude to adopt with regard to technical assistance programs, the Ministry of Foreign Affairs recommended a thorough investigation of the UN's interest in France's African territories, with special attention to any envisaged development projects.[27] Officials in Paris worried that health personnel working on the ground in the empire had fundamentally misunderstood the nature and purpose of UN technical assistance. Heads of colonial health services in Africa—operating under the constant pressure of constrained budgets and limited personnel—were attracted to the new funding opportunities that the UN presented. But technical assistance, according to the French Ministry of Public Health, was not actually about allotting funds. Instead, these programs supported "developing" regions of the world by providing technical expertise. This technical know-how, one memo explained, was "destined for under-developed countries that were, in principle, deprived of qualified technicians and specialized personnel." The goal, in effect, was to "provide these countries with men capable of guiding them."[28]

Ministry officials explained that in the case of France's African empire, funding shortages were the most serious impediment to economic and social development, not a lack of technical know-how. What France really needed, one memo argued, was "not technical assistance from the UN in its current form, but instead an international investment fund that would be infinitely more useful." While there were "obvious political reasons" for participating in international development projects, French officials found themselves "automatically deviating that assistance from its fundamental goal" of providing expert knowledge.[29] As Médecin-Colonel Georges Garcin explained in his report on the first meeting of the Regional Committee for Africa in 1951,

> The majority of African territories already have all of the necessary experts and sufficient personnel at their disposal. Financial support, however, weighs heavily on local budgets, and would do so even more if these territories wished to expand their programs for the benefit of their growing populations. Local financial resources cannot, unfortunately, always support such an expansion of activity. It would be regrettable to

> see the programs that have already achieved such positive results suddenly be left with no future. It would be equally unfortunate to be forced to exclude part of a population from the benefits of these programs.[30]

French development projects in the empire, he argued, would benefit more from the provision of costly supplies by the UN and the WHO than they would from the presence of external technical advisers.

These programs also had the added complication of committing colonial governments to long-term investments in development programs whose costs they could not afford to cover. As a memo from the Ministry of Public Health explained, UNICEF "proposes, with its limited means, through a very judiciously chosen action, to encourage those countries who have engaged its assistance to augment their efforts in favor of child health. Any program adopted [by UNICEF], which is always strictly limited in its timeframe, needs to be supported by an equal or greater financial commitment by the interested government. The goal of UNICEF is to launch aid programs for which individual governments will ultimately take sole responsibility." In other words, instead of providing a much-needed source of funding for colonial health projects, engagement with UNICEF or other UN agencies ultimately committed colonial governments to new programs that they may not have been able to afford in the long term.[31] In the case of the antimalaria campaign, the total cost of the program came to 1,383,000,000 francs, of which the French government was responsible for just under half.[32]

While the French government had requested assistance in the form of insecticides, house-spraying equipment, and transportation to carry out the project, WHO rules stipulated that materials could only compose 25 percent of the total amount requested for any technical assistance program. Thus, the majority of the required costs ultimately fell to the French government. Within the framework of UN technical assistance, priority was given to funding experts and technical personnel. Equipment and transportation, moreover, was considered to be property of the UN and could not be left under the supervision of employees of the French colonial administration, despite the French government's request that the antimalaria campaign be carried out exclusively by its own medical personnel. Foreign supplies thus inevitably came with foreign bodies—bodies that, in the eyes of the French, could operate as agents of anticolonialism on the ground in Africa. While the rules for UNICEF-sponsored technical assistance were in theory more flexible, the Ministry of Public Health noted that in all likelihood the sums required to carry out the campaign would exceed even UNICEF's means.[33]

Still wary of international inference in colonial affairs, the French delegation to the WHO lobbied the WHO's Executive Council to provide funding and supplies for local (colonial) projects that were already in place. At the first annual meeting of the WHO Regional Committee for Africa, the French delegation proposed a resolution to this effect. The resolution stated that since technical experts already existed in many African territories, the structure of technical assistance should be modified to include material and financial support for existing programs.[34] The French delegation made the case that the development efforts that had already been undertaken by the French government, with French funds, justified further financial support by the WHO.[35] The antimalaria campaigns in Madagascar and Cap Vert—the delegation explained—had already been extremely successful, and the delegates hoped that an infusion of WHO funds would allow the government to expand these campaigns to larger areas within the AOF federation. The French delegation was adamant, however, that any funds or supplies not be attached to a requirement to include foreign WHO experts in the program.[36]

Reassurances from top officials in the WHO that the organization had no intention of meddling in colonial affairs did little to allay French suspicions about the real intentions of WHO technicians who would come to work in Africa. In a letter to Garcin, a representative from the French Ministry of Foreign Affairs noted that if the provision of WHO experts was to be a requirement to accept supplies and funds, these experts would only be permitted to visit the sites before and after the fact, and only to judge the extent of malaria within these territories, not to advise on the program itself. Worried that WHO technical personnel might stir up existing anticolonial sentiments in the empire, the letter from the ministry noted that the French government would need to negotiate with the WHO on the choice of experts, stating that they "should originate, if at all possible, from other administering powers in Africa."[37] The director general of the WHO assured the delegations at the regional meeting that the principle behind technical assistance was to conform to the directives issued by the government hosting the program and that it was not the policy of the WHO to criticize existing health services or to attempt to influence policy within that country or territory. Given the fears of the colonial delegations about the expansion of WHO activities into their territories, however, this reassurance was not particularly comforting.[38]

While the French government was hesitant to accept technical assistance in the form of experts, the pressure of colonial finances was making it increasingly difficult to expand programs already in place.[39] With each passing year, rising rates of morbidity and mortality drew further negative attention to France's African empire. Indeed, the only statistic more staggering than the cost of antimalaria programs was the number of people affected by the disease in the absence of such programs. According to one report from the mid-1940s, over three hundred thousand people were treated for malaria in AOF every year, along with seventy thousand in AEF.[40] The toll exacted by the disease would ultimately prove too much for the French government, both financially and politically. The need to protect Africans from malaria weighed heavily on the colonial administration, and the French government was ultimately forced to make certain compromises vis-à-vis the UN and its specialized agencies.

In addition to cooperating with UN agencies to expand the existing antimalaria programs in AEF, the administration in AOF also launched pilot programs for the cities of Thiès, Senegal; Bobo-Dioulasso, Upper Volta; and Porto-Novo, Dahomey. A 1954 report suggested that the initial results of these pilot programs were promising, but noted that further investigation would be needed to refine and reorganize the approach.[41] In 1956, UNICEF allotted a credit of $1,387,000 to AOF for the fight against leprosy, malaria, yaws, and malnutrition. Of the total sum, over $400,000 were earmarked for supplies needed to expand AOF's malaria eradication campaign. The investment provided for 166 tons of DDT, as well as the transportation and machinery necessary for the house-spraying campaign, which had a goal of protecting more than two and a half million people over the course of the year.[42] By the mid-1950s, malaria eradication programs were operational across a range of French territories on the African continent, after years of working toward a compromise wherein the French government and the UN specialized agencies would share the financial burden of the program.

The compromise between the French colonial administration and the UN, however, ultimately came too late for the French administration in Africa to ever develop a seamlessly working relationship with the WHO or with other

Figure 6.1. Examinations being carried out in a village near Maroua, Cameroon, during a field trip organized for the participants in the malaria training course (1955). © World Health Organization, 1955.

UN agencies. Despite the WHO's staunchest efforts to halt the transmission of malaria, and despite the French colonial administration's attempts to improve health while still preserving colonial sovereignty, in the end neither succeeded. By 1956, the French government had begun to devolve more authority to local governments in France's sub-Saharan African territories, and in 1960 it relinquished control entirely. In 1969, the WHO abandoned its goal of malaria eradication, after almost a decade and a half of economic, political, and technical difficulties.

James L. A. Webb Jr. has argued that cultural misunderstandings between Africans and WHO technical personnel imposed significant limits on the organization's ability to execute the MEP. He explains, "The malariologists had been little attuned to the African social universes in whose midst their antimalarial projects unfolded, and the projects advanced largely without input from communities in the project zones."[43] Technicians working on the project were ill equipped to handle the movement of people in and out of the treatment zones, and house spraying and chemoprophylaxis were considered by some to be intolerable annoyances. If cultural miscalculation proved to be an insurmountable barrier to a malaria-free Africa, so too were the political constraints that limited the WHO's ability to institute its programs in African colonies. While colonial intransigence was only one reason among many that the WHO's MEP failed, and while international pressure was only one factor in empire's undoing, these two failures were intimately connected. Indeed, the way that postwar international organizations framed their approach to development and technical assistance was, in a certain sense, diametrically opposed to the way the French were framing their own bid to hold on to the empire. Motivated by their fears about the rising tide of global anticolonialism, the French government was reluctant to accept what the UN had to offer: international expertise and oversight for the expansion of local development programs. At the same time, the UN was unable to provide the one thing the French administration desperately needed: financial resources to support existing colonial endeavors.

Feeding Africa's Future Generations

While the politics of malaria eradication often dominated French concerns about international development programs in the 1950s, anxieties surrounding the role that UN agencies would play in promoting nutrition came in a close second. Medical experts both in the global public health community and within the French colonial administration considered malnutrition to be one of the most important health problems in postwar Africa. Because nutrition was the "bedrock for health," medical professionals saw malnutrition and malnourishment as important risk factors for numerous other diseases. Undernourished bodies, they argued, were not capable of fighting disease or healing themselves.[44] After the Second World War, public health experts recommended a two-pronged solution for addressing the crisis of malnutrition in Africa. First, local administrations—with the help of international agencies such as UNICEF—needed to set up supplemental feeding programs that could function as a stopgap measure. Second, colonial governments needed to invest in long-term nutrition research and agricultural planning that would take into account the needs of the people—especially children—living in the territories under their control.[45]

Yet while French and foreign medical experts agreed about the importance of establishing programs that would support the nutrition of African families, debates about the causes of malnutrition—and the necessary solutions—remained mired in the broader clash between imperialism and internationalism throughout the 1950s. While a broader range of international resources emerged after the war to support local governments as they addressed the problem of malnutrition, colonial officials were reluctant to rely too heavily on international development programs. They worried that drawing extensively on food resources provided by organizations such as UNICEF would demonstrate a lack of capacity on the part of the French administration to provide for the most basic needs of its African constituents. Indeed, in their accusations of colonial underdevelopment, anticolonial delegations to the UN Special Committee on Information from Non-self-governing Territories often focused on shortcomings in production. When the special committee met in 1949, several delegations noted the failure to produce a sustainable supply of protein-rich food for people living in dependent territories. The Soviet and Indian delegations, for example, accused colonial governments of using their agricultural resources for their own profit, pursuing "a policy of exploitation unrelated to the interest of the indigenous population." These delegations claimed that the focus of colonial administrations was on the production of cash crops for export rather than food crops intended for the people they were meant to be governing.[46] The resulting malnutrition and malnourishment were, among other factors, two of the most important causes of infant mortality in sub-Saharan Africa.[47] While the high incidence of malaria in Africa could always be blamed on an uncontrollable global parasite, the failure to provide nutritious food called into question the priorities of the colonial governments in Africa who claimed to be improving the quality of life for the populations living within those territories.

The most common form of malnutrition was protein deficiency, known in the African context as kwashiorkor. It was common in children between ages one and five, when no suitable substitute was available to replace breast milk after weaning. According to a 1955 UN study on social conditions in colonial territories, kwashiorkor was common in AOF and AEF, British West and East Africa, and the Belgian Congo, as well as in Malaya and certain islands in the Caribbean. While less common than protein deficiency, some African territories also saw high rates of vitamin deficiencies such as beriberi (in rice-based diets) and pellagra (in corn-based diets). In addition to the low availability of protein-rich foods in colonial territories, the special committee report also attributed poor nutrition to general poverty and the inability to buy the foods that were available.[48] Experts in the empire, however, argued that African women, either out of ignorance or because of cultural taboos surrounding certain foods, failed to include the necessary nutrients in their families' diets.[49] Parasites and other diseases then compounded the already-existing problems of poor nutrition. A 1953 report from the French nutrition research agency, ORANA, stated that the problem of kwashiorkor was equal to that of malaria in terms of the need to development prophylactic measures and effective treatments.[50]

Over the course of the 1940s and early 1950s, several UN agencies recommended a meticulous study of the nutritional needs of people living in the "developing" world, as well as a careful consideration of how to distribute agricultural resources properly in order to fulfill those needs.[51] Nutrition experts working for the UN FAO, for example, emphasized the need for technical experts to work in conjunction with government officials in order to implement a scientifically sound approach to nutritional self-sufficiency. These recommendations built on ideas that had emerged in the 1930s as a result of the League of Nations' activities in the field of nutrition but were reinforced by a growing ability to scientifically analyze both the foods themselves and the effects of malnourishment and malnutrition.[52] During this period, scientists and public health experts were only beginning to understand the exact nature of nutritional deficiencies. What made studying malnutrition so challenging, according to the 1955 special committee report, were the "wide differences in climate, land resources, traditions, the incidence of endemic diseases, economic patterns and general levels of development." It was thus difficult to assess malnutrition across a wide range of territories using the same standards or to generalize about causes and solutions. As a general rule, however, nutrition experts noted that most diets in sub-Saharan Africa were primarily starch based (rice, corn, or cassava) and that milk, meat, fruit, and vegetables were included infrequently, at best. These types of diets put young children at risk for both protein and vitamin deficiencies.[53]

The question of how to address the crisis of malnutrition in Africa was taken up by a wide range of technical experts, colonial officials, and international bureaucrats, including a joint WHO-FAO Expert Committee on Nutrition.[54] While serious efforts to understand and combat malnutrition from a global perspective had been undertaken by the League of Nations in the interwar period, the post–Second World War moment saw a new wave of collective action around the problems of food and diet. Several conferences in the late 1940s and early 1950s set the stage for new programs to combat malnutrition, including supplemental feeding programs, public information campaigns, and local research about nutritional deficiencies and supplements. The level of cross-border cooperation in the field of nutrition in the decade following the war was unprecedented. What is perhaps most significant about these meetings, however, is the concerted effort by colonial governments to carve out a domain where colonial expertise could continue to play an important role in shaping development programs, even at a time when resources to support those programs were increasingly provided by the UN and its specialized agencies. As colonial health officials gathered to share experiences and data and to discuss solutions to the crisis of malnutrition in sub-Saharan Africa, representatives from different UN agencies often attended only as observers.

In 1949, in Dschang, Cameroon, the CCTA sponsored the first postwar meeting dedicated to the problem of malnutrition in Africa. Deciding that they would benefit from a more narrow approach to the problems of nutrition, conference participants focused their discussions on infants, children, and mothers, who were the most frequent victims of malnutrition in Africa.[55] According to Dr. Benjamin Platt, professor of nutrition at the London School of Hygiene and Tropical Medicine, "Infant and child mortality rates are . . . highest . . . when the population is affected by malnutrition and malaria."[56] Since infant and maternal mortality were important indicators of the progress of colonial development, this was a sensible place to start when approaching the problem of poor nutrition. Three years later, many of the participants from the 1949 conference gathered again, this time in Fajara, the capital of the British colony of the Gambia. Fajara was a strategic choice, as it housed the Field Research Station, which the British Medical Research Council had founded in 1937 to "provide facilities for research dealing with those problems of human nutrition and food technology which . . . could only be made . . . in a colonial territory."[57] In conjunction with the Field Research Station, the London School of Hygiene and Tropical Medicine also created an applied nutrition unit, with the goal of studying and exchanging technical information on nutrition and food technology, facilitating fieldwork and laboratory research, and training colonial personnel in the field of nutrition.[58] The CCTA, in turn, took a similar approach by creating working groups and an information-sharing network for colonial nutrition. The 1949 and 1952 conferences were an early part of this effort.

The Fajara conference focused on the problem of protein deficiency, paying special attention to the way that a shortage of protein-rich foods affected the health of mothers and children. In his introductory remarks to the conference, Sir Percy Wyn-Harris suggested that kwashiorkor might be a logical point of focus both for colonial governments and for the UN, since it touched not only the "people of Africa" but also "human welfare generally." By eliminating malnutrition, he argued, colonial governments would be able to raise the standard of living for everyone in these territories.[59] In their recommendations, delegates emphasized the need to develop locally produced foodstuffs in areas where malnutrition was endemic. Governments and farmers within individual territories needed to develop agricultural production in a way that would permit the people living in those areas to achieve a balanced diet without having to rely on foreign imports or international aid. Extensive research, the conference participants argued, would be needed to determine just how to achieve that goal.[60]

The late 1940s and early 1950s saw a rapid expansion in scientific research on nutrition in Africa. In the late 1940s, the Mission anthropologique de l'Afrique Occidentale Française (Anthropological Mission of French West

Africa) conducted studies on African diets and nutrition, with a focus on protein deficiencies. In 1953, the mission was replaced by another organization charged with the study of African nutrition, ORANA, which had an even broader mandate than its predecessor. Beyond the role it would play in studying nutritional deficiencies in the African diet, this organization was also responsible for offering plans both for the prevention of malnutrition and malnourishment and for the development of protein-rich foodstuffs that would be appropriate for supplemental feeding programs.[61]

In its early years, ORANA operated under the leadership of Médecin-Lieutenant-Colonel Raoult, who also served as the French representative at the various CCTA nutrition conferences and would later collaborate with UNICEF on its supplementary feeding program in AEF.[62] In addition to his investigative tours in Senegal, Guinea, Upper Volta, and Côte d'Ivoire, Raoult also worked on developing the institution's documentation center and research laboratories. His laboratory research included investigations into the nutritional qualities of African women's breast milk, as well as of millet and sorghum, two staples of west African diets. ORANA programs also aimed to study malnutrition in conjunction with various other infections—malaria, bilharzia, tuberculosis, intestinal parasites, and syphilis—in order to study the correlation between nutritional deficiencies and the incidence of disease. These studies could then inform decisions about how best to channel public health spending in the colonies.[63]

In 1953, for example, ORANA conducted in experiments in Bobo-Dioulasso, Upper Volta, to test the relative benefits of spending colonial development funds on antimalaria medications versus supplementary feeding programs. Research teams treated one village, Sinorosso, with the antimalaria medication nivaquine and provided another, Kokroué, with dried milk. Researchers chose a third village, Borodoungou, as a control site and provided its inhabitants with neither antimalaria medication nor dried milk. ORANA teams conducted another set of experiments in the Senegalese village of Popenguine, south of Dakar. There they created a center where doctors and technicians ran nutrition analyses, distributed milk for mothers and children, and worked to develop other sources of protein based on local food sources. Beyond simply providing supplementary food sources, the researchers based at the Popenguine center kept careful records of the way that local families—including 3,500 children—used the center's resources.

Center personnel established a medical file for each child and encouraged families to bring their children as often as they were able. ORANA researchers carefully tracked the physical development of the local children, as well as the rates of illness. Teams reported success both for the program itself—reporting lowered rates of morbidity and mortality—and for the particular method of study they used.[64]

Although the French colonial administration expanded its commitment to research in the field of nutrition after 1945, its ability to remedy widespread malnourishment and malnutrition in Africa remained severely hampered by budgetary constraints. Colonial doctors and officials were thus forced to look to international agencies to shoulder much of the financial burden for launching supplemental nutrition programs in their African territories. In 1952, shortly after the joint FAO-WHO committee on nutrition published its report on kwashiorkor in Africa, both the French administration in equatorial Africa and the Belgian administration in the Congo began negotiations with UNICEF to launch supplementary nutrition programs in those territories.[65] The goal of these programs was twofold. First, they aimed to increase the production and distribution of protein-rich foods, and second, they worked to educate people and encourage them to consume new foods that were not traditionally part of their diet. Because efforts were especially directed at women and children, these programs were often run out of schools or maternity clinics.[66] While school lunch programs, milk stations, and other supplementary nutrition schemes had existed in some form since the early twentieth century, UNICEF officially endorsed these programs at the 1947 meeting of the WHO Interim Commission. Experts at the meeting promoted dried skim milk as the most economically efficient source of protein for infants and young children.[67] While supplementary feeding programs were ultimately aimed to draw on locally produced items, for an interim period they operated with stocks of dried skim milk provided by UNICEF, supplemented by a supply of cheese, butter, and vitamin tablets.[68]

UNICEF launched its first supplemental nutrition program in Africa in the Belgian Congo. Although the program reached an average of thirty thousand women and children a month, it encountered numerous difficulties, including low school attendance, a lack of trained personnel, and transportation shortages. The biggest obstacle, however, was the extremely high cost of the foods being distributed. Such programs were thus only cost effective in areas with very high rates of malnutrition and with a high population density.[69] UNICEF piloted a similar program in AEF shortly after the launch of the Congo program. While the program was intended to run from 1952 to 1954, it was discontinued early due to the high cost of importing dried milk from Europe. Rates of malnutrition were slightly lower in AEF, and because the pilot program could only reach ten thousand mothers and pre-school-age children and five thousand schoolchildren a month, UNICEF officials deemed that it was not cost effective.[70] In addition to UNICEF-sponsored milk distribution programs, local governments in AEF and AOF worked to develop school lunch programs throughout the 1950s. Although these programs were often constrained by a lack of funding, they attempted to provide the basic nutrients needed by schoolchildren in order to prevent kwashiorkor and vitamin deficiencies.[71]

Beyond their support for supplemental nutrition programs, international organizations also collaborated on nutrition research with colonial governments. UNICEF, the WHO, and the FAO worked with French and African researchers, for example, on developing protein-rich food products that could be locally sourced. The FAO supported experiments in Dakar, Bamako, and Bobo-Dioulasso to test the digestibility, palatability, and nutritive value of biscuits made from a combination of fish flour and corn or cassava. UNICEF and the FAO also worked with governments to increase local milk production in order to avoid reliance on costly powdered milk imported from Europe. UN agencies also worked with colonial administrations on training personnel to put new knowledge about nutrition and health into action.[72] In response to criticisms at the UN that one of the primary causes of malnutrition in colonial territories was a lack of trained personnel, the WHO and the FAO jointly sponsored nutrition-training programs in Marseille in 1952 and 1955 for francophone medical workers who planned to work in AOF, AEF, Cameroon, and the Belgian Congo.[73] In 1958, the FAO created a training program to prepare Dakarois schoolteachers to assist in the execution of a UNICEF-sponsored supplementary new nutrition program that had been launched two years earlier.[74]

Although in many ways the path to collaboration between international and colonial entities was marked by fewer political obstacles in the field of nutrition than in the domain of malaria eradication, colonial officials remained profoundly skeptical about the broader implications of relying on international aid for nutrition programs. In a 1952 memo from the French Ministry of Health and Population to the Ministry of Overseas France, for example, the Minister of Health warned of the danger of committing to a UNICEF-sponsored supplemental nutrition program. Such programs, he cautioned, would ultimately be insufficient to achieve the task of permitting the French colonial administration enough time for the "sufficient development of locally-sourced foodstuffs that can respond to the protein needs of mothers and their children." Given the unlikelihood of success, it seemed undesirable, argued the memo, to provoke a "dissociation between France and its African territories" or to create a "predominance of financial aid emanating from international organizations."[75] Although French authorities would ultimately reach a workable compromise with the WHO and UNICEF—receiving some funding for both malaria eradication and supplementary nutrition campaigns—the relationship between the French government and UN agencies in Africa would continue to be colored by these deeply entrenched tensions through the end of the colonial era.

~

When it came to working with the UN's technical assistance programs, French experts in Africa continually emphasized France's long history of contributing to the technical and scientific development of the African continent. If international support was needed to ensure a certain standard of health and well-being for Africans in the French Union, it was not—according to French officials—because the French lacked the necessary expertise. Instead, French delegates to the UN and the WHO argued that it was the incredible success of the French colonial health system that had resulted in the budgetary challenges of the 1950s. Ultimately the French government was able to strike a compromise between the UN and its colonial administration in Africa, with UNICEF ultimately providing the materials for both malaria eradication campaigns and supplementary nutrition programs. As these programs took shape on the African continent, however, they did so under the pressure of extreme suspicion and uncertainty on the part of the French government. While the French ultimately succeeded in procuring some of the financial support that they had sought, the tensions that emerged over the provision of technical expertise were yet another destabilizing factor in the precarious edifice of Franco-international cooperation in postwar Africa.

When we think about the shortcomings of global health programs in 1950s Africa, we must consider not only the logistical limitations of these efforts but also the perceived threat to colonial sovereignty that French administrators and doctors saw in these international initiatives. If financial need forced colonial doctors and officials to accept international aid, the programs that this aid supported remained inextricably bound to the broader debates about the legitimacy of empire that had prompted French opposition to the WHO in the first place. As the French government fought to defend colonial autonomy and to protect France's empire from an expanding system of international oversight, it also struggled to defend the value of the scientific and technical expertise that French doctors and scientists had garnered over decades of colonial rule. It was one thing to be short of funds in the wake of a massive global conflict, but for the French to accept technical advice related to the governance of their empire would have been another matter entirely. This became all the more important in the final years of colonial rule, when the scientific, technical, and social connections between colony and metropole would remain as the only tenable defense of empire.

Epilogue

In November 1972, Robert Debré—now ninety years old—stepped off an airplane in Abidjan. It was his third visit, and he was there to attend two important medical conferences: the Journées médicales d'Abidjan (Abidjan Medical Conference) and the Colloque international sur l'allaitement maternel (International Colloquium on Breastfeeding). Debré—"a long-time friend of the Ivory Coast"—was accompanied on his flight by Ivorian president Félix Houphouët-Boigny. Both men were arriving in Abidjan after a trip to Niamey, where they had consulted with the government of Niger on the implementation of a new public health policy. As they disembarked, they were greeted by the French ambassador to Côte d'Ivoire, the dean of the Faculté de Médecine d'Abidjan, and Professor Hyppolite Ayé, who was serving as the minister of public health and population. The International Colloquium on Breastfeeding, sponsored by the CIE, was important news in Côte d'Ivoire. Several major newspapers featured photos of Debré sitting with both Ayé and Mamadou Coulibaly, the president of Côte d'Ivoire's Economic and Social Council. Ayé proclaimed that the CIE, in choosing Abidjan as the location for the conference, was conferring a "great honor" on his country. Attended by representatives from Australia, Africa, Europe, Latin America, and the United States, as well as from various international agencies, the conference was described by Ayé as having both an "interregional character" and an "international reach." In his opening remarks he thanked Debré for his years of contributions to the field of social pediatrics and for his role in creating an organization that continued to serve as a "global beacon of child protection."[1]

Both the conference itself and Debré's presence there highlight several important continuities in this story, not least of which was the enduring influence of French doctors in the ever-changing landscape of health and medicine in postindependence Africa. At the same time, the strong presence of

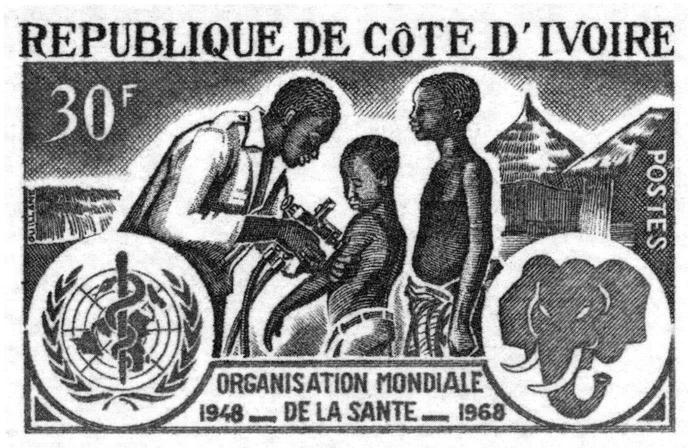

Figure 7.1. Postage stamp commemorating the twentieth anniversary of the WHO, Côte d'Ivoire, 1968. Designed and engraved by Cécile Guillame, 1968. Reproduction from author's collection.

African representatives among the conference attendees points to a significant shift from the late colonial period, when European physicians and scientists still dominated the field of African health despite postwar reforms that gave colonial citizens a greater role in shaping their own political, economic, and social destinies. The formal end of the French empire, however, brought real change to the landscape of medicine and public health in sub-Saharan Africa. Compared to the violent process of decolonization that was taking place in French Algeria, the end of empire in France's territories south of the Sahara was a relatively peaceful process.[2] In 1958, Guinea was the first territory to become independent. In 1960, the other territories in AEF and AOF—including Côte d'Ivoire—followed suit.[3] The decade-and-a-half-long battle to prevent international "interference" in the French empire dissolved quietly alongside the structures of colonial governance, now passed on to independent African hands. But just as the legacies of colonial rule left a significant imprint on postcolonial Africa, so too did the fifteen years of tension between the colonial administration and international organizations.

Historians are quite familiar with the many visible ways in which decolonization marked a major turning point in African history. Numerous studies, for example, have investigated the sometimes violent, sometimes peaceful processes that accompanied the creation of independent African states. Historians have also interrogated the way that Africans navigated the thorny terrain of establishing new national identities after decades—and, in some cases, centuries—of colonial violence and inequality.[4] But the end of empire shaped the world in myriad other ways, and not just for Africans. Explorations of the end of empire can also illuminate important aspects of the role that global institutions have played over the last fifty years, and they can also tell us something about the relationships between former colonial governments and the rest of the world. We can ask, for example, in what ways was decolonization a turning point for the relationship between former European colonial powers in Africa? How did organizations that began as a way to promote cooperation between Europeans in Africa fare after African independence? And finally, what role did international organizations such as the UN and the WHO play as a forum for Europeans and Africans to forge new relationships in the context of a decolonizing world?

In the following two sections I explore these questions by considering the work of the CIE on the eve of African independence and France's role in the WHO Regional Office for Africa after decolonization. In the final section of this epilogue I then turn to broader questions of French expertise and national identity in a globalizing and decolonizing world.

The CIE on the Eve of African Independence

As colonial territories on the African continent made the transition to independent statehood, the CIE served as an important forum for French and African doctors to build new relationships both during and after the process of decolonization.[5] Unlike the CCTA—which would eventually be transferred to independent African governments—the CIE continued to work in Africa under French leadership for several decades after the end of French rule.[6] In 1959, as a reprise to the 1952 conference on child health in Africa, doctors, government officials, and representatives from different international organizations met once again to continue their discussion of health and social problems affecting the African family. While the 1952 meeting had provided a space for colonial doctors to discuss and coordinate medical and social action in sub-Saharan Africa—away from the prying eyes of the

UN—by 1959 most colonial territories in Africa had already achieved a significant degree of autonomy. Indeed, many were well on their way to full political independence. This conference, sponsored by the CIE and the CCTA, thus provided a forum where European and African medical personnel could begin to cultivate new relationships in the era of African independence.

In January 1958, representatives from both the CIE and the CCTA met with colonial doctors and administrators at the Château de Longchamp to discuss the possibility of hosting a second conference on child health in Africa. Attendees of the meeting, which was chaired by Debré, decided to hold the conference the following year and settled on Lagos, Nigeria, as the location. In 1952, the primary goal of the conference had been to provide a "broad view" of the problems of child health in order to prioritize them according to their extent and severity. The goal of the 1959 conference, in contrast, was to "assess the methods used and the tasks still ahead." The meeting would focus on three primary topics: nutrition, maternal and child health services, and the adaptation of the African child to different social environments. Unlike the first conference on African child health, the 1959 meeting in Lagos included delegates not only from colonial health administrations but also from newly independent African states, such as Ghana, and included many African doctors. Like the first meeting, however, the number of government health officials far outnumbered representatives from international organizations. The WHO and UNICEF sent only one observer each, while the British colonial administration sent thirteen delegates, the French sent twelve, and the Belgians five.[7]

In the opening session, the Nigerian Federation's minister of labor and welfare welcomed the conference participants, lauding their commitment to a field of study that is "so near to the hearts of all men and women, be they scientists or illiterates." He continued, "In the countries from whence we come, maternity and child health services are at various stages of development. One thing is agreed, however, and that is that every mother and every child is entitled to a place, as a right, in the family and in the community in addition to the care and advice appropriate to the physical, mental, and social needs of the child." The minister's speech emphasized the importance of improving nutrition for pregnant women and breastfeeding mothers and suggested that careful attention be paid to the problem of kwashiorkor, or protein deficiency. It was up to the state and medical and social experts, he argued, to determine the best way to provide that care given "prevailing circumstances" and the need to respect "traditional and other beliefs." He then outlined the health and social challenges that Nigeria was facing on the eve of decolonization, most notably the high incidence of malnutrition and the social problems incumbent on a society undergoing rapid political and economic change. According to the minister, these problems were becoming even more pressing in the context of Nigeria's transition to independence, when the government would need to safeguard the lives of the "new citizens of Africa." He concluded by expressing his excitement at welcoming delegates from the independent nations of Sierra Leone and Liberia, as well as his hope that the meeting would foster the "great spirit of unity that exists amongst us" as "equal partners of the world community."[8]

Debré expanded on these ideas in his own opening address, noting the significant changes that had occurred in the relationship between African states and their youngest citizens. Until recently, Debré argued, states had only concerned themselves with children "insofar as they have understood that [states] might disappear unless they could replace the dead by the newborn." While national governments across the globe were beginning to grasp the importance of children as the future of humanity, nowhere was this more true than on the African continent. Debré emphasized the importance of expanding social pediatrics in sub-Saharan Africa, arguing that healthy children make for healthy future citizens. Medical and social services, however, needed to grapple not only with the problems of infectious disease and nutrition, but also with the broader social and psychological consequences of a rapidly changing society. African children needed to be able to integrate themselves into a world that was, in many ways, not of their own making.[9] The 1959 symposium was a moment to take stock of the situation of the African child—the "new citizens" of a decolonizing continent—in order to set an agenda for the immediate postindependence years.

Yet the meeting also had another crucial—if unstated—goal: to lay the initial foundations of Franco-African medical cooperation for a postcolonial future. By hosting a major medical conference in decolonizing Nigeria, the CIE was staking a claim for French medicine in independent Africa, and not only in countries that had once been colonies of the French empire.[10] Despite these efforts, in the postcolonial period former imperial boundaries would become, in a sense, even more rigid. Throughout the 1960s, French delegates to the WHO Regional Office for Africa would tirelessly work to promote "French" expertise, advocating for the selection of French or francophone African doctors for important posts, and doggedly insisting on the preservation of the French language as the lingua franca of medicine and diplomacy. These physicians, social experts, and politicians would often find themselves disappointed, however, as they witnessed increasingly clear lines drawn between the francophone and anglophone camps within the office. In the wake of decolonization, French doctors found themselves facing a growing marginalization of French medicine within the most important international health organization working on the African continent.

Intercolonial Cooperation Unraveled

Even after the majority of their African territories had acceded to independence, British and French officials continued to participate in the annual sessions of the WHO Regional Office for Africa under the rubric of "member states still having responsibilities in the region."[11] While most French territories in sub-Saharan Africa had gained their independence through relatively peaceful means, elsewhere on the African continent, violent conflict persisted. In both French Algeria and the Belgian Congo, confrontations between colonial and nationalist forces drew international attention.[12] Yet in the immediate postindependence period, instead of focusing on the health ramifications this violence could have in areas that bordered newly independent countries, French diplomatic correspondence was dominated by another concern: the need to secure a prominent place for French medicine, the French language, and francophone doctors—both French and African—in the WHO.

The technical coalition between the French and the British—forged under the threat of international "interference"—would come undone after 1960 just as easily as it had been created in the wake of the war. Whereas the WHO Africa office had once served as a battleground for the struggle between colonial regimes and international organizations, in the postindependence period it would rapidly become the scene of a new standoff, as French and British doctors battled to extend their respective influence in postcolonial Africa.[13]

The first post-1960 meeting of the WHO Regional Committee for Africa—held in Brazzaville in September 1961—serves as a window into these rapidly changing relationships. The meeting began with a few tense moments between the French delegation and the delegations from France's former colonial territories. In his opening remarks, for example, the Malian minister of public health, Dr. Sominé Dolo, stated: "21 African states, compared to only 5 last year, are now constitutionally able to defend the interests of their countries in the Regional Committee. In the sanitary domain, however, the current picture remains obscured by the presence of a certain number of people who wrongfully claim a right to represent certain African territories. I hope they will not be present in 1962." Yet despite these occasional flickers of tension between the French delegation and those from France's former colonies, the French report on the meeting emphasized the camaraderie that developed between the different francophone representatives, as African delegations sought French support for their various proposals.[14]

The driving source of conflict, according to the French delegation's report on the meeting, was not the hostility of delegations from former French colonies, but rather the rapidly growing divide between English- and French-speaking states in Africa. French delegates argued that nowhere was the degree to which anglophone Africa had gained the advantage in the international sphere more obvious than in the WHO Regional Committee for Africa. According to the French report, "The francophone delegations left Brazzaville with the impression that there are only two African states that count for the WHO and the UN." The first was Nigeria, "because of its resources and its population density, and because it serves as an anchoring point for American interests on the African continent." The second was the Belgian Congo, whose rapidly progressing breakdown offered the WHO an unprecedented opportunity for a "vast demonstration of assistance."[15]

Much of the French delegation's anxiety crystallized around Dr. C. M. Norman-Williams, the Nigerian deputy director of the WHO Regional Office for Africa. At the time of African independence, Portuguese doctor and known francophile Francisco J. C. Cambournac was head of the WHO Africa office, but by the early 1960s Cambournac had been all but officially displaced by Norman-Williams. The primary French complaint against Norman-Williams concerned his inability to communicate in French. The deputy director's lack of French language skills was indicative, the French

Table 7.1. Countries and Territories Represented at the Annual Meeting of the Regional Committee for Africa, 1958–1961

1958	1959	1960	1961
Belgium	Belgium	Republic of Cameroon	Belgium
France	France	France	Cameroon
Ghana	Ghana	Republic of Ghana	Central African Republic
Liberia	Republic of Guinea	Republic of Guinea	Chad
Portugal	Liberia	Liberia	Congo (Brazzaville)
Spain	Portugal	Portugal	Congo (Léopoldville)
Union of South Africa	Spain	Republic of Togo	Dahomey
United Kingdom	Union of South Africa	United Kingdom	France
Federation of Nigeria*	United Kingdom	Central African Republic*	Gabon
Federation of Rhodesia and Nyasaland*	Federation of Nigeria*	Republic of the Congo*	Ghana
Sierra Leone*	Federation of Rhodesia and Nyasaland*	Republic of Gabon*	Guinea
	Sierra Leone*	Federation of Nigeria*	Côte d'Ivoire
		Federation of Rhodesia and Nyasaland*	Liberia
		Sierra Leone*	Malagasy Republic
		Republic of Côte d'Ivoire**	Mali
		Republic of Dahomey**	Mauritania
		Federation of Mali**	Niger
		Republic of the Niger**	Nigeria
		Republic of Upper Volta**	Portugal
			Senegal
			South Africa
			Togo
			United Kingdom
			Upper Volta
			Federation of Rhodesia and Nyasaland*
			Ruanda Urundi*
			Sierra Leone*

Data Source: World Health Organization Library.
*Associate member status
**Observer status

delegation argued, of the displacement of French as the language of internationalism. The delegation's report lamented the fact that francophone doctors working for the bureau were sent to the United States to practice their English, while no such provision existed to train anglophone employees of the office to work in French. The francophone delegations to the

WHO Regional Committee for Africa were now relegated to the role of the "poor relations."[16]

Another memo suggested that the abandonment of the French language and the increasingly important role played by Nigeria and Ghana in the WHO Regional Office for Africa were akin to a "veritable colonization" of the WHO by Anglo-Saxon forces.[17] Officials at the French Ministry of Foreign Affairs were fearful of French marginalization at the WHO and worried that new African leaders were failing to take the issue seriously. In the wake of the meeting, the ministry sent a delegate to approach the presidents of Senegal and Côte d'Ivoire—Léopold Sédar Senghor and Houphouët-Boigny—to impress upon them the gravity of the Anglo-African threat.[18] Tensions between the French and the British at the WHO thus managed to trump even the conflict between the French and the most hesitant of the francophone African delegations.

At the close of the 1961 session, the delegations from Mali and Togo—the staunchest opponents to ongoing European involvement in the committee—expressed their enthusiasm for the results that Franco-African cooperation had produced in the meeting. They noted that they looked forward to the even more "spectacular" collaboration that they hoped would take place at the 1962 meeting, "once the Algerian drama had had time to wrap up."[19]

If the year 1960 was a turning point for France's relationship to its former African territories, it was also a watershed moment with regard to French relationships with other former colonial powers and with global institutions that would play an important role in developing infrastructure in these new states. While the French had once viewed international organizations as a significant threat to empire, after 1960 these institutions became privileged spaces for negotiating new relationships with independent African territories and with the broader world. Scientific, technical, and political friendships that had been an easy answer to international anticolonialism in the late colonial period quickly soured after 1960. Former colonial allies quickly became postcolonial opponents as European states renegotiated their relationship to their former colonies in the context of international spaces. This battle against the marginalization of French medicine, language, culture, and personnel at the WHO was one that would captivate French doctors and officials in the French Ministry of Foreign Affairs well into the

1960s, a testament to how decolonization shaped relationships on the African continent in often-unexpected ways.

Internationalism, Decolonization, and the Particular Universalism of Global France

A book about French doctors, scientists, and social reformers in the empire naturally raises questions about the expertise they generated and about the nature of the places, polities, and societies where they deployed that knowledge. Was there indeed something specifically *French* about the expertise that these individuals had to offer?[20] And was France's approach to governing its overseas territories really as unique as the characters in this book wanted the world to believe? The answer, in some regards, is yes. Certain aspects of this story are, in fact, uniquely French. France's vast network of overseas Pasteur Institutes, for example, played an important role in promoting the scientific research that shaped the medical services explored in this book. The Pasteur Institute in Paris developed the BCG vaccine in the early twentieth century, and this vaccine later proved to be crucial in the fight against tuberculosis in the empire in the 1940s and 1950s. There were also elements of the French Union that proved to be exceptional. The fact that African politicians like Senghor and Houphouët-Boigny held positions in the French government was, as Jan C. Jansen and Jürgen Osterhammel have argued, "something inconceivable in the British empire."[21] The potential for Africans to participate in the French political system on an equal footing with colleagues from metropolitan France was indeed a unique feature of France's postwar empire.

In others respects, however, the "Frenchness" of this story existed only in the imaginations of the politicians, doctors, and social reformers who fill the pages of this book. Medical and social programs in French Africa were indeed much more similar to those of their British and Belgian counterparts than they were different. As for the distinctiveness of French colonial rule, one need not look beyond the ongoing inequalities in Brazzaville to understand the ways that the legacies of colonial racism, segregation, and violence persisted in the post-1945 era, at a time when French authorities had purportedly transformed the empire into an entirely new kind of political and social entity. As the American journalist writing under the pseudonym Geneva put it on the eve of the San Francisco Conference, "Imperialism is imperialism whether it is old or new, and the daily routine violence necessary to maintain old tyrannies is almost as inexcusable as new aggression."[22]

Yet despite the similarities between French modes of colonial rule and scientific investigation and those of the rest of the world, the one common thread that unites this story is the near obsession with French uniqueness, or what Sudhir Hazareesingh has aptly termed a "fetish for singularity."[23] While French history certainly abounds with particularities, what is perhaps most interesting for the historian of twentieth-century France is not the idiosyncrasies themselves but rather the French preoccupation with imagining them, cultivating them, and making them known to the world.[24] This book is not the story of a set of health programs or a body of scientific knowledge that were—at their hearts—quintessentially French. It is, instead, the story of a group of individuals who wanted to fortify a sense of French national identity at a moment of profound psychic uncertainty about France's place in the world.

Historians of contemporary France have tended to think of Americanization as the most significant threat to France's national identity in the postwar era.[25] But the French did not define the universalism of the French Republic against the United States alone. After 1945, the French also defined themselves against another form of universalism: the rapidly expanding internationalism of the postwar period. Many French politicians, doctors, and scientists perceived the UN, and all that it came to represent, to be just as dangerous to French identity as the looming presence of the United States. It was in this context that medical expertise, social policy, and scientific theories of disease became political tools to recraft that identity. As historian Jessica Reinisch has succinctly argued, "Expertise is always political."[26] At a moment when the possibilities for global engagement seemed to have multiplied exponentially, the stakes for the French nation seemed higher than ever.

The empire proved to be a crucial component in this quest to define French identity in the twentieth century, both before and after decolonization. As historians of contemporary France have tried to understand the impact that France's global reach had on the rest of the world, they have also explored the ways in which France's international presence has allowed the French to conceive of themselves in a particular way. In this book I have shown that in the postwar period, French doctors, scientists, and politicians mobilized France's entire imperial apparatus against the universalizing impulse of postwar internationalism. Moreover, as France's ongoing involvement in the CIE and the WHO Regional Office for Africa demonstrates, the battle to promote French expertise on a global scale outlasted even France's efforts to hold on to its empire. As former colonies on the African continent were passed to independent African governments, French politicians and experts continued to use international health organizations as a way to promote France's presence abroad, to forge new relationships with former colonial subjects, and to define a unique French identity in a globalizing world.

If this book has provided a foundation for rethinking the history of France's role in the world since the Second World War, it also offers a framework for understanding the connections between expertise, internationalism, and decolonization. Just as European governments in Africa deployed particular bodies of scientific, medical, and social expertise to undergird colonial rule, so too would African governments seek to establish their own authority in these fields in the era that followed political independence. While the transfer of political power may have taken place over the course of a relatively short period of time, the *longue durée* process of decolonization is, in many senses, still ongoing. As African governments begin to make new archives available to scholars looking to investigate this long and complex process, there will be myriad opportunities for historians to explore the end of empire and its aftermath from a variety of angles and through a wide range of lenses.[27] By engaging the various forms of expertise that have transformed the way bodies and environments were governed in decolonizing Africa, we will have a better understanding not only of the ways that European colonialism has left a lasting imprint on the continent but also of the ways that Africans have seized opportunities to shape their own medical, scientific, and political destinies.[28]

Notes

Introduction

1. Archives de l'Institut de médecine tropicale du Service de santé des armées (hereafter IMTSSA) 238, Organisation des Nations Unies (ONU), Organisation mondiale de la Santé (OMS), RC2 / AFR / Min / 1, Comité régional de l'Afrique, deuxième session, procès-verbal de la première séance, Monrovia, Liberia, 31 July 1952, 10 h 00, 9–10. All translations from French are my own.

2. While the term *developing world* was used with considerable frequency (in addition to *Third World*) in the period under examination here, this term has since fallen out of use. For recent debates about these terms, see Dayo Olopade, "The End of the 'Developing World,'" *New York Times,* 28 February 2014; Marc Silver, "If You Shouldn't Call It the Third World, What Should You Call It?," *Goats and Soda* (blog), NPR, 4 January 2015, https://www.npr.org/sections/goatsandsoda/2015/01/04/372684438/if-you-shouldnt-call-it-the-third-world-what-should-you-call-it; and B. R. Tomlinson, "What Was the Third World?," *Journal of Contemporary History* 38, no. 2 (April 2003): 307–321.

3. For a broad analysis of the history of internationalism and international organizations, see Akira Iriye, *Global Community: The Role of International Organizations in the Making of the Contemporary World* (Berkeley: University of California Press, 2002); Sandrine Kott, "Les organisations internationales, terrains d'étude de la globalisation: Jalons pour une approche socio-historique," *Critique internationale* 52 (July–September 2011): 9–16; and Mark Mazower, *Governing the World: The History of an Idea* (New York: Penguin, 2012).

4. See John Charles, "Origins, History, and Achievements of the World Health Organization," *British Medical Journal* 2 (May 1968): 293–296.

5. Sunil S. Amrith, *Decolonizing International Health: India and Southeast Asia, 1930–1965* (Basingstoke, UK: Palgrave Macmillan, 2006), 2. On India's enthusiasm for WHO assistance, also see WHO, *First World Health Assembly, Geneva, 24 June–24 July 1948,* Official Records of the World Health Organization 13 (Geneva: World Health Organization, 1948), 263.

6. Frederick Cooper, *Citizenship between Empire and Nation: Remaking France and French Africa, 1945–1960* (Princeton, NJ: Princeton University Press,

2014); C. A. Julien, "From the French Empire to the French Union," *International Affairs* 26, no. 4 (October 1950): 487–502; and Archives diplomatiques du Ministère des Affaires Etrangères, La Courneuve (hereafter ADLC), Série Afrique (1945–1965), Généralités 31, "Note pour la délégation française à la 10ème session du Conseil économique et social à Lake Success (7 février 1950): Préparation d'une étude sur la situation économique en Afrique et intérêt qu'il y aurait à créer une Commission économique pour l'Afrique," 4–5.

7. Amrith, *Decolonizing International Health*, 2. On the intersection of health and politics, see Didier Fassin, *L'espace politique de la santé: Essai de généalogie*, Sociologie d'aujourd'hui (Paris: Presses universitaires de France, 1996); and Didier Fassin and Dominique Memmi, *Le gouvernement des corps* (Paris: Editions de l'Ecole des hautes études en sciences sociales, 2004).

8. Theodore Brown, Marco Cueto, and Elizabeth Fee, "At the Roots of the World Health Organization's Challenges: Politics and Regionalization," *American Journal of Public Health* 106, no. 11 (November 2016): 1912–1917.

9. On the earliest antimalaria efforts of the WHO, see WHO, *Annual Report of the Director-General to the World Health Assembly and the United Nations, 1948*, Official Records of the World Health Organization 16 (Geneva: World Health Organization, 1949), 9–11; and WHO, *Annual Report of the Director-General to the World Health Assembly and the United Nations, 1949*, Official Records of the World Health Organization 24 (Geneva: World Health Organization, 1950), 3–4.

10. See Jessica Pearson-Patel, "How Today's Ebola Response Reflects the History of Colonialism in Africa," interview by Jason Steinhauer, *Time Magazine Online*, 13 February 2015, http://time.com/3707158/ebola-colonialism-history/. Also see Adia Benton, "Race and the Immune-Logics of Ebola Response in West Africa," *Somatosphere: Science, Medicine and Anthropology*, 19 September 2014; Laura Seay and Kim Yi Dionne, "The Long and Ugly Tradition of Treating Africa as a Dirty, Diseased Place," *Washington Post*, 25 August 2014; and Siobhán O'Grady, "Colonial Lines Drawn Again for Ebola Aid," *Foreign Policy*, 22 September 2014.

11. Susan Pedersen, *The Guardians: The League of Nations and the Crisis of Empire* (Oxford: Oxford University Press, 2015).

12. Both the British and the French used the term *anticolonial delegations* broadly to refer to any representatives to the UN who spoke out against any aspect of colonial rule. Although they pointed most often to delegations from the Soviet Union, Latin America, the Middle East, India, and the Philippines, one British official went as far as to say that out of the eighty nations that belonged to the UN at the time, "57 could be considered as generally 'anti-colonial.'" Alan Burns, *In Defence of Colonies: British Colonial Territories in International Affairs* (New York: Macmillan, 1957), 8.

13. ADLC, Série Afrique (1945–1965), CCTA 2, "Réunion tenue chez M. Parodi sur la préparation des entretiens coloniaux de Londres," 22 April 1949, 8–9.

14. Loi 46-940 du 7 mai 1946 tendant à proclamer citoyens tous les ressortissants des territoires d'outre-mer. Also see James E. Genova, "Constructing Identity in Post-war France: Citizenship, Nationality, and the Lamine Guèye Law, 1946–1953," *International History Review* 26, no. 1 (March 2004): 56–79.

15. French Constitution of 1946, Preamble.

16. Cooper, *Citizenship between Empire.*

17. Geneva [pseud.], "America's Plan for the Colonial World," *American Mercury* 60, no. 254 (February 1945): 135–136.

18. ADLC, Série Afrique (1945–1965), Généralités 1, "Aide-mémoire sur la thèse coloniale française à San-Francisco," 27 March 1945, 1–2.

19. On Smuts's position, see Mark Mazower, *No Enchanted Palace: The End of Empire and the Ideological Origins of the United Nations* (Princeton, NJ: Princeton University Press, 2009).

20. United Nations Charter, Chapter XI, "Declaration regarding Non-self-governing Territories."

21. On the League of Nations mandates system, see Pedersen, *Guardians.* On the UN trusteeship system, see Meredith Terretta, *Nation of Outlaws, State of Violence: Nationalism, Grassroots Tradition, and State-Building in Cameroon* (Athens, OH: Ohio University Press, 2010); Meredith Terretta, *Petitioning for Our Rights, Fighting for Our Nation: The History of the Democratic Union of Cameroonian Women, 1949–1960* (Bamenda, Cameroon: Langaa Research and Publishing, 2013); and Meredith Terretta, "'We Had Been Fooled into Thinking That the UN Watches over the Entire World': Human Rights, UN Trust Territories, and Africa's Decolonization," *Human Rights Quarterly: A Comparative and International Journal of the Social Sciences, Philosophy, and Law* 34, no. 2 (2012): 329–360.

22. Jessica Pearson, "O império francês vai a S. Francisco: A criação das Nações Unidas e os limites da reforma colonial," in *Os impérios do internacional: Perspectives, genealogias e processos,* ed. Miguel Bandeira Jerónimo and José Pedro Monteiro (Lisbon: Almedina, forthcoming).

23. On human rights and decolonization, see Roland Burke, *Decolonization and the Evolution of International Human Rights* (Philadelphia: University of Pennsylvania Press, 2010); Ullrich Lohrmann, *Voices from Tanganyika: Great Britain, the United Nations and the Decolonization of a Trust Territory, 1946–1961* (Berlin: Lit, 2007); Charles Parkinson, *Bills of Rights and Decolonization: The Emergence of Domestic Human Rights Instruments in Britain's Overseas Territories* (Oxford: Oxford University Press, 2007); and Robert A. Hill and Edmond J. Keller, eds., *Trustee for the Human Community: Ralph J. Bunche, the United Nations, and the Decolonization of Africa* (Athens, OH: Ohio University Press, 2010).

24. Mazower, *No Enchanted Palace,* 8.

25. On the role of international public opinion in another colonial context, see Matthew Connelly, *A Diplomatic Revolution: Algeria's Fight for Independence and the Origins of the Post–Cold War Era* (Oxford: Oxford University Press, 2003).

26. See Yassin El-Ayouty, *The United Nations and Decolonization: The Role of Afro-Asia* (The Hague: Martinus Nijhoff, 1971); and Vrushali Patil, *Negotiating Decolonization in the United Nations: Politics of Space, Identity, and International Community* (New York: Routledge, 2008).

27. On the history of the International Sanitary Conferences, see David P. Fidler, *International Law and Infectious Diseases* (Oxford: Oxford University Press, 1999); and Valeska Huber, "The Unification of the Globe by Disease? The International Sanitary Conferences on Cholera, 1851–1894," *Historical Journal* 49, no. 2 (2006): 453–476.

28. Séance du 5 août 1851, in Ministère des Affaires Etrangères, *Procès-verbaux de la Conférence sanitaire internationale ouverte à Paris le 27 juillet 1851* (Paris: Imprimerie Nationale, 1852), 3–4.

29. Séance du 14 août 1851, in ibid., 10.

30. Séance du 23 juillet 1851, in ibid., 5.

31. See Iris Borowy, *Coming to Terms with World Health: The League of Nations Health Organisation, 1921–1946* (Frankfurt: Peter Lang, 2014); Martin Dubin, "The League of Nations Health Organisation," in *International Health Organisations and Movements, 1918–1939*, ed. Paul Weindling (Cambridge: Cambridge University Press, 1995), 56–80; Norman Howard-Jones, *International Public Health between the Two World Wars: The Organizational Problems* (Geneva: World Health Organization, 1978); Carol Miller, "The Social Section and Advisory Committee on Social Questions of the LNHO," in Weindling, *International Health Organisations*, 154–175; Amy L. S. Staples, *The Birth of Development: How the World Bank, Food and Agriculture Organization, and World Health Organization Changed the World, 1945–1965* (Kent, OH: Kent State University Press, 2007), 129–132; and Paul Weindling, "Social Medicine at the League of Nations Health Organisation and the International Labour Office Compared," in Weindling, *International Health Organisations*, 134–153.

32. See John Farley, *To Cast Out Disease: A History of the International Health Division of the Rockefeller Foundation (1913–1951)* (Oxford: Oxford University Press, 2004); and Jean-François Picard and William Schneider, "From the Art of Medicine to Biomedical Science in France: Modernization or Americanization?," in *Rockefeller Philanthropy and Modern Biomedicine: International Initiatives from World War I to the Cold War*, ed. William Schneider (Bloomington: Indiana University Press, 2002), 106–124.

33. On the origins of the WHO and its mission, see United Nations, World Health Organization Interim Commission, *Minutes of the Technical Preparatory Committee for the International Health Conference Held in Paris from 18 March to 5 April 1946*, Official Records of the World Health Organization 1 (New York: United

Nations, World Health Organization Interim Commission, 1947); and United Nations, World Health Organization Interim Commission, *Summary Report on Proceedings and Final Acts of the International Health Conference Held in New York from 19 June to 22 July 1946,* Official Records of the World Health Organization 2 (New York: United Nations, World Health Organization Interim Commission, 1948). Also see Yves Beigbeder, Mahyar Nashat, Marie-Antoinette Orsini, and J. F. Tiercy, *The World Health Organization* (The Hague: M. Nijhoff, 1998).

34. World Health Organization Constitution, 1946, 1.

35. See Randall Packard, "Malaria Dreams: Postwar Visions of Health and Development in the Third World," *Medical Anthropology: Cross-cultural Studies in Health and Illness* 17, no. 3 (1997): 279–296; Javed Siddiqi, *World Health and World Politics: The World Health Organization and the UN System* (Columbia: University of South Carolina Press, 1995); Staples, *Birth of Development;* and James L. A. Webb Jr., *The Long Struggle against Malaria in Tropical Africa* (New York: Cambridge University Press, 2014). For a nuanced study of the WHO in the postcolonial period, see Nitsan Chorev, *The World Health Organization Between North and South* (Ithaca, NY: Cornell University Press, 2012).

36. United Nations, World Health Organization Interim Commission, *Minutes,* 11.

37. On the political constraints that shaped the work of the League of Nations Health Organization, see ibid., 23.

38. On the embrace of the WHO by newly independent countries, see Staples, *Birth of Development,* 137.

39. On the regionalization of the WHO, see *First World Health Assembly,* 262–274.

40. ADLC, Série Afrique (1945–1965), CCTA 1, "Note pour le ministre, objet: création éventuelle d'un organisme de coopération technique coloniale en Afrique occidentale et centrale," 1947, 5.

41. ADLC, Nations Unies—Organisations internationales (hereafter NUOI) 323, "La politique régionaliste de l'Organisation mondiale de la Santé—état de la question à la veille de la 2ème assemblée mondiale," 1949, 5.

42. Ibid., 19.

43. Jessica Pearson-Patel, "Remapeando as fronteiras da saúde imperial: A Organização Mundial da Saúde e os debates internacionais sobre a regionalização no Norte de África Francês, 1945–1956," trans. Luís Domingos, in *Os passados do presente: Internacionalismo, imperialismo e a construção do mundo contemporâneo,* ed. Miguel Bandeira Jerónimo and José Pedro Monteiro (Lisbon: Almedina, 2015), 295–322.

44. While French authorities briefly considered proposing all of their sub-Saharan African territories for membership in the Europe Region, this idea was quickly rejected, as it was unlikely to be accepted by other members of the WHO. See "La politique régionaliste," 1949, 15–16.

45. Deborah J. Neill, *Networks in Tropical Medicine: Internationalism, Colonialism, and the Rise of a Medical Specialty, 1890–1930* (Stanford, CA: Stanford University Press, 2012).

46. On the history of the CCTA, see John Kent, *The Internationalization of Colonialism: Britain, France, and Black Africa, 1939–1956* (New York: Oxford University Press, 1992). On the origins of the CIE, see Robert Debré, *L'honneur de vivre: Témoignage* (Paris: Stock / Hermann, 1974); Robert Debré, *Ce que je crois* (Paris: Grasset, 1976); Etienne Berthet and Michel Manciaux, *Le Centre international de l'enfance,* Notes et études documentaires 4527–4528 (Paris: Documentation française, 1979); International Children's Centre, *International Children's Centre 1955* (Paris: Château de Longchamp, 1956) and *Activities of the International Children's Centre in 1958* (Paris: Château de Longchamp, 1959). Also see Jessica Pearson-Patel, "Promoting Health, Protecting Empire: Inter-colonial Medical Cooperation in Postwar Africa," *Monde(s): Histoire, espaces, relations* 7 (May 2015): 213–230. On the internationalization of the protection of childhood, see Joëlle Droux, "L'internationalisation de la protection de l'enfance: Acteurs, concurrences et projets transnationaux (1900–1925)," *Critique internationale* 52 (July–September 2011): 17–33.

47. See Thomas Neville Bonner, *Becoming a Physician: Medical Education in Britain, France, Germany and the United States, 1750–1945* (New York: Oxford University Press, 1995); Abraham Flexner, *Medical Education in Europe* (New York: Carnegie Foundation, 1912) and *Medical Education in the United States and Canada: A Report to the Carnegie Foundation for the Advancement of Teaching* (New York: Carnegie Foundation, 1910); L. Harrison Mettler, "Medical Paris—Notes from My Sketchbook," *Journal of the American Medical Association* 27, no. 9 (1896): 487–490; William Osler, "Impressions of Paris," *Journal of the American Medical Association* 52, no. 9 (1909): 701–703; "Paris: The New Site for the Paris Faculty of Medicine," *Journal of the American Medical Association* 99, no. 11 (1932): 927–928; "Paris: Reform of Medical Teaching," *Journal of the American Medical Association* 132, no. 12 (22 July 1950): 1110–1111; David Wilsford, *Doctors and the State: The Politics of Health Care in France and the United States* (Durham, NC: Duke University Press, 1991); and Doris T. Zallen, "Louis Rapkine and the Restoration of French Science after the Second World War," *French Historical Studies* 17, no. 1 (Spring 1991): 6–37.

48. For a broader treatment of France's position in the postwar world, especially France's relationship with the United States, see Alessandro Brogi, *A Question of Self-Esteem: The United States and the Cold War Choices in France and Italy, 1944–1958* (Westport, CT: Praeger, 2002); Philip H. Gordon, *A Certain Idea of France: French Security Policy and the Gaullist Legacy* (Princeton, NJ: Princeton University Press, 1993); William I. Hitchcock, *France Restored: Cold War Diplomacy and the Quest for Leadership in Europe, 1944–1954* (Chapel Hill: University

of North Carolina Press, 1998); and Richard F. Kuisel, *Seducing the French: The Dilemma of Americanization* (Berkeley: University of California Press, 1993).

49. See, for example, Commission pour la Coopération Technique en Afrique au Sud du Sahara, *Malnutrition chez la mère, le nourrisson et le jeune enfant en Afrique: Le rapport de la deuxième Conférence inter-africaine sur la nutrition, Fajara, Gambie, 19–27 novembre 1952* (London: HMSO, 1956); and Centre international de l'enfance et la Commission de coopération technique en Afrique au sud du Sahara, *Le bien-être de l'enfant en Afrique au Sud du Sahara: Colloque organisé à Lagos (Nigéria) du 25 au 31 mars 1959 par le Centre international de l'enfance et la Commission de coopération technique en Afrique au sud du Sahara, sous la présidence de M. le Professeur Robert Debré* (Paris: Centre international de l'enfance, 1959). Also see Etienne Berthet, "Problèmes de pédiatrie sociales dans les pays en voie de développement," *Revue médicale du Moyen-Orient* 12, no. 3 (1955): 328–337.

50. ADLC, Série Afrique (1945–1965), CCTA 1, "Conversations anglo-franco-belges," 21 May 1947, 26.

51. ADLC, NUOI 528, Assemblée générale, Quatrième commission, XIVème session, "Intervention de M. Kosciusko-Morizet, représentant permanent de la France au Conseil de tutelle, sur la cessation des renseignements concernant les territoires devenus autonomes (Point 36 de l'ordre du jour)," 3 December 1959. Also see Gregory Mann, *From Empires to NGOs in the West African Sahel: The Road to Nongovernmentality* (New York: Cambridge University Press, 2015); and Rachel Kantrowitz, "'So That Tomorrow Would Be Better for Us': Developing French-Funded Catholic Schools in Dahomey and Senegal, 1946–1975" (PhD diss., New York University, 2015).

52. For an excellent overview of new approaches to the study of colonial public health, see Jennifer Johnson, "New Directions in the History of Medicine in European, Colonial and Transimperial Contexts," *Contemporary European History* 25, no. 2 (2016): 387–399.

53. See Matthew M. Heaton, *Black Skin, White Coats: Nigerian Psychiatrists, Decolonization, and the Globalization of Psychiatry* (Athens: Ohio University Press, 2013); and Jennifer Johnson, *The Battle for Algeria: Sovereignty, Healthcare, and Humanitarianism* (Philadelphia: University of Pennsylvania Press, 2016). Also see Warwick Anderson, "Where Is the Postcolonial History of Medicine?," *Bulletin of the History of Medicine* 72, no. 3 (1998): 529.

54. Alice Conklin, *A Mission to Civilize: The Republican Idea of Empire in France and West Africa, 1895–1930* (Stanford, CA: Stanford University Press, 1997). Also see Ellen Amster, *Medicine and the Saints: Science, Islam, and the Colonial Encounter in Morocco, 1877–1956* (Austin: University of Texas Press, 2013); Megan Vaughan, *Curing Their Ills: Colonial Power and African Illness* (Stanford, CA: Stanford University Press, 1991); and Shula Marks, "What Is Colonial about

Colonial Medicine? And What Has Happened to Imperialism and Health?," *Social History of Medicine* 10, no. 2 (1997): 205–219.

55. On the history of epidemic disease control efforts in colonial Africa, see Philip Curtin, "Medical Knowledge and Urban Planning in Colonial Tropical Africa," in *The Social Basis of Health and Healing in Africa,* ed. Steven Feierman and John M. Janzen (Berkeley: University of California Press, 1992), 235–255; Myron Echenberg, *Black Death, White Medicine: Bubonic Plague and the Politics of Public Health in Colonial Senegal, 1914–1945* (Portsmouth, NH: Heinemann, 2002); Myron Echenberg, *Africa in the Time of Cholera: A History of Pandemics from 1817 to the Present* (New York: Cambridge University Press, 2011); John Farley, *Bilharzia: A History of Imperial Tropical Medicine* (New York: Cambridge University Press, 1991); Maryinez Lyons, *The Colonial Disease: A Social History of Sleeping Sickness in Northern Zaire, 1900–1940* (Cambridge: Cambridge University Press, 1992); and Randall Packard, *White Plague, Black Labor: Tuberculosis and the Political Economy of Health and Disease in South Africa* (Berkeley: University of California Press, 1989).

56. On the questionable ethical standards of colonial medicine, see Guillaume Lachenal, *Le médicament qui devait sauver l'Afrique: Un scandale pharmaceutique aux colonies* (Paris: La Découverte, 2014); and Clifford Rosenberg, "The International Politics of Vaccine Testing in Interwar Algiers," *American Historical Review* 117, no. 3 (2012): 671–697.

57. See Lynn M. Thomas, *Politics of the Womb: Women, Reproduction, and the State in Kenya* (Berkeley: University of California Press, 2003); Nancy Rose Hunt, *A Colonial Lexicon of Birth Ritual, Medicalization, and Mobility in the Congo* (Durham, NC: Duke University Press, 1999); and Nancy Rose Hunt, "'Le bébé en brousse': European Women, African Birth Spacing, and Colonial Intervention in Breastfeeding in the Belgian Congo," in *Tensions of Empire: Colonial Cultures in a Bourgeois World,* ed. Frederick Cooper and Ann Laura Stoler (Berkeley: University of California Press, 1997), 287–321.

1. War, Citizenship, and the Limits of French Civilization

Epigraph: Archives nationales d'outre-mer (hereafter ANOM), 2 G 45 (11), Guinea, 1945 health services report, Conakry, 10 August 1946, medical section, 34.

1. See, for example, Robert Gildea, *Marianne in Chains: Daily Life in the Heart of France during the German Occupation* (New York: Picador, 2003); Julian Jackson, *France: The Dark Years, 1940–1944* (Oxford: Oxford University Press, 2003); Ian Ousby, *Occupation: The Ordeal of France, 1940–1944* (New York: Cooper Square, 2000); and Robert Paxton, *Vichy France: Old Guard and New Order, 1940–1944* (New York: Columbia University Press, 2001). For a popular

contemporary portrayal of the exodus and occupation, see Irène Némirovsky, *Suite Française* (New York: Knopf, 2006).

2. Archives nationales de France (hereafter ANF), F1a-3859, CFLN, Commissariat à l'intérieur, "La situation sanitaire en France: Beaucoup de prisonniers rapatriés souffrent de tuberculose, 13 April 1944; ANF, F1a-3859, CFLN, Commissariat à l'information, Centre d'information et de documentation, "Pillage et santé," 28 November 1943, 1; ANF, F1a-3859, CFLN, Commissariat à l'intérieur, "Etude concernant la malnutrition et ses répercussions sur la santé publique en Europe," October 1943, 1; and ANF, F1a-3859, France-Politique, "Manifeste du Front national pour l'indépendance de la France—aux médecins," 9 September 1943, 2.

3. For a general history of the empire at war, see Ruth Ginio, *French Colonialism Unmasked: The Vichy Years in French West Africa* (Lincoln: University of Nebraska Press, 2006); Eric Jennings, *Free French Africa in World War II: The African Resistance* (Cambridge: Cambridge University Press, 2015); and Eric Jennings, *Vichy in the Tropics: Pétain's National Revolution in Madagascar, Guadeloupe, and Indochina, 1940–1944* (Stanford, CA: Stanford University Press, 2001).

4. Guinea, 1945 health services report, 33.

5. République Française, *Conférence africaine française, Brazzaville, 30 janvier 1944 à 8 février 1944* (Paris: Ministère des Colonies, 1945).

6. Frederick Cooper, "A Constitution for an Empire of Citizens," chap. 2 in *Citizenship between Empire and Nation: Remaking France and French Africa, 1945–1960* (Princeton, NJ: Princeton University Press, 2014).

7. In 1947–1948, for example, a series of violent strikes rocked the territories of Senegal and Niger as railway workers rose up against unfair and exploitative working conditions. See Frederick Cooper, *Decolonization and African Society: The Labor Question in French and British Africa* (Cambridge: Cambridge University Press, 1996); and Frederick Cooper, "'Our Strike': Equality, Anticolonial Politics, and the 1947–48 Railway Strike in French West Africa," *Journal of African History* 36 (1996): 81–118. The strike was also the subject of Ousmane Sembène's 1960 novel *Les bouts de bois de Dieu* (Paris: Le Livre Contemporain, 1960).

8. On health care and medical advice for Europeans living in tropical regions, see F. Hénaff, "Hygiène de l'européen aux pays chauds," in *Exposition coloniale de Marseille, 1906: Compte rendu des travaux du Congrès colonial de Marseille*, ed. J. Charles-Roux (Paris: Challamel, 1907), 313–335. Also see Eric Jennings, *Curing the Colonizers: Hydrotherapy, Climatology, and French Colonial Spas* (Durham, NC: Duke University Press, 2006).

9. Alice Conklin, *A Mission to Civilize: The Republican Idea of Empire in France and West Africa, 1895–1930* (Stanford, CA: Stanford University Press, 1997).

10. Abel Lahille, *Mes impressions sur l'Afrique Occidentale Française: Étude documentaire au pays du tam-tam* (Paris: A. Picard, 1910), 221.

11. See, for example, Guillaume Lachenal, "Le médecin qui voulut être roi: Médecine coloniale et utopie au Cameroun," *Annales, histoire, sciences sociales* 65, no. 1 (2010): 121–156; Clifford Rosenberg, "The International Politics of Vaccine Testing in Interwar Algiers," *American Historical Review* 117, no. 3 (2012): 671–697; and Helen Tilley, *Africa as a Living Laboratory: Empire, Development, and the Problem of Scientific Knowledge, 1870–1950* (Chicago: University of Chicago Press, 2011).

12. Conklin, *Mission to Civilize*, 38–52.

13. For a comparative study of indigenous medical services throughout the French empire, see M. le Docteur Grall, "L'Assistance médicale indigène aux colonies," in Charles-Roux, *Exposition coloniale de Marseille*, 268–281.

14. Conklin, *Mission to Civilize*, 48–52.

15. Jules Carde, "Instructions sur le fonctionnement des services de l'Assistance médicale indigène: Instructions relatives à l'orientation et au développement des services de l'Assistance médicale indigène," Dakar, 15 February 1926, in Gouvernement Général de l'Afrique Occidentale Française, *Instructions du Gouverneur Général Carde sur le développement de l'Assistance médicale indigène sociale et sur la protection sanitaire des travailleurs en A.O.F.* (Paris: Librairie Larose, 1931), 1.

16. There is a vast literature on the topic of gender and population policy in metropolitan France. On pronatalism and positive eugenics in France, see Joshua Cole, *The Power of Large Numbers: Population, Politics, and Gender in Nineteenth-Century France* (Ithaca, NY: Cornell University Press, 2000); Alisa Klaus, *Every Child a Lion: The Origins of Maternal and Infant Health Policy in the United States and France, 1890–1920* (Ithaca, NY: Cornell University Press, 1993); Cheryl Koos, "Gender, Anti-individualism, and Nationalism: The Alliance Nationale and the Pronatalist Backlash against the Femme Moderne, 1933–1940," *French Historical Studies* 19, no. 3 (Spring 1996): 699–723; Francine Muel-Dreyfus, *Vichy et l'éternel féminin* (Paris: Editions de Seuil, 1996); Susan Pedersen, *Family, Dependence and the Origins of the Welfare State: Britain and France, 1914–1945* (Cambridge: Cambridge University Press, 1993); Karen Offen, "Depopulation, Nationalism, and Feminism in Fin-de-Siècle France," *American Historical Review* 89, no. 3 (June 1984): 648–676; Miranda Pollard, *Reign of Virtue: Mobilizing Gender in Vichy France* (Chicago, University of Chicago Press, 1998); Andres Horacio Reggiani, "Procreating France: The Politics of Demography, 1919–1945," *French Historical Studies* 19, no. 3 (Spring 1996): 725–754; Mary Louise Roberts, *Civilization without Sexes: Reconstructing Gender in Postwar France, 1917–1927* (Chicago: University of Chicago Press, 1994); William H. Schneider, "The Eugenics Movement in France, 1890–1940," in *The Wellborn Science*, ed. Mark Adams (Oxford: Oxford University Press, 1990), 69–109; and William H. Schneider, *Quality and Quantity: The Quest for Biological Regeneration in Twentieth-Century France* (Cambridge: Cambridge University Press, 1990). On the study of demography in France, see Paul-André

Rosental, *L'intelligence démographique: Sciences et politiques des populations en France (1930–1960)* (Paris: Jacob, 2003). On pronatalism in the empire, see Alice Conklin, "Faire Naître v. Faire du Noir: Race Regeneration in France and French West Africa, 1895–1940," in *Promoting the Colonial Idea: Propaganda and Visions of Empire in France,* ed. Tony Chafer and Amanda Sackur (Basingstoke, UK: Palgrave, 2002), 143–155.

17. Conklin, *Mission to Civilize,* 69–71.

18. Lahille, *Mes impressions,* 223.

19. Report of 1905, quoted in ibid., 224.

20. Conklin, *Mission to Civilize,* 218.

21. Jules Carde, "Instructions relatives a.) à l'orientation d'Assistance médicale indigène b.) à l'hygiène et à la protection sanitaire des travailleurs recrutés par les particuliers," in Gouvernement Général de l'Afrique Occidentale Française, *Instructions du Gouverneur Général Carde,* 38.

22. ANF, F1a-3859, "Note sur la création et l'organisation d'un ministère de la population et de l'hygiène," 15 November 1943. On the CMR, see Anne Simonin, "Le Comité médical de la résistance: Un succès différé," *Mouvement social* 180 (1997): 159–178.

23. Robert Debré, *Médecine, santé publique, population: Rapports présentés au Comité médical de la résistance et au Comité national des médecins français: Transmis au Comité français de la libération nationale, à Alger, en janvier 1944* (Paris: Editions du Médecin Français, 1944), 71.

24. Ibid.,8.

25. ANOM, 2 G 41 (5), AOF, Inspection générale des services sanitaires et médicaux, 1941 report, appendix: "Projet de création d'une direction générale du service de santé et de réorganisation des services sanitaires et médicaux en Afrique française," Dakar, 10 December 1943, 3.

26. Ibid., 6.

27. Ibid., 3–4.

28. On the legal and administrative status of the DGSP in AOF, see ANOM, 2 G 42 (7), Inspection générale des services sanitaires et médicaux, 1942 report, appendix: "De la réorganisation des services sanitaires et médicaux de l'Afrique Occidentale Française," 8–9.

29. Inspection générale, 1941 report, 5.

30. IMTSSA 106, "L'œuvre sanitaire de la France en AOF," 11.

31. This organizational format in turn would serve as a model for other hospitals throughout the colonies of AOF. See Inspection générale, 1941 report, 19–20.

32. Ibid., 5–6.

33. Ibid., 12–15. As this report explained, the standardization of medical supplies was not a new idea in 1943, but it had never been implemented properly.

34. Inspection générale, 1941 report, 9–12.

35. Ibid., 11–12.

36. Ibid., 6.
37. Ibid., 7.
38. On the relationship between AOF and the Vichy government, see Ginio, *French Colonialism Unmasked.* On Vichy and the empire more broadly, see Jennings, *Vichy in the Tropics.*
39. ANOM, 2 G 41 (3), "Rapport sur le fonctionnement technique de l'Institut Pasteur de l'Afrique Occidentale Française en 1941," 5–6.
40. ANOM, G 44 (4), C. Durieux, "Rapport sur le fonctionnement technique de l'Institut Pasteur de l'Afrique Occidentale Française en 1944," 6.
41. "Rapport sur le fonctionnement technique de l'Institut Pasteur (1941)," 5–6.
42. ANOM, 2 G 41 (10), Côte d'Ivoire, 1941 health services report, Abidjan, 30 May 1942, administration section, 2.
43. ANOM, 2 G 50 (9), DGSP, 1950 report 128.
44. ANOM, 2 G 41 (11), Dahomey, 1941 health services report, administrative section, 53.
45. ANOM, 2 G 41 (16), French Sudan, 1941 health services report, administrative section, 38–39. Also see ANOM, 2 G 45 (8), Senegal, 1945 health services report, 1 October 1946, administrative section, 89.
46. ANOM, 2 G 41 (9), HCI, 1941 report, medical section, 42.
47. ANOM, 2 G 44 (64), DGSP, Service général autonome de la maladie du sommeil en AOF et au Togo, 1944 report, Bobo-Dioulasso, 3 June 1945, 6.
48. ANOM, 2 G 42 (6), "Rapport sur le fonctionnement technique de l'Institut Pasteur de l'Afrique Occidentale Française en 1942," 5–6; and Durieux, "Rapport sur le fonctionnement technique," 5.
49. ANOM, 2 G 43 (9), Côte d'Ivoire, 1943 health services report, Abidjan, 30 July 1944, pharmacy section, 40.
50. ANOM, 2 G 44 (15), Institut Pasteur de Kindia (Guinea), 1944 report, 31 January 1945, 3.
51. ANOM, 2 G 42 (57), DGSP, 1942 report, 37; ANOM, 2 G 43 (56), DGSP, Service autonome de la maladie du sommeil en AOF et au Togo, 1943 report, Bobo-Dioulasso, 25 September 1944, 6; ANOM, 2 G 44 (5), DGSP, 1944 report, pharmacy section, 52.
52. ANOM, 2 G 43 (61), DGSP, 1943 report, 1.
53. For a general history of the idea of "degeneration" in the European context, see Daniel Pick, *Faces of Degeneration: A European Disorder, c. 1848–1918* (Cambridge: Cambridge University Press, 1999).
54. Côte d'Ivoire, 1941 health services report, 57.
55. "De la réorganisation," 5. Also see "L'œuvre sanitaire de la France en AOF," 9.
56. Dahomey, 1941 health services report, 53.
57. "De la réorganisation," 7.

58. Cooper, *Citizenship between Empire.*

59. "Discours prononcé par M. Pleven, commissaire aux colonies, le dimanche janvier 1944 à l'ouverture de la Conférence africaine française," in République Française, *Conférence africaine française,* 22.

60. For a broader historical context on the "assimilation" debate, see Raymond Frederick Betts, *Assimilation and Association in French Colonial Theory, 1890–1914* (Lincoln: University of Nebraska Press, 2005).

61. ANOM, 2 G 41 (14), Niger, 1941 health services report, medical section, 82–83. Also see ANOM, 2 G 42 (17), Niger, 1942 health services report.

62. ANOM, 2 G 42 (7), Médecin-Inspecteur Ricou, "Les maladies vénériennes en Afrique Occidentale Française," 1942, 15. Also see Philippa Levine, *Prostitution, Race, and Politics: Policing Venereal Disease in the British Empire* (New York: Routledge, 2003).

63. See Desprez, "Les maternités rurales en régions libérées," *Revue médico-social de l'enfance* 1, no. 6 (November–December 1933): 418; Klaus, *Every Child a Lion,* 52–53; and M. A. Piffault, "Préjugés et Superstitions," in *Premier Congrès international d'éducation et de protection* (Namur, Belgium: Auguste Godenne, 1905), 127–130. On the increasing govermentalization of child health provisions, and of social services for families more generally, see Bonnenfant, "Treize années de service social rural par l'Association d'hygiène sociale de l'Aisne, 1923–1926," *Revue médico-social de l'enfance* 5, no. 3 (May–June 1937): 168–184; and Bonnenfant, "Treize années de service social rural (suite et fin)," *Revue médico-social de l'enfance* 5, no. 4 (July–August 1937): 283–306. Also see Laura Lee Downs, *Childhood in the Promised Land: Working-Class Movements and the Colonies de Vacances in France, 1880–1960* (Durham, NC: Duke University Press, 2002); and Ivan Jablonka, *Ni père ni mère: Histoire des enfants de l'Assistance publique, 1874–1938* (Paris: Seuil, 2006).

64. HCI, 1941 report, 20–21.

65. Ibid.

66. Ibid., 51.

67. Ibid., 20–21.

68. DGSP, 1950 report, 128.

69. ANOM, 2 G 50 (11), Service générale de l'inspection médicale des écoles, 1949–1950 report.

70. United Nations, "The Universal Declaration of Human Rights," 1948, Article 25, http://www.un.org/en/documents/udhr/.

71. On labor rights, see Fredrick Cooper, *Africa since 1940: The Past of the Present* (Cambridge: Cambridge University Press, 2002); and Cooper, *Decolonization and African Society.* Also see Tony Chafer, *The End of Empire in French West Africa: France's Successful Decolonization?* (Oxford: Berg, 2002), 19.

72. ANOM, 2 G 46 (15), Côte d'Ivoire, 1946 health services report, 242.

73. On African resistance to French medical services, see Guillaume Lachenal, *Le médicament qui devait sauver l'Afrique: Un scandale pharmaceutique aux colonies* (Paris: La Décoverte, 2014).

74. Côte d'Ivoire, 1946 health services report; ANOM, 2 G 47 (16), Côte d'Ivoire, 1947 health services report, Abidjan, 1 September 1948.

75. Côte d'Ivoire, 1946 health services report, 259.

76. Ibid., 65.

77. Ibid., 260–262.

78. Ibid., 262–264.

79. ANOM, 2 G 48 (76), Dahomey, "Rapport sur l'enfance malheureuse ou deficient," 1948, 6.

80. Côte d'Ivoire, 1946 health services report, 260.

81. ANOM, 2 G 48 (25), Upper Volta, 1948 health services report, 80. Also see ANOM, 2 G 54 (85), Niger, health services, 1954 annual report, medical section, 22. For more general perspectives on the colony of Upper Volta, see Gabriel Massa and Y. Georges Madiéga, *La Haute-Volta coloniale: Témoignages, recherches, regards* (Paris: Karthala, 1995).

82. Robert Debré, *L'honneur de vivre: Témoignage* (Paris: Stock/Hermann, 1974), 382.

83. ANOM, 2 G 50 (18), French Sudan, 1950 health services report, 552.

84. Côte d'Ivoire, 1947 health services report, 62.

85. World Health Organization Constitution, 1946.

2. The United Nations and the Politics of Health

Epigraph: ANOM, 2 G 50 (124), AOF, Direction du Cabinet, "Synthèse périodique d'informations no. 2, Annexe: Les politiques française et britannique dans l'Ouest africain," March–April 1950, 99.

1. ADLC, Série Afrique (1945–1965), Généralités 32, telegram from Jean Chauvel (French ambassador to the UN), 7 November 1949.

2. Works by scholars such as Guillaume Lachenal and Clifford Rosenberg have demonstrated, however, the extent to which even public health programs were intimately bound up with colonial violence and coercion. See Guillaume Lachenal, *Le médicament qui devait sauver l'Afrique: Un scandale pharmaceutique aux colonies* (Paris: La Découverte, 2014); and Clifford Rosenberg, "The International Politics of Vaccine Testing in Interwar Algiers," *American Historical Review* 117, no. 3 (2012): 671–697.

3. For a broader exploration of propaganda and French imperialism, see Tony Chafer and Amanda Sackur, eds., *Promoting the Colonial Idea: Propaganda and Visions of Empire in* France (Basingstoke, UK: Palgrave Macmillan, 2002).

4. Jennifer Johnson, *The Battle for Algeria: Sovereignty, Healthcare, and Humanitarianism* (Philadelphia: University of Pennsylvania Press, 2016).

5. On the anticolonialism of the US, Soviet, Indian, and Indonesian delegations, see ADLC, NUOI 471, "Historique: Renseignements provenant des territoires non-autonomes," 1956.

6. On the Soviet position, see ADLC, Série Afrique (1945–1965), Généralités 1, letter from Pierre Charpentier (temporary French ambassador to Moscow) to Georges Bidault (president of the provisional government), 24 June 1945, 1–3. On the Indian position, see ADLC, Série Afrique (1945–1965), Généralités 31, letter from Christian Fouchet (French consul general, Calcutta) to Bidault, 23 September 1946, 1–2.

7. ADLC, Série Afrique (1945–1965), Généralités 1, "Aide-mémoire sur la thèse coloniale française à San-Francisco," 27 March 1945, 4. Also see "Colonial Issue," *Economist* 147, no. 5301 (31 March 1945): 402. On the British position, see ADLC, Série Afrique (1945–1965), Généralités 1, letter from René Massigli (French ambassador to the United Kingdom) to Bidault, 12 April 1945.

8. See William Roger Louis, *Imperialism at Bay: The United States and the Decolonization of the British Empire, 1941–1945* (New York: Oxford University Press, 1978); and Elizabeth Borgwardt, *A New Deal for the World: America's Vision for Human Rights* (Cambridge, MA: Belknap Press of Harvard University Press, 2005). Also see Geneva [pseud.], "America's Plan for the Colonial World," *American Mercury* 60, no. 254 (February 1945): 135–136; ADLC, NUOI 5, Provisional Government of the French Republic, delegation to the United States, office of postwar studies, "Rapport no. 15: Les vues du gouvernement des Etats-Unis sur les questions coloniales et l'administration des territoires sous mandat," 20 December 1944, 1–2; and ADLC, NUOI 521, "Note sur l'attitude de la délégation des Etats-Unis aux Nations Unies en ce qui concerne les territoires non autonomes et les territoires sous tutelle," 5 January 1949.

9. See, for example, George Padmore, "'New Deal' for Colored Races," *Pittsburgh Courier,* 29 January 1944, 11; Hugh Weston, "End of Vast French Empire Looms," *Pittsburgh Courier,* 11 May 1946, 16; and "South Africa, France Balk on Giving Up Colonies to UNO," *Chicago Defender,* 19 January 1946, 4. For a broader perspective on the French government's diplomatic approach to the San Francisco Conference, see Jessica Pearson, "O império francês vai a S. Francisco: A criação das Nações Unidas e os limites da reforma colonial," in *Os Impérios do Internacional: Perspectivas, Genealogias e Processos,* ed. Miguel Bandeira Jerónimo and José Pedro Monteiro (Lisbon: Almedina, forthcoming).

10. ADLC, Série Afrique (1945–1965), Généralités 31, "L'Organisation des Nations Unies et les questions coloniales," May 1948, 9.

11. On the connection between the mandates system and the system of colonial oversight that evolved at the San Francisco Conference, see United Nations,

Department of Public Information, ST/DPI/SER.A/73/Rev.1, "Background Paper on Chapter XI of the Charter concerning Non-self-governing Territories," 1 April 1957, 2. Also see Susan Pedersen, *The Guardians: The League of Nations and the Crisis of Empire* (Oxford: Oxford University Press, 2015). On the achievements of the international trusteeship system, see US Department of State, *The United States and Non-self-governing Territories: A Summary of Information regarding the United States and Non-self-governing Territories with Particular Reference to Chapters XI, XII, and XIII of the Charter of the United Nations* (Washington, DC: US Government Printing Office, 1947), 1.

12. United Nations, Department of Public Information, "Background Paper on Chapter XI," 2. Also see United Nations, Department of Public Information, *What the United Nations Is Doing for Non-self-governing Territories* (Lake Success, NY: Department of Public Information, 1948), 10; and ADLC, NUOI 521, letter from Chauvel to Robert Schuman (minister of foreign affairs), 30 December 1949.

13. United Nations Charter, Chapter XI, Article 73(e). Also see Anne Winslow, *International Responsibility for Colonial Peoples,* International Conciliation 458 (New York: Carnegie Endowment for International Peace, 1950).

14. "Historique: Renseignements," 1956. For a British perspective on the dangers of Article 73(e) specifically and of UN colonial oversight in general, see Alan Burns, *In Defence of Colonies: British Colonial Territories in International Affairs* (New York: Macmillan, 1957). On the Belgian stance toward the UN and the colonial question, see Fernand van Langenhove, *The Question of Aborigines before the United Nations: The Belgian Thesis* (Brussels: Institut Royal Colonial Belge, 1954). Also see Belgian Information Center, *The Sacred Mission of Civilization: To Which Peoples Should the Benefits Be Extended?* (New York: Belgian Information Center, 1953). For an American perspective, see "Matters Arising under Chapters XI, XII, and XIII of the Charter of the United Nations (Trusteeship and Non-self-governing Territories)," in *Foreign Relations of the United States, 1952–1954,* vol. 3, *United Nations Affairs,* ed. Ralph R. Goodwin and William Z. Slany (Washington, DC: US Government Printing Office, 1979), 434–508.

15. See United Nations, Department of Public Information, *What the United Nations,* 4–5; and "Historique: Renseignements," 1956, 2–3. For a more extended discussion of the Special Committee and the role of colonial reporting in the process of decolonization, see Jessica Lynne Pearson, "Defending Empire at the United Nations: The Politics of International Colonial Oversight in the Era of Decolonisation," *Journal of Imperial and Commonwealth History* 45, no. 3 (2017): 525–549.

16. "International Responsibility."

17. See ADLC, Série Afrique (1945–1965), Généralités 31, letter from the minister of overseas France to the minister of foreign affairs, 24 May 1946, 2; ADLC, NUOI 521, *Notes documentaires et études* no. 545, "Documents concernant les

territoires non autonomes et les territoires sous tutelle," 12 February 1947, 21–22; and ADLC, NUOI 521, "Note a / s définition des territoires non autonomes," Paris, 2 October 1948. On the changing juridical status of France's overseas empire after the war, see Frederick Cooper, *Citizenship between Empire and Nation: Remaking France and French Africa, 1945–1960* (Princeton, NJ: Princeton University Press, 2014).

18. "International Responsibility," 73.

19. André Mathiot, *Les Territoires Non Autonomes et la Charte des Nations Unies* (Paris: Librairie générale du droit et du jurisprudence, 1949), 59–60.

20. "Historique: Renseignements," 1956, 1.

21. United Nations, Department of Public Information, *What the United Nations,* 19.

22. United Nations, General Assembly, *Report of the Special Committee on Information Transmitted under Article 73e of the Charter,* Official Records: Third Session, Supplement 12 (A / 593) (Lake Success, NY: United Nations 1948), 8. Also see United Nations, Department of Public Information, *What the United Nations,* 20.

23. The French delegation claimed they were not opposed to the principles embodied in the UN Declaration of Human Rights, simply the manner in which the committee was attempting to implement them. "Historique: Renseignements," 1956, 15, 23.

24. United Nations, General Assembly, *Report of the Special Committee* (1948), 8. Also see United Nations, Department of Public Information, *What the United Nations,* 20.

25. IMTSSA 222, letter from the minister of overseas France (health services division) to the minister of foreign affairs, 24 February 1953, 2.

26. See Frederick Cooper, *Decolonization and African Society: The Labor Question in French and British Africa* (Cambridge: Cambridge University Press, 1996), 176.

27. United Nations, General Assembly, *Report of the Special Committee on Information Transmitted under Article 73e of the Charter,* Official Records: Sixth Session, Supplement 14 (A / 1836) (Geneva: United Nations, 1951), 12.

28. United Nations, General Assembly, *Report of the Special Committee* (1948), 4; United Nations, General Assembly, *Report of the Special Committee on Information Transmitted under Article 73e of the Charter,* Official Records: Fifth Session, Supplement 17 (A / 1303) (New York: United Nations, 1950), 4.

29. "L'Organisation des Nations Unies," May 1948, 29.

30. United Nations, General Assembly, *Report of the Special Committee on Information Transmitted under Article 73e of the Charter,* Official Records: Fourth Session, Supplement 14 (A / 923) (Lake Success, NY: United Nations,1949), 4.

31. United Nations, General Assembly, *Report of the Special Committee* (1950), 5.

32. United Nations, General Assembly, Committee on Information from Non-self-governing Territories, third session (1952), item 6 of the provisional agenda,

A / AC.35 / L.89, "Public Health Administration in Non-self-governing Territories, Report Prepared by the Secretariat," 28 July 1952, 44. Also see United Nations, General Assembly, *Report of the Committee on Information from Non-self-governing Territories,* Official Records: Tenth Session, Supplement 16 (A / 2908) (New York, 1955), 18.

33. United Nations, General Assembly, "Public Health Administration," 3.

34. United Nations, General Assembly, *Report of the Committee on Information from Non-self-governing Territories,* Official Records: Seventh Session, Supplement 18 (A / 2219) (New York, 1952), 3, 16. See Chapter 5 for more on juvenile delinquency and social problems.

35. United Nations, General Assembly, *Report of the Committee on Information from Non-self-governing Territories,* Official Records: Eighth Session, Supplement 15 (A / 2465) (New York, 1953), 9. Also see United Nations, General Assembly, *Report of the Committee on Information* (1955), 18.

36. United Nations, General Assembly, *Report of the Committee on Information* (1952), 19. Also see United Nations, Department of Public Information, "Background Paper on Chapter XI," 67. The 1952 report also emphasized the role that grassroots participation in health programs could play in supplementing the lack of funding for "the costly paraphernalia which they need." By "enlist[ing] the support of those in the villages who are influential in everyday life," health administrations in dependent territories could extend their reach in a different way, thereby obviating the need for more sophisticated equipment and facilities. See United Nations, General Assembly, *Report of the Committee on Information* (1952), 21.

37. United Nations, General Assembly, *Report of the Committee on Information* (1952), 216.

38. United Nations, General Assembly, "Public Health Administration," 43.

39. United Nations, General Assembly, *Report of the Committee on Information* (1952), 3, 16–17.

40. Ibid., 23.

41. Ibid., 7. On the use of technical assistance programs by the British and French colonial administrations, see United Nations, General Assembly, *Report of the Committee on Information* (1955), 5.

42. "Historique: Renseignements," 2–3; ADLC, NUOI 521, United Nations, Department of Public Information (research section), "Non-self-governing Territories, Background Paper No. 73," 1 January 1953, 19–21. Also see Pearson, "Defending Empire."

43. United Nations, General Assembly, *Report of the Committee on Information* (1952), 2.

44. United Nations, General Assembly, *Report of the Special Committee* (1951), 2. Also see United Nations, General Assembly, *Report of the Special Committee* (1949), 6.

45. "Historique: Renseignements," 1956.

46. On the use of indigenous languages, see ADLC, NUOI 521, Nations Unies, Assemblée Générale, "Langue de l'enseignement dans les territoires non autonomes, résolutions adoptées par l'Assemblée générale à sa 263ème séance plénière," 3 December 1949.

47. United Nations, General Assembly, *Report of the Committee on Information* (1955), 19–20.

48. Randall Packard, "Visions of Postwar Health and Development and Their Impact on Public Health Interventions in the Developing World," in *International Development and the Social Sciences: Essays on the History and Politics of Knowledge,* ed. Frederick Cooper and Randall Packard (Berkeley: University of California Press, 1997), 95–115.

49. On the French government's disapproval of the expanding role of the UN in colonial matters, see ADLC, NUOI 521, "Note sur les dix résolutions adoptées par l'Assemblée générale des Nations Unies concernant les territoires non autonomes," 5 December 1949.

50. For a broader history of French participation in the Special Committee, and of the decisions to stop the transmission of 73(e) reports after the passage of the *loi cadre* (framework law) in 1956, see ADLC, NUOI 528, Assemblée générale, Quatrième commission, XIVème Session, "Intervention de M. Kosczíusko-Morizet, représentant permanent de la France au Conseil de tutelle, sur la cessation des renseignements concernant les territoires devenus autonomes (Point 36 de l'ordre du jour)," 3 December 1959. Also see ADLC, NUOI 528, Ministère des Affaires Etrangères, "Note pour le ministre a / s de cessation de la communication aux Nations Unies des renseignements sur les territoires non autonomes," 21 August 1959.

51. United Nations, Department of Public Information, *What the United Nations,* 23.

52. NUOI 521, Nation Unies, Assemblée générale, quatrième session, "Compte rendu sténographique de la deux cent soixante-troisième séance tenue à Flushing Meadow (New York)," 2 December 1949, 10 h 45, 89.

53. United Nations, Department of Public Information, *What the United Nations,* 23.

54. Mathiot, *Les Territoires Non Autonomes,* 48, 62, 75.

55. "Historique: Renseignements," 1956, 2, 10, 18.

56. AOF, Direction du Cabinet, "Synthèse périodique d'informations no. 2," March–April 1950, 99.

57. ADLC, NUOI 521, "Note pour le secrétaire générale a / s de résolutions adoptées par l'Assemblée générale des Nations Unies au sujet des territoires non autonomes, 4ème session," 28 September to 29 November 1949, 4–7. Also see ADLC, NUOI 521, letter from M. Jousselin (conseiller de l'Union Française) to the minister of foreign affairs, 8 January 1950.

58. ADLC, NUOI 521, "Note pour le ministre a / s de résolutions adoptées," 20 December 1949.

59. Archives nationales du Sénégal (hereafter ANS), 1 H 49 (163), letter from the minister of overseas France to the high commission of the republic in AOF, 17 December 1953, 5.

60. ADLC, NUOI 521, Ministry of Foreign Affairs (Afrique-Levant), "Note pour le secrétaire général a / s de recommandations anticolonialistes à l'Assemblée des Nations Unies," 6 December 1949.

61. ADLC, NUOI 521, "Interview donnée à la Radio des Nations Unies par M. Laurentie, délégué-adjoint au Conseil de tutelle," 9 December 1949.

62. Léon Blum, "Le colonialisme devant l'ONU," *Le Populaire,* 5 December 1949.

63. ANS, 1 H 49 (163), letter from the Government General of French Africa (political, social, and administrative affairs division) to the director of public health; the director of public instruction; the director of economic services (agriculture); the director of public works; and the director of the Institut Français d'Afrique Noire, 28 June 1948. Also see ANS, 1 H 49 (163), letter from the minister of overseas France to the high commissioner of the republic in AOF, Paris, 6 December 1952.

64. ANS, 1 H 49 (163), minister of overseas France (political affairs division), "Circulaire: renseignements fournis au titre de l'Article 73," 4.

65. Letter from the minister of overseas France to the high commissioner of the republic in AOF, 17 December 1953, 4.

66. ANS, 1 H 49 (163), Direction général de l'intérieur, Service des affaires politiques, "Circulaire: Renseignements ONU," Dakar, 23 December 1952, 2.

67. ANOM, 2 G 52 (3), "Rapport bisannuel sur la protection de la collectivité, de la famille et de l'enfance," 1951–1952, 138.

68. ANS, 1 H 49 (163), "Situation et évolution de la santé publique en AOF pendant l'année 1949." On medical research in the colonies, see Constant Mathis, *L'oeuvre des pastoriens en Afrique noire, Afrique Occidentale Français* (Paris: Presses Universitaires de France, 1946). Also see Aro Velmet, "Pasteur's Empire: French Expertise, Colonialism, and Transnational Science, 1890–1940" (PhD diss., New York University, 2017).

69. ANS, 1 H 49 (163), Médecin-Colonel Sanner, "Documentation concernant la santé publique en AOF, année 1952, établie en exécution des circulaires no. 975 / INT / AP. 2 du 17.12.1952 et no. 997 / INT / AP. 2 du 23.12.1952 et conformément au schéma-guide de l'ONU (Article 73 / e de la Charte)," Dakar, 17 February 1953, 1.

70. "Rapport bisannuel," 1951–1952, 16.

71. "Arrêté 6341 / APA du 30 décembre 1950," in ibid.

72. Nation Unies, Assemblée générale, quatrième session, 2 December 1949, 10 h 45, 88.

73. On the charges leveled against the colonial administrations, see United Nations, General Assembly, *Report of the Special Committee* (1949), 6.

74. Mathiot, *Les Territoires Non Autonomes,* 76.

3. Between Colonial Knowledge and International Expertise

Epigraph: IMTSSA 238, Note for the director of political affairs, 4 July 1951, 1.

1. ADLC, Série Afrique (1945–1965), CCTA 1, "Commentaires de l'ordre du jour de la conférence tripartite," 20 February 1947.

2. ADLC, Série Afrique (1945–1965), CCTA 1, "Note pour le ministre sur la création éventuelle d'un organisme de coopération technique coloniale en Afrique occidentale et centrale," 1947, 5.

3. On the CCTA in the context of broader Franco-British colonial cooperation, see John Kent, *The Internationalization of Colonialism: Britain, France, and Black Africa, 1939–1956* (New York: Oxford University Press, 1992).

4. David P. Fidler, *International Law and Infectious Diseases* (Oxford: Oxford University Press, 1999); Valeska Huber, "The Unification of the Globe by Disease? The International Sanitary Conferences on Cholera, 1851–1894," *Historical Journal* 49, no. 2 (2006): 453–476.

5. See Iris Borowy, *Coming to Terms with World Health: The League of Nations Health Organisation, 1921–1946* (Frankfurt: Peter Lang, 2014); Martin Dubin, "The League of Nations Health Organisation," in *International Health Organisations and Movements, 1918–1939,* ed. Paul Weindling (Cambridge: Cambridge University Press, 1995), 56–80; and Norman Howard-Jones, *International Public Health between the Two World Wars: The Organizational Problems* (Geneva: World Health Organization, 1978).

6. World Health Organization Constitution, 1946, Preamble.

7. For the earliest discussions of the principles of regionalization and decentralization, see United Nations, World Health Organization Interim Commission, *Minutes of the Technical Preparatory Committee for the International Health Conference Held in Paris from 18 March to 5 April 1946,* Official Records of the World Health Organization 1 (New York: United Nations, World Health Organization Interim Commission, 1947), 29–31, 66–69; and United Nations, World Health Organization Interim Commission, *Summary Report on Proceedings, Minutes, and Final Acts of the International Health Conference Held in New York from 19 June to 22 July 1946,* Official Records of the World Health Organization 2 (New York: United Nations, World Health Organization Interim Commission, 1948), 23–25.

8. World Health Organization Constitution, 1946, Chapter XI, Article 44.

9. Marcos Cueto, *The Value of Health: A History of the Pan American Health Organization* (Washington, DC: Pan American Health Organization, 2007).

10. ADLC, NUOI 323, Délégation française à l'Organisation mondiale de la Santé, 7ème session du Conseil éxécutif, "Note sur les tendances actuelles de l'Organisation mondiale de la Santé: Régionalisation et décentralisation," Geneva, 11 January 1951.

11. On the assignment of different countries and territories to the different regions, see ADLC, NUOI 323, United Nations, World Health Organization Interim Commission, "Cinquième session: rapport du secrétaire exécutif, Siège de l'OMS et bureaux régionaux," 8 January 1948. Also see ADLC, NUOI 323, United Nations, World Health Organization Interim Commission, "Enquête relative à la détermination des régions géographiques, note du secrétariat," 4 August 1947; and WHO, *First World Health Assembly, Geneva, 24 June to 24 July 1948,* Official Records of the World Health Organization 13 (Geneva: World Health Organization, December 1948), 262–274.

12. On the issue of remapping the imperial world, see Aiyaz Husain, *Mapping the End of Empire: American and British Strategic Visions in the Postwar World* (Cambridge, MA: Harvard University Press, 2014). Also see James R. Akerman, ed., *Decolonizing the Map: Cartography from Colony to Nation* (Chicago: University of Chicago Press, 2017).

13. ADLC, NUOI 330, World Health Organization, "Establishment of African Region, Position at 1950," 2 May 1950, appendix 2.

14. IMTSSA 222, "Note au sujet de la région africaine du Comité régional africain et Bureau régional africain de l'OMS," n.d., 1. Also see ADLC, NUOI 323, United Nations, World Health Organization, "Première Assemblée mondiale de la santé: Deuxième rapport de la commission du siège et de l'organisation régionale," 8 July 1948. French North Africa was not included in the African region, and its regional placement would later be the subject of an entirely different set of political debates. See Jessica Pearson-Patel, "Remapeando as fronteiras da saúde imperial: A Organização Mundial da Saúde e os debates internacionais sobre a regionalização no Norte de África Francês, 1945–1956," trans. Luís Domingos, in *Os passados do presente: Internacionalismo, imperialismo e a construção do mundo contemporâneo,* ed. Miguel Bandeira Jerónimo and José Pedro Monteiro (Lisbon: Almedina, 2015), 295–322.

15. The position of British colonies was, however, slightly more flexible than the French overseas territories. As one 1951 French memo explained, "England has the possibility of being represented . . . in the regional offices either directly or through associate members. Such a possibility is not open to us because our constitution considers our overseas territories not as Associated states, but as an integral part of the Republic." See ADLC, NUOI 323, "OMS: Questions d'ordre régional," January 1951, 8. Also see ADLC, Série Afrique (1945–1965), CCTA 2, "Conclusions provisoires adoptées au cours des conversations à trois (belgo-anglo-française) tenues au Ministère des Colonies à Bruxelles du 30 mai au 1 juin 1949," appendixes 1 and 2.

16. IMTSSA 238, note from the Union of South Africa, 1949, and IMTSSA 238, Organisation Mondiale de la Santé, "Création d'une région africaine, situation en avril 1950," 5–7. Also see ADLC, NUOI 330, Ministry of Foreign Affairs (political affairs division), "Création d'un Bureau régional africain de l'Organisation mondiale de la Santé," n.d.

17. Note from the Union of South Africa, 1949, 2. Also see World Health Organization, "Establishment of African Region," 2 May 1950, appendix 1, 2; and ADLC, NUOI 323, "La politique régionaliste de l'Organisation mondiale de la Santé—état de la question à la veille de la 2ème Assemblée mondiale," 1949, 1.

18. WHO, *Annual Report of the Director-General to the World Health Assembly and the United Nations, 1949,* Official Records of the World Health Organization 24 (Geneva: World Health Organization, 1950), 23.

19. Ibid., 32.

20. Ibid., 37.

21. For an extensive discussion of French participation in regional cooperation in Latin America, see ADLC, NUOI 323, "OMS: Questions d'ordre régional," January 1951, 10–11. India, among other states, contested France's claim to belong to all six regions. See "La politique régionaliste," 1949, 3.

22. ADLC, NUOI 323, untitled and undated memo. On the creation of markets for French drugs and medical technology, see ADLC, NUOI 323, "Compte rendu de la réunion interministérielle tenue au département le 21 juillet à 17h," n.d., 2.

23. On the commercial and cultural possibilities offered by the WHO regional offices, see ADLC, NUOI 323, note for the direction of cultural relations, 17 July 1952. Also see "OMS: Questions d'ordre régional," January 1951, 12–14.

24. See ADLC, Série Afrique (1945–1965), CCTA 2, letter from the minister of foreign affairs to the minister of overseas France (political affairs division), 2 April 1949, 3. On the growth of African nationalism after the Second World War, see Tony Chafer, *The End of Empire in French West Africa: France's Successful Decolonization?* (Oxford: Berg, 2002); and Patrick Manning, *Francophone Sub-Saharan Africa, 1880–1995* (Cambridge: Cambridge University Press, 1998). On increasing US involvement in African development as part of the postwar European reconstruction, see Kent, *Internationalization of Colonialism,* 263–266; and ADLC, Série Afrique (1945–1965), CCTA 2, "Note pour le ministre sur l'organisation de la coopération technique en Afrique," 18 May 1949.

25. "Note pour le ministre sur la création éventuelle," 1947, 10.

26. ADLC, Série Afrique (1945–1965), CCTA 1, "Mémoire pour les conversations que le Gouverneur Laurentie et M. Monod doivent avoir à Londres le 19 février," 18 February 1947. Also see "Commentaires de l'ordre du jour," 20 February 1947.

27. ADLC, Série Afrique (1945–1965), CCTA 1, Ministry of Foreign Affairs (Africa division) and Ministry of Overseas France (political division), "Mémorandum pour la conférence coloniale franco-anglo-belge de mai 1947," 2.

28. ADLC, Série Afrique (1945–1965), CCTA 3, "Agreed Conclusions of the Anglo-Belgian Colonial Discussions Held at the Colonial Office, London," 26–28 June 1946.

29. ADLC, Série Afrique (1945–1965), CCTA 1, "Conversations franco-anglo-belges de 20, 21, et 22 mai 1947," 1. Also see "Mémorandum pour la conférence coloniale franco-anglo-belge de mai 1947," 9. On earlier interimperial medical cooperation, see Deborah J. Neill, *Networks in Tropical Medicine: International, Colonialism, and the Rise of a Medical Specialty* (Stanford, CA: Stanford University Press, 2012).

30. "Mémorandum pour la conférence coloniale franco-anglo-belge de mai 1947," 12–13.

31. ADLC, Série Afrique (1945–1965), CCTA 1, letter from René Massigli to Georges Bidault, 20 February 1947, 3; ADLC, Série Afrique (1945–1965), CCTA 1, letter from Massigli to Marius Moutet, 10 March 1947.

32. ADLC, Série Afrique (1945–1965), CCTA 1, letter from Moutet to Massigli, 17 April 1947, 1–2. On Moutet's perspectives on imperial reform, see Jean-Pierre Gratien, *Marius Moutet: Un socialiste à l'outre-mer* (Paris: L'Harmattan, 2006). Also see Frederick Cooper, *Citizenship between Empire and Nation: Remaking France and French Africa, 1945–1960* (Princeton, NJ: Princeton University Press, 2014), 68–69.

33. Kent, *Internationalization of Colonialism,* 154. Also see Martin Shipway, "Thinking like an Empire: Governor Henri Laurentie and Postwar Plans for the Late Colonial French 'Empire State,'" in *The French Colonial Mind,* ed. Martin Thomas (Lincoln: University of Nebraska Press, 2011), 219–250; and Martin Shipway, "Madagascar on the Eve of Insurrection, 1944–1947," in *The Decolonization Reader,* ed. James Le Sueur (New York: Routledge, 2003), 82–83.

34. "Conversations franco-anglo-belges de 20, 21, et 22 mai 1947," 1.

35. ADLC, Série Afrique (1945–1965), CCTA 1, Ministre des Affaires Etrangères, Service d'information et de presse, "Circulaire no. 98, a/s conversations franco-anglo-belges sur les problèmes de l'Afrique occidentale et centrale," 9 May 1947.

36. "Conversations franco-anglo-belges de 20, 21, et 22 mai 1947," 4.

37. Ibid., 11.

38. Ibid., 22–24.

39. "Mémorandum pour la conférence coloniale franco-anglo-belge de mai 1947," 5.

40. Ibid., 3. On the history of the Caribbean Commission, see Bernard L. Poole, *The Caribbean Commission: Background of Cooperation in the West Indies* (Columbia: University of South Carolina Press, 1951); and Willis Grafton Nealley,

"The Caribbean Commission as an International Instrument for Regional Collaboration" (PhD diss., Stanford University, 1951).

41. ADLC, Série Afrique (1945–1965), CCTA 2, "Sujets justifiant des futures conférences et reunions," n.d.

42. On early discussions of whether to include Portugal and South Africa, see letter from Massigli to Bidault, 20 February 1947, 3–4. Also see ADLC, Série Afrique (1945–1965), CCTA 1, "Commission anglo-franco-belge," 20 May 1947, 15 h 30, 3–4.

43. Both Britain and France developed their own internal approaches to funding colonial development in the postwar era. See Frederick Cooper, *Decolonization and African Society: The Labor Question in French and British Africa* (Cambridge: Cambridge University Press, 1996). On FIDES, see ADLC, Série Afrique (1945–1965), Généralités 31, "Note pour la délégation française à la 10ème session du Conseil économique et social à Lake Success (7 février 1950): Préparation d'une étude sur la situation économique en Afrique et intérêt qu'il y aurait à créer une Commission économique pour l'Afrique," 7.

44. ADLC, Série Afrique (1945–1965), CCTA 2, "Réunion tenue chez M. Parodi sur la préparation des entretiens coloniaux de Londres," 22 April 1949, 8–9.

45. ADLC, NUOI 528, Assemblée générale, Quatrième commission, XIVème session, "Intervention de M. Kosciusko-Morizet (représentant permanent de la France au Conseil de tutelle) sur la cessation des renseignements concernant les territoires devenus autonomes (Point 36 de l'ordre du jour)," 3 December 1959, 1–3.

46. "Réunion tenue chez M. Parodi," 22 April 1949, 8–9.

47. ADLC, Série Afrique (1945–1965), CCTA 3, "Rapport au ministre: Conférence tenue à Londres les 7 et 8 septembre 1949 sur la coopération technique en Afrique," 13 September 1949.

48. "Réunion tenue chez M. Parodi," 22 April 1949, 7. On the dangers of including South Africa in a permanent organization for technical cooperation, see ADLC, Série Afrique (1945–1965), CCTA 3, letter from the minister of overseas France to the minister of foreign affairs (Africa division), 16 September 1949, 5.

49. "Truman's Inaugural Address," 20 January 1949, Harry S. Truman Library, https://www.trumanlibrary.org/whistlestop/50yr_archive/inagural20jan1949.htm. Also see Kent, *Internationalization of Colonialism*, 198.

50. David Owen, "The United Nations Program of Technical Assistance," *Annals of the American Academy of Political and Social Science* 270 (1950): 109–117. Also see Bart J. Bok, "The United Nations Expanded Program for Technical Assistance," *Science* 117, no. 3030 (1953): 67–70.

51. "Rapport au ministre," 13 September 1949, 5–6. On the problem of foreign technicians, see ADLC, Série Afrique (1945–1965), CCTA 3, note from 26 September 1949, 8.

52. "Rapport au ministre," 13 September 1949, 16–18.

53. ADLC, Série Afrique (1945–1965), CCTA 3, letter from Henri Laurentie to Robert Schuman (minister of foreign affairs), 4 October 1949, 1–2.

54. ADLC, Série Afrique (1945–1965), CCTA 3, "Compte-rendu de la réunion interministérielle tenue le 16 décembre chez l'ambassadeur secrétaire général concernant la coopération technique en Afrique," n.d., 2. On the possibility of creating an economic commission for Africa, see "Note pour la délégation française (7 février 1950)."

55. "Compte-rendu de la réunion interministérielle (21 juillet)," 3. On the danger presented by certain UN delegates such as Benegal Shiva Rao, see ADLC, Série Afrique (1945–1965), CCTA 3, "Etude des points qu'il conviendrait de porter à l'ordre du jour de la première réunion du comité inter-gouvernemental pour la coopération technique en Afrique," n.d., 2. For a more general explanation of India's approach to the colonial question at the UN, see ADLC, Série Afrique (1945–1965), Généralités 31, letter from Christian Fouchet (French consul general, Calcutta) to Georges Bidault (president of the provisional government) 23 September 1946. Also see Mark Mazower, "Jawaharlal Nehru and the Emergence of the Global United Nations," chap. 4 in *No Enchanted Palace: The End of Empire and the Ideological Origins of the United Nations* (Princeton, NJ: Princeton University Press, 2009). On the possibility of including Liberia and Ethiopia in the CCTA, see ADLC, Série Afrique (1945–1965), CCTA 3, "Réunion du 15 décembre," 2.

56. Commission de cooperation technique en Afrique au sud du Sahara, preface to *Coopération scientifique et technique en Afrique au sud du Sahara, 1948–1955* (London: S. Austin and Sons, 1956), i-ii. The CCTA consisted of two separate organizations that were eventually merged, the Commission de coopération technique en Afrique au sud du Sahara and the Conseil scientifique pour l'Afrique au sud du Sahara. The latter was originally created to serve as a liaison between different intergovernmental scientific organizations in Africa, facilitate cooperation between researchers, facilitate exchanges for scientific workers, and work with the CCTA to convene scientific conferences. In 1954 these two organizations were joined. See ibid., xi.

57. CCTA, *Coopération Scientifique,* v.

58. See, for example, Neill, *Networks in Tropical Medicine.*

59. CCTA, *Coopération Scientifique,* 1.

60. Ibid., 43.

61. Ibid., 44.

62. Note from the Union of South Africa, 1949, 6.

63. ADLC, NUOI 330, "Communiqué à Ministère de la France d'Outre-Mer, direction du service de santé, Ministère de la France d'Outre-Mer, Direction des affaires politiques, Direction d'Afrique Levant, a/s 11ème session du Conseil économique et social, extrait d'une lettre du chef de la délégation française no. 120 du 8 août, concernant une intervention du délégué de l'Inde en faveur de la créa-

tion d'un Bureau régional africain de l'Organisation mondiale de la Santé," 11 August 1950, 1. Also see ADLC, NUOI 330, Colonial Office, Memo 25512/35/1/50, 8 March 1950; and "Création d'un Bureau régional africain."

64. Note from the Union of South Africa, 1949, 13.

65. Ibid., 11.

66. World Health Organization, "Establishment of African Region," 2 May 1950, 7.

67. Ibid., appendix 2. A telegram dated 5 May 1950 from the government of South Africa to its embassy in Paris claimed that the government in fact agreed with many of the reasons the French government gave for delaying the creation of a regional office but stated that "our hand had been forced by insistence by Liberia on early establishment of an African region and that although we could not say so in our paper we felt it might be dangerous to leave the initiative to Liberia in this matter." They noted that if the French delegation were to find some way to convince Liberia to delay the dispersal of funds until the following year, they "should only be too happy to fall into line." See ADLC, NUOI 330, "Démarquage d'un télégramme adressé par le gouvernement sud-africain à son ambassade à Paris et remis le 19 mai [illegible] par l'ambassade à Afrique-Levant, objet: Bureau africain de l'OMS," n.d.

68. ADLC, NUOI 330, Ministry of Foreign Affairs (Africa division), "Bureau africain de l'OMS," 5 May 1950, 2.

69. The French delegation proposed the possibility of working out a situation analogous to that of the Pan American Sanitary Bureau, which was a previously independent organization brought into the WHO framework in lieu of a regional organization. See "Communiqué à Ministère de la France d'Outre-Mer," 11 August 1950, 2. Also see ADLC, NUOI 330, letter from Bernard Toussaint (permanent representative of France to the UN) to Schuman, 14 September 1950, 2.

70. "Création d'un bureau régional africain," 2–3.

71. ADLC, NUOI 330, telegram, Lisbon, 6 May 1950, 17 h 45, no. 194.

72. ADLC, NUOI 330, telegram, London, 8 May 1950, 21 h 40, no. 1625.

73. "Communiqué à Ministère de la France d'Outre-Mer," 11 August 1950, 3–4. Also see NUOI 323, "OMS: Questions d'ordre régional," January 1951, 13.

4. The World Health Organization Comes to Brazzaville

Epigraph: ADLC, NUOI 323, "La politique régionaliste de l'Organisation mondiale de la Santé—état de la question à la veille de la 2ème Assemblée mondiale," 1949, 12.

1. World Health Organization Library (hereafter WHOL), WHO Regional Committee for Africa, RC2 / AFR / 5, second session, statement by the president of Liberia, Mr. William V. S. Tubman, 31 July 1952, 4.

2. IMTSSA 238, UN, WHO, EB8 / Min / 4, provisional minutes of the fourth meeting, 4 June 1951, 7. Also see IMTSSA 238, ONU, OMS, Conseil éxécutif, huitième session, "Extrait in extenso des débats de la quatrième séance," 4 June 1951, 14 h 30, 16–21. Also see IMTSSA 238, "Preparatory Meeting of African Governments (Geneva)," 11 June 1951, 5.

3. Ibid., 9. Also see IMTSSA 238, OMS, Comité régional de l'Afrique, RC1 / AFR / Min / 2, première session, procès-verbal provisoire de la deuxième séance, Geneva, 24 September 1951, 14 h 00, 12–14.

4. IMTSSA 238, OMS, Organisation régionale de l'Afrique, AFR / Min / 1, "Réunion préparatoire des gouvernements africains, procès-verbal provisoire de la réunion tenue au Palais des Nations," Geneva, 11 June 1951, 10 h 00, 7.

5. IMTSSA 222, Ministry of Overseas France, direction of health services, "Rapport du Médecin-Colonel Garcin, chef de la section technique à la Direction du service de santé du Ministère de la France d'Outre-Mer et délégué à la réunion préparatoire pour l'Organisation régionale de l'Afrique, à Monsieur le Ministre des Affaires Etrangères, Secrétariat des conférences, Direction Afrique-Levant, objet: réunion préparatoire des gouvernements africains pour l'organisation régional de l'Afrique," n.d., 5.

6. Edward Berenson, "Brazza and the Scandal of the Congo," chap. 6 in *Heroes of Empire: Five Charismatic Men and the Conquest of Africa* (Berkeley: University of California Press, 2010). Also see Pierre Paul François Camille Savorgnan de Brazza and Napoléon Ney, *Conférences et lettres de P. Savorgnan de Brazza sur ses trois explorations dans l'Ouest africain, de 1875 à 1886* (Paris, 1887); and "A. E. F.: Brazzaville," *Le courrier colonial illustré,* 15 September 1929.

7. Phyllis M. Martin, *Leisure and Society in Colonial Brazzaville* (Cambridge: Cambridge University Press, 1995), 12. On resource development in French Congo, see, for example, "Les bois de l'Afrique Equatoriale Française," *Le courrier colonial illustré,* 31 December 1931. For an earlier colonial perspective on the Congo region, see "Le Congo français," *La dépêche coloniale illustrée,* 30 November 1908; and "Afrique équatoriale—Moyen Congo," *La dépêche coloniale illustrée,* 15 April 1911.

8. Air France, "Richesses agricoles," *Echos de l'air: Bulletin mensuel* 38 (July 1950): 6 and Air France "De Dakar à Brazzaville," *Echos de l'air: Bulletin mensuel* 38 (July 1950): 12.

9. R. L. Pont, "Brazzaville," *Air France revue,* Winter 1952–1953, 86–88. On postwar construction and modernization in Brazzaville, also see Georges Balandier, *Sociologie des Brazzavilles noires* (Paris: Presses de la Fondation nationale des sciences politiques, 1985), viii–x.

10. Air France, "Air France en Afrique Occidentale Française et en Afrique Equatoriale Française," *Echos de l'air: Bulletin mensuel* 38 (July 1950): 3.

11. Pont, "Brazzaville," 86–88. For a more extensive discussion of transportation in AEF, see "Voies de transports et moyens de communication en A. E. F.," *Les annales coloniales,* December 1933.

12. On the expansion of medical infrastructure in postwar Brazzaville, see IMTSSA 103, "Discours prononcé par Monsieur le Gouverneur Général Soucadeaux à la séance d'ouverture du Conseil du Gouvernement de l'Afrique Equatoriale Française," 23 December 1946, 22–23. On the Pasteur Institute in Brazzaville, see Deborah J. Neill, *Networks in Tropical Medicine: Internationalism, Colonialism, and the Rise of a Medical Specialty, 1890–1930* (Stanford, CA: Stanford University Press, 2012), 95. Also see Pratik Chakrabarti, "Bacteriology and the Civilizing Mission," chap. 9 in *Medicine and Empire, 1600–1960* (Basingstoke, UK: Palgrave Macmillan, 2014). Much of the medical infrastructure centered on French efforts to combat sleeping sickness in the region. See "Prophylaxie de la maladie du sommeil en Afrique Equatoriale Française," *La dépêche coloniale illustrée,* 31 July 1911; and "La maladie du sommeil en AEF," *La presse coloniale illustrée,* July 1922.

13. Pont, "Brazzaville," 88.

14. Eric Jennings, *Free French Africa in World War II: The African Resistance* (Cambridge: Cambridge University Press, 2015), 2–5. Also see Jerôme Ollandet, *Brazzaville, capitale de la France libre: Histoire de la résistance française en Afrique, 1940–1944* (Paris: L'Harmattan, 2013).

15. Martin Shipway, "The Brazzaville Conference and Its Origins: Policy Formation and Myth Making on the Congo," chap. 1 in *The Road to War: France and Vietnam, 1944–1947* (New York: Berghahn, 2003). Also see Harry Gamble, "Gaullist Hesitations: From the Brazzaville Conference to the Liberation," chap. 7 in *Contesting French West Africa: Battles over Schools and the Colonial Order, 1900–1950* (Lincoln: University of Nebraska Press, 2017); and Peo Hansen and Stefan Jonsson, *Eurafrica: The Untold History of European Integration and Colonialism* (London: Bloomsbury, 2015), 95–96.

16. Neill, *Networks in Tropical Medicine,* 100–101.

17. Gilbert Houlet, *Les guides bleus illustrés: Brazzaville, Léopoldville, Pointe-Noire* (Paris: Librarie Hachette, 1958), 11–12. On conditions in Bacongo and Poto-Poto in the 1950s, also see Marcel Soret, *Démographie et problèmes urbains en A. E. F.: Poto-Poto, Bacongo, Dolisie* (Montpellier: Imprimerie Charité, 1954); and Martin, *Leisure and Society,* 35–44.

18. Balandier, *Sociologie des Brazzavilles noires.*

19. "Preparatory Meeting," 11 June 1951, 8–9. On the history of colonial violence and racism in the Belgian Congo, see Adam Hochschild, *King Leopold's Ghost: A Story of Greed, Terror, and Heroism in Colonial Africa* (Boston: Houghton Mifflin, 1998).

20. "Réunion préparatoire des gouvernements africains," 11 June 1951, 10 h 00, 10. Also see "Rapport du Médecin-Colonel Garcin, objet: réunion préparatoire

des gouvernements africains pour l'Organisation régional de l'Afrique," 2–3. For more on the connections between Brazzaville and other locales, see Houlet, *Les guides bleus illustrés,* 3–6.

21. See IMTSSA 238, memorandum on the conditions of establishment in Brazzaville of the World Health Organization's Regional Office for Africa, n.d.; IMTSSA 238, DGSP, letter from the high commissioner of the republic to the minister of overseas France, 31 August 1952; and WHOL, Regional Committee for Africa, RC1 / AFR / Min / 2, first session, provisional minutes for the second meeting, 24 September 1951, 4–12.

22. Regional Committee for Africa, first session, provisional minutes for the second meeting, 24 September 1951, 11–12.

23. "Rapport du Médecin-Colonel Garcin, objet: réunion préparatoire des gouvernements africains pour l'Organisation régional de l'Afrique," 5–6.

24. IMTSSA 238, letter from the minister of foreign affairs to Médecin-Colonel Garcin, 19 September 1951, 1–2.

25. IMTSSA 238, Note for the director of political affairs, 4 July 1951, 1–2.

26. ANS, 1 H 50 (163), "Accord entre le Gouvernement français et l'Organisation mondiale de la Santé sur les privilèges et immunités (région Afrique), signé les 23 juillet et 1 août 1952."

27. ADLC, NUOI 330, letter from the minister of overseas France to the high commissioner of the republic in AEF, Brazzaville, 28 January 1952.

28. "Rapport du Médecin-Colonel Garcin, objet: réunion préparatoire des gouvernements africains pour l'Organisation régional de l'Afrique," 3. Also see "Réunion préparatoire des gouvernements africains," 11 June 1951, 10 h 00, 19.

29. WHOL, Regional Committee for Africa, first session, provisional minutes of the third meeting, 25 September 1951, 6–9.

30. IMTSSA 222, "Rapport du Médecin-Colonel Garcin, chef de la section technique à la Direction du service de santé du Ministère de la France d'Outre-Mer, représentant de la France à la 1ère session du Comité régional africain de l'OMS, à Monsieur le Ministre des Affaires Etrangères (Secrétariat des conférences)," Geneva, September 1951, 10.

31. Regional Committee for Africa, first session, provisional minutes of the third meeting, 25 September 1951, 9.

32. IMTSSA 238, ONU, OMS, Comité régional de l'Afrique, RC1 / AFR / Min / 3, première session, procès-verbal provisoire de la troisième séance, Geneva, 25 September 1951, 9 h 30, 10–12.

33. IMTSSA 238, ONU, OMS, Comité régional pour l'Afrique, RC3 / AFR / 5, troisième session, rapport du directeur du Bureau régional d'Afrique, 13 August 1953, 9.

34. ANS, 1 H 50 (163), "Compte-rendu sur la 2ème session du Comité régional pour l'Afrique de l'Organisation mondiale de la Santé (Monrovia, 31 juillet–7 août 1952)," 6.

35. Ibid., 6.

36. IMTSSA 238, ONU, OMS, Comité régional de l'Afrique, RC2 / AFR / Min / 5 Rev. 1, deuxième session, procès-verbal de la cinquième séance, Monrovia, Liberia, 5 August 1952, 16 h 30, 3.

37. United Nations, General Assembly, *Report of the Special Committee on Information Transmitted under Article 73e of the Charter,* Official Records: Fifth Session, Supplement 17 (A / 1303) (New York, 1950), 4.

38. "Compte-rendu sur la 2ème session," 6–7. Also see Comité régional de l'Afrique, deuxième session, procès-verbal de la cinquième séance, 5 August 1952, 16 h 30, 4–5; and IMTSSA 238, ONU, OMS, Comité régional de l'Afrique, RC2 / AFR / Min / 6 Rev. 1, deuxième session, procès-verbal de la sixième séance, Liberia, 6 August 1952, 9 h 30, 7.

39. IMTSSA 238, letter from the minister of overseas France to the director of health services, 6 October 1953, 1. Also see "Compte-rendu sur la 2ème session," 4.

40. "La politique régionaliste," 1949, 5. On Chisholm's career, see John Farley, *Brock Chisholm, the World Health Organization, and the Cold War* (Vancouver: University of British Columbia Press, 2008).

41. "Compte-rendu sur la 2ème session," 4.

42. Ibid., 6–7. Also see Comité régional de l'Afrique, deuxième session, procès-verbal de la cinquième séance, 5 August 1952, 4–5; and Comité régional de l'Afrique, deuxième session, procès-verbal de la sixième séance, 6 August 1952, 9 h 30, 7.

43. "Rapport du Médecin-Colonel Garcin," 13 August 1952, 5–8. Also see Comité régional de l'Afrique, deuxième session, procès-verbal de la cinquième séance, 5 August 1952, 5.

44. IMTSSA 222, "Note pour servir éventuellement au membre français du Conseil éxécutif de l'OMS," 5 January 1953, 2.

45. The French delegation warned of future trouble in the case that Liberia were to join the CCTA, despite the benefit its participation would have for "the equilibrium [of the committee] . . . and a more equitable participation of the African territories." In "Compte-rendu sur la 2ème session," 9.

46. Ibid., 10. The French noted on more than one occasion the silence of their colleagues in many of the important debates. "Without exaggeration, it is possible to affirm that the French delegation was always at the head of the discussion and the majority of the decisions undertaken have been through French initiative, and that the French propositions have always been followed by the majority, if not the entirety, of the committee." From "Rapport du Médecin-Colonel Garcin, objet: 2ème session du Comité régional africain," 13 August 1952, 11.

47. "Rapport du Médecin-Colonel Garcin, objet: 2ème session du Comité régional africain," 13 August 1952, 13.

48. Ibid., 10.

49. "Compte-rendu sur la 2ème session," 14.

50. World Health Organization, "General François Daubenton (Obituary)," *Chronicle of the World Health Organization* 19, no. 10 (1965): 419.

51. ADLC, NUOI 330, United Nations Office, Geneva, Centre d'Information, Communiqué de Presse OMS / 103, "Organisation mondiale de la Santé: Création d'un bureau de l'OMS pour l'Afrique," 24 October 1950.

52. "Rapport du Médecin-Colonel Garcin, objet: réunion préparatoire des gouvernements africains pour l'Organisation régional de l'Afrique," 6.

53. WHOL, Comité régional de l'Afrique, première session, procès-verbal provisoire de la troisième séance, 25 September 1951, 9 h 30, 4. Also see "Compte-rendu sur la 2ème session," 8.

54. ANS, 1 H 52 (163), "Note sur la réunion du comité spécial du Comité régional pour l'Afrique de l'Organisation mondiale de la Santé (Brazzaville, 15 à 19 décembre 1953)," 1. Daubenton was far from the first European physician to complain about the unsuitability of Brazzaville's housing stock. Concerns about Brazzaville's suitability as a site for scientific and medical research date back to the interwar period and the founding of the Pasteur Institute there. See Neill, *Networks in Tropical Medicine,* 94–95.

55. Comité régional pour l'Afrique, troisième session, "Rapport du Directeur du Bureau régional d'Afrique," 13 August 1953, 6–13.

56. IMTSSA 238, report and letter from Médecin-Colonel Garcin to the minister of foreign affairs, 24 October 1953, 5–6.

57. "Note sur la réunion," December 1953, 6–7.

58. Report and letter from Garcin to the ministry of foreign affairs, 24 October 1953, 5.

59. "Note sur la réunion," December 1953, 6–7.

60. IMTSSA 238, letter from the Ministry of Foreign Affairs to the Ministry of Overseas France, 30 October 1952, 1.

61. "Note sur la 3ème session," 6 October 1953, 10.

62. "Note sur la réunion," December 1953, 2.

63. Ibid., 3.

64. Ibid., 12.

65. IMTSSA 222, "Rapport du Médecin-Colonel Garcin, chef de la section technique à la Direction du service de santé du Ministère de la France d'Outre-Mer, chef de la délégation Française à la 2ème Session du Comité africain de l'OMS, à Monsieur le Ministre des Affaires Etrangères (Secrétariat des conférences), objet: 2ème session du Comité régional africain," 13 August 1952, 5. Also see IMTSSA 238, OMS, Comité Régional de l'Afrique, deuxième session, procès-verbal de la deuxième séance, Monrovia, Liberia, 4 August 1952, 9 h 00, 21–22. On the Africanization of the office and of the medical profession in general, see IMTSSA 238, OMS, Comité régional de l'Afrique, RC3 / AFR / Min / 1 Rev. 1, procès-verbal de la première séance, Kampala, Uganda, 21 September 1953, 10 h 30, 7.

66. "Note sur la réunion," December 1953, 4–5.

67. Ibid., 1.

68. "Rapport du Médecin Colonel Garcin, Objet: 3ème session du Comité régional de l'OMS pour l'Afrique," 24 October 1953, 7.

69. "Note sur la 3ème session," 6 October 1953, 9.

70. "Note sur la réunion," December 1953, 7.

71. "Rapport du Médecin Colonel Garcin, objet: 3ème session du Comité régional de l'OMS pour l'Afrique," 24 October 1953, 14–15.

72. Ibid., 15.

73. Ibid., 15–16.

74. Ibid., 16–17.

75. The WHO Regional Office for Africa was temporarily moved from Brazzaville to Harare, Zimbabwe, following the outbreak of civil war in the Congo in 1997. The office was then reinstalled in Brazzaville in 2001. See "29th Regional Programme Meeting Opens in Brazzaville," World Health Organization, Regional Office for Africa, accessed February 6, 2018, http://www.afro.who.int/news/29th-regional-programme-meeting-opens-brazzaville.

76. On the work of the ad hoc committee during 1953–1954, see ANS, 1 H 52 (163), "Note sur la 4ème session du Comité régional de l'Afrique de l'Organisation mondiale de la Santé," n.d., 3. The committee's work was accomplished without any difficulty, and it was able to successfully devise a plan to address the problems raised at the 1953 regional meeting, including a visit to the Cité du Djoué to work out the details of the housing arrangements.

5. Family Health, France, and the Future of Africa

Epigraph: "Address Delivered by Dr. W. Bonne, Representing the World Health Organization," in International Children's Centre, *Statutes of the International Children's Centre, and Addresses Delivered at the Ceremony of Inauguration 18 January 1950 in the Salon de l'Horloge, Ministry of Foreign Affairs* (Paris: International Children's Centre, 1950), 21–22.

1. Centre international de l'enfance, *Les problèmes de l'enfance dans les pays tropicaux de l'Afrique: Colloque organisé par le Centre international de l'enfance, Brazzaville, 8–13 décembre 1952* (Paris: Centre international de l'enfance, Impr. de Villain et Bar, 1953).

2. On the history of medical research and education and public health in France, as well as postwar reform of medical education, see Thomas Neville Bonner, *Becoming a Physician: Medical Education in Britain, France, Germany, and the United States, 1750–1945* (New York: Oxford University Press, 1995); Matthew Ramsey, "Public Health in France," in *The History of Public Health and the Modern State*, ed. Dorothy Porter (Amsterdam: Editions Rodopi, 1994), 45–118; and George Weisz, *The Medical Mandarins: The French Academy of Medicine*

in the Nineteenth and Early Twentieth Centuries (New York: Oxford University Press, 1995).

3. See Robert Debré, *L'honneur de vivre: Témoignage* (Paris: Stock / Hermann, 1974) and *Ce que je crois* (Paris: Grasset, 1976). Also see Robert Debré, *Hommage au professeur Robert Debré: 1882–1978* (Paris: B. Grasset, 1980); and Jessica Pearson-Patel, "Promoting Health, Protecting Empire: Inter-colonial Medical Cooperation in Postwar Africa" in *Monde(s): Histoire, espaces, relations* 7 (May 2015): 213–230. Robert Debré was also the father of Michel Debré, who served as Prime Minister under Charles de Gaulle from 1959 to 1962.

4. See, for example, Charles de Gaulle's descriptions of France throughout his *Mémoires de Guerre* (Paris: Librarie Plon, 1999).

5. See George Rosen, "Approaches to a Concept of Social Medicine: A Historical Survey," *Milbank Memorial Fund Quarterly* 26, no. 1 (January 1948): 7–21. Also see Dorothy Porter and Roy Porter's classic overview of the history of social medicine, "What Was Social Medicine? An Historiographical Essay," *Journal of Historical Sociology* 1, no. 1 (March 1988): 90–106; and Dorothy Porter, "How Did Social Medicine Evolve and Where Is It Heading?," *PLoS Med* 3, no. 10 (October 2006) : e399. On the distinction between social medicine and biomedicine, see "Introducing *Social Medicine,*" *Social Medicine* 1, no. 1 (February 2006): 1–4.

6. On the history of social pediatrics, see Cheryl Krasnick Warsh and Veronica Jane Strong-Boag, eds., *Children's Health Issues in Historical Perspective* (Waterloo, ON: Wilfrid Laurier University Press, 2005). On child health in metropolitan France, see Jean-Paul Martineaud, *De Vincent de Paul à Robert Debré: Des enfants abandonnés et des enfants malades à Paris* (Paris: L'Harmattan, 2006).

7. For an exploration of the idea of "saving the children" in different geographic contexts, see Pearl S. Buck, "Save the Children for What?," *Journal of Educational Sociology* 17, no. 4 (December 1943): 195–199; and Linda Mahood and Vic Satzewich, "The Save the Children Fund and the Russian Famine of 1921–1923: Claims and Counter-claims about Feeding 'Bolshevik' Children," *Journal of Historical Sociology* 22, no. 1 (March 2009): 55–83. Also see Michael Barnett, *Empire of Humanity: A History of Humanitarianism* (Ithaca, NY: Cornell University Press, 2013), 2.

8. On earlier international efforts in favor of childhood, see Joëlle Droux, "L'internationalisation de la protection de l'enfance: Acteurs, concurrences et projets transnationaux (1900–1925)," *Critique internationale* 52 (July–September 2011): 17–33. On the role of children and the family in the French empire, see Julia Ann Clancy-Smith and Frances Gouda, *Domesticating the Empire: Race, Gender, and Family Life in French and Dutch Colonialism* (Charlottesville: University Press of Virginia, 1998); Ivan Jablonka, *Enfants en exil: Transfert de pupilles réunionnais en métropole, 1963–1982* (Paris: Seuil, 2007); and Owen White, *Children of the French Empire: Miscegenation and Colonial Society in French West Africa, 1895–1960* (New York: Oxford University Press, 1999).

9. Nancy Rose Hunt, *A Colonial Lexicon of Birth Ritual, Medicalization, and Mobility in the Congo* (Durham, NC: Duke University Press, 1999), 3–4. Also see Soyer, "Congo belge: Bien-être familial et équipement sociale," *Familles dans le monde* 11, no. 4 (1958): 299–309; and A. Tricot-Guisen, "Comment faut-il envisager au Congo belge le problème des jardins d'enfants pour les petits noirs?," *Bulletin trimestriel du Centre d'étude des problèmes sociaux indigènes* 34 (1954): 7–35. Another important competitor in the field of African social medicine was South Africa. See Shula Marks, "Doctors and the State: George Gale and South Africa's Experiment in Social Medicine," in *Science and Society in Southern Africa,* ed. Saul Dubow (Manchester: Manchester University Press, 2000), 188–211.

10. L. Harrison Mettler, "Medical Paris—Notes from My Sketchbook," *Journal of the American Medical Association* 27, no. 9 (1896): 487–490.

11. William Osler, "Impressions of Paris," *Journal of the American Medical Association* 52, no. 9 (1909): 701.

12. Debré, *L'honneur de vivre,* 171.

13. See Bonner, *Becoming a Physician,* 241.

14. Ibid., 255.

15. See Abraham Flexner, *Medical Education in the United States and Canada: A Report to the Carnegie Foundation for the Advancement of Teaching* (New York: Carnegie Foundation for the Advancement of Teaching, 1910) and *Medical Education in Europe: A Report to the Carnegie Foundation for the Advancement of Teaching* (New York: Carnegie Foundation for the Advancement of Teaching, 1912).

16. William H. Schneider, "The Men Who Followed Flexner," in *Rockefeller Philanthropy and Modern Biomedicine: International Initiatives from World War I to the Cold War,* ed. William H. Schneider (Bloomington: Indiana University Press, 2002), 9.

17. Jean-François Picard and William Schneider, "From the Art of Medicine to Biomedical Science in France: Modernization or Americanization?," in Schneider, *Rockefeller Philanthropy,* 109.

18. Flexner, *Medical Education in Europe,* 15.

19. See Henry S. Pritchett, introduction to *Medical Education in Europe,* by Flexner, xx.

20. Debré, *L'Honneur de vivre,* 138, 169.

21. Ibid., 187.

22. Ibid., 188.

23. Ibid., 318.

24. Etienne Berthet, "Activities of the International Children's Centre," *American Journal of Public Health* 48, no. 4 (April 1958): 458–467.

25. In the first six years of its existence, UNICEF covered 60 percent of the CIE's budget, with the remainder made up of contributions from the French government. In addition to the base funding from UNICEF, the WHO also provided aid to the CIE in the form of grants for doctors and auxiliary medical personnel (both

toward participation in CIE courses and toward participation in specialized health teams). For an explanation of the types of scholarships offered by both the CIE and the WHO, see 1 Archives du Centre international de l'enfance (hereafter CIDEF) 11, "Rapport au Conseil d'administration sur l'activité du Centre international de l'enfance pendant l'année 1951," 12–13. All participants in CIE courses were recipients of either a CIE grant or a WHO grant. The WHO also provided experts to help in CIE research and teaching initiatives. Funding from UNICEF and the WHO was subject to the condition that a technical consultative committee be created that would include representatives from the UN and its various specialized agencies (UNESCO, UNICEF, the International Labour Organization, and FAO) in addition to members of the CIE. The committee would be responsible for formulating general directives and for giving advice on the execution of the CIE's various programs. The UN also required that the CIE submit an annual report of its activities to the Secretary-General to be transmitted in turn to UNICEF, the WHO, and the Economic and Social Council of the UN. See ADLC, NUOI 441, "Recommandation du comité spécial sur le Centre international de l'enfance de Paris adoptée par le Conseil éxécutif," 4 November 1949, 1–5.

26. Debré, *L'honneur de vivre,* 329.

27. Ibid., 335.

28. ADLC, NUOI 441, letter from the minister of foreign affairs to Robert Debré, 9 November 1949.

29. ADLC, NUOI 441, Robert Debré, untitled memo, 15 July 1949, 1. Also see ADLC, NUOI 441, telegram from the French embassy in London to the Ministry of Foreign Affairs, 1 November 1949.

30. On the bureaucratic obstacles to the CIE's creation, see International Children's Centre, *International Children's Centre: Structure and Activities, Extracts from the Report Presented by Dr. Etienne Berthet at the Meeting of the ICC Executive Board (Paris, May 30–31, 1960)* (Paris: Château de Longchamp, 1960), 3–5; and International Children's Centre, *Activities of the International Children's Centre and Plan of Work for the Years 1962–1966: Report Presented by Dr. Etienne Berthet, Director General of the International Children's Centre, at the Meeting of the Executive Board of the United Nationals Children's Fund, June 1961* (Paris: Centre international de l'enfance, 1961), 2–3. Also see "Recommandation du comité spécial," 4 November 1949, 1.

31. International Children's Centre, *Statutes,* 45. For background on the history of puericulture in France, see Adolphe Pinard, *La puériculture du premier âge* (Paris: A. Colin, 1919); Jules Rouvier, *Hygiène de la première enfance* (Paris: Doin, 1889); Gaston Variot, *Comment sauvegarder les bébés: Enseignement de l'hygiène infantile donné à l'Institut de puériculture et à la Goutte de lait de Belleville* (Paris: Gaston Doin, 1922); and Gaston Variot, *La puériculture pratique; ou, l'art d'élever les enfants du premier âge* (Paris: Doin, 1930).

32. "Address Delivered by Madame Georges-Picot, Vice-President of the Municipal Council of Paris," in International Children's Centre, *Statutes,* 25.

33. "Address Delivered by Mr. P. Schneiter," in International Children's Centre, *Statutes,* 11.

34. International Children's Centre, introduction to *Statutes.*

35. "Address Delivered by Mr. P. Schneiter," 9.

36. There is an extensive literature on the role of prestige in France's postwar diplomatic relations. See William I. Hitchcock, *France Restored: Cold War Diplomacy and the Quest for Leadership in Europe, 1944–1954* (Chapel Hill: University of North Carolina Press, 1998); and Alessandro Brogi, *A Question of Self-Esteem: The United States and the Cold War Choices in France and Italy, 1944–1958* (Westport, CT: Praeger, 2002). While scholars have historically understood prestige to be a by-product of power, Brogi reverses this relationship, stating that prestige can actually produce, or at least serve as a stand-in for, actual coercive power. Although historians such as Hitchcock and Brogi have discussed the rehabilitation of France in terms of high political issues such as economic recovery and military security, I argue that these concepts and frameworks can also be applied to medicine and international health cooperation. Political theorist Hans Morgenthau has argued that prestige is "particularly important as a political weapon in an age in which the struggle for power is fought not only with the traditional methods of political pressure and military force, but in large measure as the struggle for the minds of men." Quoted in Brogi, *Question of Self-Esteem,* 4. This was a particularly important perspective for the French government in the wake of the war, when France's empire was threatened from both within and without.

37. "Address Delivered by Mr. P. Schneiter," 11.

38. "Address Delivered by Professor A. Wallgren, Member of the Executive Board of the International Children's Centre," in International Children's Centre, *Statutes,* 27–28.

39. "Rapport au Conseil d'administration (1951)," 1.

40. In 1951, 163 participants came from thirty-eight countries and territories, including AEF, Algeria, Germany, AOF, Argentina, Austria, Belgium, Bolivia, Brazil, Canada, Chile, Denmark, Egypt, Spain, Finland, France, Great Britain, Greece, Haiti, Iran, Ireland, Israel, Italy, Lebanon, Luxembourg, Madagascar, Morocco, Mexico, Norway, the Netherlands, Portugal, Sweden, Switzerland, Syria, Tunisia, Turkey, and Yugoslavia. Sessions were offered by professors from Belgium, Denmark, the United States, France, Great Britain, Italy, Norway, and Switzerland. UNICEF sponsored the first social pediatrics course in Paris in 1948, with a second course offered in 1949. The program was taken over by the CIE in 1950 once the center opened. See "Rapport au Conseil d'administration (1951)," 10.

41. 1 CIDEF 11, Centre international de l'enfance, "Rapport sur les activités des services au cours de l'année 1952," Paris, December 1952, 17–20.

42. In 1952, the on-site visits that were offered as part of the social pediatrics course included the Clinique obstétricale Baudelocque, Ecole de puériculture de la Faculté de médecine de Paris, Centre de prématurés de l'école de puériculture, Centre de protection maternelle et infantile de Nanterre, Centre national de transfusion sanguine, les laboratoires de la tuberculose de l'Institut Pasteur de Paris, and l'Institut national d'études démographiques. See ibid.

43. "Rapport au Conseil d'administration (1951)," 12.

44. The timing was also connected to a CCTA conference on nutrition in Fajara, the capital of the Gambia. Since many of the meetings' participants were traveling from Europe rather than from Africa—and were attending both meetings—holding the conference in December allowed them to avoid making two separate long-haul voyages. See Commission pour la coopération technique en Afrique au sud du Sahara, *Malnutrition chez la mère, le nourrisson et le jeune enfant en Afrique: Le rapport de la deuxième Conférence inter-africaine sur la nutrition, Fajara, Gambie, 19–27 novembre 1952* (London: HMSO, 1956). The conference was an effort to follow up on a previous meeting that took place in Dschang, Cameroon. See Inter-African Conference on Nutrition, *Conférence interafricaine sur l'alimentation et la nutrition, Dschang, Cameroun, 3–9 octobre 1949* (Paris: Documentation française, 1949).

45. Centre international de l'enfance, *Les problèmes de l'enfance,* 1.

46. On the 1931 conference, see Evelyn Sharp, *The African Child: An Account of the International Conference on African Children, Geneva* (Westport, CT: Negro Universities Press, 1970).

47. Centre international de l'enfance, *Les problèmes de l'enfance,* iii–iv.

48. While Liberian physicians such as Dr. Joseph Togba served as a counterbalance to the European delegations to the WHO Regional Committee for Africa, Liberia was not represented at the 1952 child health conference.

49. "Allocution de M. J. Cédile," in Centre international de l'enfance, *Les problèmes de l'enfance,* 1.

50. Ibid., 1.

51. For a broader look at Sicé's perspectives on AEF during the war, see Adolphe Sicé, *L'Afrique équatoriale au service de la France* (Paris: Presse Universitaire, 1946).

52. "Allocution de M. J. Cédile," 2.

53. Ibid., 3.

54. Ibid., 1–2.

55. "Allocution de Mme Eboué," in Centre international de l'enfance, *Les problèmes de l'enfance,* 5.

56. Ibid., 5.

57. Ibid., 6. On the idea of the "évolué" in French colonial history, see Catherine Coquéry-Vidrovitch, "Nationalité et citoyenneté en Afrique Occidentale Française: Originaires et citoyens dans le Sénégal colonial," *Journal of African*

History 42, no. 2 (2001): 285–305; James E. Genova, *Colonial Ambivalence, Cultural Authenticity, and the Limitations of Mimicry in French-Ruled West Africa, 1914–1956* (New York: Peter Lang, 2004); and Gary Wilder, *The French Imperial Nation-State: Negritude and Colonial Humanism between the Two World Wars* (Chicago: University of Chicago Press, 2005).

58. "Allocution de Mme Eboué," 6. For a broader exploration of the crisis of health in Brazzaville, see Marcel Soret, *Démographie et problèmes urbains en A. E. F.: Poto-Poto, Bacongo, Dolisie* (Montpellier: Imprimerie Charité, 1954), 125–127.

59. "Allocution de M. J. Cédile," 3.

60. 1 CIDEF 233, Centre international de l'enfance, "Cours sur la pathologie tropicale de l'enfant et ses incidences sociales," 19 September to 30 October 1955. See IMTSSA 291 for the transcripts of the various sessions offered in the 1955 course on tropical pathology.

61. Dr. Jean Sénécal, professor of infant medicine at the Faculté de médecine de Dakar, was one of the most notable presenters, speaking on "problems of adaptation in the somatic and physiological development of the child." For more on Sénécal's work in child health in AOF, see Jean Sénécal, "La protection maternelle et infantile en Afrique Occidentale Française," *Bulletin de l'Académie nationale de médecine* 141, no. 34 (December 1957): 780–785.

62. 1 CIDEF 233, Centre international de l'enfance, "Cours de pédiatrie sociale," Dakar, 5 November to 15 December 1956, 2.

63. Ibid., 10. On Cambournac's involvement with the fight against malaria in sub-Saharan Africa, see WHOL, WHO/Mal/58, Afr/Mal/Conf/14.26, F. J. C. Cambournac and the World Health Organization, "Report on Malaria in Tropical Africa," October 1950.

64. "Cours de pédiatrie sociale (1956)," 10. Also see G. Dulphy, "Le problème d'enfance outre-mer," *Chronique d'outre-mer* 4 (April 1954): 3–16.

65. Centre international de l'enfance, *Etude des conditions de vie de l'enfant africain en milieu urbain et de leur influence sur la délinquance juvénile: Enquête entreprise à Madagascar, au Cameroun et en Côte d'Ivoire de 1954 à 1957 par le Centre international de l'enfance, avec l'aide des services sociaux de la France d'outre-mer* (Paris: Centre international de l'enfance, 1959).

66. See Martin Shipway, "Madagascar on the Eve of Insurrection, 1944–1947," in *The Decolonization Reader,* ed. James Le Sueur (New York: Routledge, 2003), 82–83; and Meredith Terretta, *Nation of Outlaws, State of Violence: Nationalism, Grassroots Tradition, and State-Building in Cameroon* (Athens: Ohio University Press, 2010).

67. United Nations, General Assembly, *Report of the Committee on Information from Non-self-governing Territories,* Official Records: Seventh Session, Supplement 18 (A/2219) (New York, 1952), 16. Also see ANOM, 2 G 41 (10), Côte d'Ivoire,

1941 health services report, Abidjan, 30 May 1942, 56; ANOM, 2 G 43 (9), Côte d'Ivoire, 1943 health services report, Abidjan, 30 July 1944, 76; ANOM, 2 G 45 (12), Côte d'Ivoire, 1945 health services report, Abidjan, 22 September 1946, 172; and ANOM, 2 G 50 (20), Côte d'Ivoire, 1950 health services report, Abidjan, December 1951, 156. Also see Pierre Aubin, "A propos des prestations familiales dans les territoires français d'Afrique noire," *Population* 9, no. 1 (1954): 51–60; Bros, "Organisation des services sociaux d'outre-mer," *Les cahiers du Musée sociale* 3 (1955): 78–83; and "Les centres sociaux en Côte d'Ivoire," *Informations sociales* 11, no. 8 (1957): 921–925.

68. Côte d'Ivoire, 1941 health services report, 56; Côte d'Ivoire, 1943 health services report, 76; Côte d'Ivoire, 1945 health services report, 172.

69. ANOM, 2 G 49 (11), Senegal, 1949 health services report, Saint Louis, 15 September 1950, 114. Also see ANOM, 2 G 49 (16), Upper Volta, 1949 health services report, Ouagadougou, 1 December 1950; and ANOM, 2 G 50 (21), Upper Volta, 1950 health services report, Ouagadougou, 23 November 1951, 198.

70. Jeanne Maddox Toungara, "Inventing the African Family: Gender and Family Law Reform in Cote d'Ivoire," *Journal of Social History* 28, no. 1 (Autumn 1994): 37–61.

71. Côte d'Ivoire, 1950 health services report, 156.

72. ANOM, 2 G 52 (3), "Rapport bisannuel sur la protection de la collectivité, de la famille et de l'enfance," 1951–1952, 1–2. Also see Simone Crapuchet, *Politique sociale d'outre-mer: Un devoir de mémoire à l'égard des pionnières* (Ramonville Saint-Agne, France: Erès, 1999).

73. "Rapport bisannuel sur la protection," 1951–1952, 1–2.

74. United Nations, General Assembly, *Report of the Committee* (1952), 15.

75. Ibid., 23; United Nations, General Assembly, *Report of the Committee on Information from Non-self-governing Territories,* Official Records: Eighth Session, Supplement 15 (A / 2465) (New York, 1953), 9.

76. Centre international de l'enfance, foreword to *Etude des conditions.*

77. Centre international de l'enfance, *Etude des conditions,* 15.

78. Ibid., 94.

79. See Sarah Fishman, *The Battle for Children: World War II, Youth Crime, and Juvenile Justice in Twentieth-Century France* (Cambridge, MA: Harvard University Press, 2002).

80. Centre international de l'enfance, *Etude des conditions,* 144.

81. "Rapport bisannuel sur la protection, 1951–1952," 142.

6. Fighting Illness, Battling Decolonization

Epigraph: World Health Organization, *Report on the Malaria Conference in Equatorial Africa Held under the Joint Auspices of the World Health Organization and the Commission for Technical Co-operation in Africa South of the Sahara, Kampala, Uganda, 27 November to 9 December 1950,* Technical Report Series 38 (Geneva: World Health Organization, 1951), 56–57. For an exploration of the theme of "underdevelopment" in AOF in an earlier context, see Catherine Coquéry-Vidrovitch, "L'Afrique coloniale française et la crise de 1930: Crise structurelle et genèse du sous-développement," *Revue française d'histoire d'outre-mer* 63, nos. 3–4 (1976): 386–424. Also see Frederick Cooper and Randall Packard, eds., *International Development and the Social Sciences: Essays on the History and Politics of Knowledge* (Berkeley: University of California Press, 1997). On the broader history of public health and the battle against epidemic diseases in Europe and in France, see Peter Baldwin, *Contagion and the State in Europe, 1830–1930* (Cambridge: Cambridge University Press, 1999); David S. Barnes, *The Making of a Social Disease: Tuberculosis in Nineteenth-Century France* (Berkeley: University of California Press, 1995); William Coleman, *Death Is a Social Disease: Public Health and Political Economy in Early Industrial France* (Madison: University of Wisconsin Press, 1982); Ann La Berge, *Mission and Method: The Early Nineteenth-Century French Public Health Movement* (Cambridge: Cambridge University Press, 1992); Lion Murard and Patrick Zylberman, *L'hygiène dans la république: La santé publique en France ou l'utopie contrariée* (Paris: Fayard, 1996); Robert Fox and George Weisz, eds., *The Organization of Science and Technology in France, 1808–1914* (New York: Cambridge University Press, 1980); and Matthew Ramsey, *Professional and Popular Medicine in France, 1770–1830: The Social World of Medical Practice* (New York: Cambridge University Press, 1988).

1. World Health Organization, *Report on the Malaria Conference,* 57.

2. On the cost of materials for DDT house-spraying campaigns, for example, see IMTSSA 234, DGSP, "Commandes de produits insecticides et chimioprophylactiques de matériel," 15 November 1951.

3. On colonial expertise and scientific knowledge in the French and British empires, see Raoul Combes, *La recherche scientifique dans les territoires d'outre-mer* (Paris: Université de Paris, 1948); Jean-Paul Moreau, *Un pasteurien sous les tropiques: 1963–2000* (Paris: L'Harmattan, 2006); Anne-Marie Moulin, "The Pasteur Institutes between the Two World Wars: The Transformation of the International Sanitary Order," in *International Health Organisations and Movements, 1918–1939,* ed. Paul Weindling (Cambridge: Cambridge University Press, 1995), 244–265; Emmanuelle Sibeud, *Une science impériale pour l'Afrique? La construction des savoirs africanistes en France, 1878–1930* (Paris: Ecole des hautes études en sciences sociales, 2002); and Helen Tilley, *Africa as a Living Laboratory: Empire, Development,*

and the Problem of Scientific Knowledge, 1870–1950 (Chicago: University of Chicago Press, 2011).

4. Randall Packard, "Malaria Dreams: Postwar Visions of Health and Development in the Third World," *Medical Anthropology: Cross-cultural Studies in Health and Illness* 17, no. 3 (1997): 279–296.

5. See, for example, ANOM, 2 G 46 (29), Togo, 1946 health services report, 36–43. Also see Pascale Barthélemy, *Africaines et diplômées à l'époque coloniale, 1918–1957* (Rennes: Presses universitaires de Rennes, 2010).

6. IMTSSA 232, "Rapport sur le problème du paludisme à Dakar," 1. Also see IMTSSA 232, Gouvernement Général de l'AEF, DGSP, "Etude sur le paludisme humain en Afrique Equatoriale Française," 1955.

7. On the unreliability of colonial statistics, see United Nations, General Assembly, *Report of the Committee on Information from Non-self-governing Territories*, Official Records: Tenth Session, Supplement 16 (A/2908) (New York, 1955), 85.

8. ANS, 1 H 50, Nations Unies, Conseil économique et social, Fonds des Nations Unies pour l'enfance, Conseil d'administration, "Rapport du directeur général sur l'état des travaux: Exécution des programmes en Afrique," E/ICEF/300/Add.2, 26 July 1955, 4.

9. For an extremely thorough study of the etiology of African malaria, see James L. A. Webb Jr., "An Introduction to African Malaria," chap. 1 in *The Long Struggle against Malaria in Tropical Africa* (New York: Cambridge University Press, 2014).

10. On the battle against sleeping sickness in France's African colonies, see Deborah J. Neill, *Networks in Tropical Medicine: Internationalism, Colonialism, and the Rise of a Medical Specialty, 1890–1930* (Stanford, CA: Stanford University Press, 2012); Jean-Paul Bado, *Les conquêtes de la médecine moderne en Afrique*, Collection tropiques (Paris: Editions Karthala, 2006); Jean-Paul Bado, *Eugène Jamot, 1879–1937: Le médecin de la maladie du sommeil ou trypanosomiase* (Paris: Editions Karthala, 2011); and Jean-Paul Bado, *Médecine coloniale et grandes endémies en Afrique 1900–1960: Lèpre, trypanosomiase humaine et onchocercose* (Paris: Editions Karthala, 1996).

11. On the history of the MEP, see Amy L. S. Staples, "Exercising International Authority: The Malaria Eradication Program," chap. 10 in *The Birth of Development: How the World Bank, Food and Agriculture Organization, and World Health Organization Changed the World, 1945–1965* (Kent, OH: Kent State University Press, 2007). Also see Nancy Leys Stepan, *Eradication: Ridding the World of Diseases Forever?* (Ithaca, NY: Cornell University Press, 2011).

12. United Nations, *Special Study on Social Conditions in Non-self-governing Territories, Analyses of Information Transmitted to the Secretary-General during 1957–1958* (New York: United Nations, 1958), 189.

13. Local governments, some alone and some in conjunction with early WHO technical assistance, sponsored the initial malaria-control programs. Early anti-

malaria efforts in AOF and AEF were led by French colonial health services that had been reorganized as a result of the political restructuring of the French empire in 1944 and 1945. See, for example, ANOM, 2 G 45 (4), Dakar, 1945 health services report, 215.

14. Staples, *Birth of Development,* 162–163. Also see Webb, *Long Struggle against Malaria,* 69–73.

15. United Nations, *Special Study on Social Conditions* (1957–1958), 175.

16. Packard, "Malaria Dreams."

17. WHOL, United Nations, World Health Organization Interim Commission, Fifth Session, "Malaria Programme," WHO.IC/159 and WHO.IC/Mal/12, 26 January 1948, 1. Emphasis in original.

18. E. J. Pampana and P. F. Russel, "Malaria: A World Problem," *Chronicle of the World Health Organization* 9 (1955): 35.

19. World Health Organization, *Sixth Report of the WHO Expert Committee on Malaria,* Technical Report Series 123 (Geneva: World Health Organization, 1957), cited in United Nations, *Special Study on Social Conditions* (1957–1958), 175.

20. United Nations, *Special Study on Social Conditions in Non-self-governing Territories, Summaries and Analyses of Information Transmitted to the Secretary-General during 1955* (New York: United Nations, 1956), 85.

21. See, for example, United Nations, *Special Study on Social Conditions* (1957–1958); and United Nations, *Special Study on Social Conditions* (1955), 91. According to the 1955 report, "Malaria, among the diseases prevalent in Non-Self-Governing Territories, is still the outstanding contributor to the mortality rate. The effect on productivity and general health is at least as important. In many parts of the world the amount of crop harvested is determined by the amount of land that can be ploughed and sown during a brief period when soil and climatic conditions are right. Disease, during this period, whether it produces actual invalidism or only debility, will affect the final crop to a major extent."

22. World Health Organization, *Report on the Malaria Conference.* On the Kampala malaria conference, also see Webb, *Long Struggle against Malaria,* 73–77.

23. IMTSSA 232, "La lutte contre le paludisme en AEF: Bilan de l'endémie," 5–6. For a detailed description of house-spraying procedures in French Africa, see IMTSSA 232, "Instructions aux chefs d'équipe de lutte contre les insectes adultes."

24. IMTSSA 234, Gouvernement Général de l'AEF, DGSP, "Instruction générale sur l'organisation d'une lutte contre et le paludisme et sur l'application qui peut être faite actuellement en Afrique Equatoriale Française," Brazzaville, 10 November 1950, 1–2.

25. IMTSSA 222, "Note au sujet de la région africaine du Comité régional africain et Bureau régional africain de l'OMS, n.d., 2.

26. Ibid.

27. IMTSSA 238, letter from the Ministry of Foreign Affairs to the Ministry of Overseas France (attention: Mademoiselle Guelfi, inspector general of labor and workforce), Paris, 21 November 1950.

28. IMTSSA 238, Ministry of Public Health and Population (social hygiene division), "Note au sujet du programme d'aide aux territoires africains," Paris, 13 February 1952.

29. Ibid.

30. IMTSSA 222, "Rapport du Médecin-Colonel Garcin," 19 September 1951, appendix 2, 2.

31. "Note au sujet du programme d'aide," 13 February 1952.

32. See ANS, 1 H 50, UNICEF, "L'UNICEF ouvre un crédit de 500 millions à l'AOF," 2 November 1956, 3.

33. The 1956 UNICEF investment in AOF, for example, required a complementary investment from the French government of almost one billion francs. See ibid.

34. "Rapport du Médecin-Colonel Garcin," 19 September 1951, appendix 2, 1. Also see IMTSSA 238, letter from the Ministry of Public Health and Population to the Ministry of Overseas France (health services division), Paris, 18 October 1951.

35. IMTSSA 238, ONU, OMS, Comité régional de l'Afrique, RC1 / AFR / Min / 4, première session, procès-verbal provisoire de la quatrième séance, Geneva, 25 September 1951, 14 h 30, 13–14.

36. "Rapport du Médecin-Colonel Garcin," 19 September 1951, appendix 2, 2.

37. IMTSSA 238, letter from the minister of foreign affairs to Médecin-Colonel Garcin (head of the technical division of health services for the Ministry of Overseas France), Paris, 19 September 1951, 6. On the house-spraying and supplementary nutrition programs, also see "Rapport du Médecin-Colonel Garcin," 19 September 1951, 11–12.

38. IMTSSA 238, OMS, Organisation régionale de l'Afrique, AFR / Min / 1, "Réunion préparatoire des gouvernements africains, procès-verbal provisoire de la réunion tenue au Palais des Nations," Geneva, 11 June 1951, 10 h 00, 20.

39. On the financial constraints on expanding malaria control and malaria eradication programs, see "Instruction générale sur l'organisation, 10 November 1950, 2; and IMTSSA 234, Haut-Commissaire de la République en Afrique Equatoriale Française à Monsieur le Secrétaire d'Etat à la France d'Outre-Mer," 4 July 1952, 3.

40. IMTSSA 232, "La lutte contre le paludisme dans nos colonies," n.d., 1.

41. ANOM, 2 G 54 (8), Médecin-Général Inspecteur Talec, DGSP, letter no. 9462 / DSS.4, Dakar, 16 December 1955, 1, 4, in Haut Commissariat de l'Afrique Occidentale Française, DGSP, "Rapport annuel sur le fonctionnement du service de santé en Afrique Occidentale Française (1954)," administrative and statistical sections, Dakar, 26 July 1955.

42. Fonds des Nations Unies pour l'enfance (UNICEF), "L'UNICEF ouvre un crédit," 1.

43. Webb, *Long Struggle against Malaria,* 91.

44. United Nations, General Assembly, *Report of the Committee on Information from Non-self-governing Territories,* Official Records: Seventh Session, Supplement 18 (A / 2219) (New York, 1952), 20.

45. Food and Agriculture Organization of the United Nations, *Nutrition Conference, Montevideo, 1948* (Montevideo: Comisión de Alimentación, 1950), 228. Also see Food and Agriculture Organization of the United Nations, *Joint FAO / WHO Expert Committee on Nutrition, Report on the Second Session, Rome, 10–17 April 1951* (Rome: Food and Agriculture Organization, 1951), 26.

46. United Nations, General Assembly, *Report of the Special Committee on Information Transmitted under Article 73e of the Charter,* Official Records: Fourth Session, Supplement 14 (A / 923) (New York, 1949), 6. In the 1955 UN Special Study on Social Conditions in Non-self-governing Territories, the final report acknowledged that conditions in independent countries in the developing world would show similar instances of malnutrition but also warned about the necessity of striking a balance between export crops and crops intended for local consumption. See United Nations, *Special Study on Social Conditions* (1955), chap. 10.

47. ANS, 1 H 50, Léon Pales, "Les problèmes de l'alimentation en Afrique noire," Journée mondiale de la santé: "Nourriture et santé," 7 April 1957, 3. On the difference between malnutrition and malnourishment, see ANS, 1 H 50, Dr. Cambournac, AFRO / PR / 100, "L'alimentation en Afrique et la santé des enfants," 7 April 1957, 1.

48. United Nations, *Special Study on Social Conditions* (1955), 127. Also see ANS 1 H 52, R. F. A. Dean (Director of Medical Research Council Group for Research in Infantile Malnutrition, Mulago Hospital, Kampala, Uganda), "De quelques problèmes nutritionnels de l'enfant d'âge préscolaire en Afrique," n.d.

49. ANS 1 H 50, W. R. Aykroyd, "Ce que mangent les gens et les raisons de leur choix," Journée mondiale de la santé: "Nourriture et santé," 7 April 1957, 3–4.

50. ANOM, 2 G 53 (95), AOF, DGSP, ORANA, "Rapport sur l'activité de recherches sur l'alimentation et la nutrition africaine (1953)," Dakar, 15 June 1954, 23.

51. United Nations, General Assembly, *Report of the Special Committee* (1949). In 1950, the delegate from the Philippines went as far as suggesting that the FAO conduct an in-depth study to determine whether colonial economic interests were indeed responsible for the imbalance between cash crops and food crops. See United Nations, General Assembly, *Report of the Special Committee on Information Transmitted under Article 73e of the Charter,* Official Records: Fifth Session, Supplement 17 (A / 1303) (New York, 1950), 6.

52. Food and Agriculture Organization of the United Nations, *Nutrition Conference,* 217–218. Also see Staples, *Birth of Development.*

53. United Nations, *Special Study on Social Conditions* (1955), 127.

54. For example, see Food and Agriculture Organization of the United Nations, *Nutrition Conference;* Food and Agriculture Organization of the United Nations, *Report of the Second Conference on Nutrition Problems in Latin America, Rio de Janeiro, Brazil, 5–13 June 1950* (Washington: Food and Agriculture Organization, 1950); and Food and Agriculture Organization of the United Nations, *Report of the Nutrition Committee for South and East Asia, Third Meeting, Bandung, Indonesia, 23–30 June 1953* (Rome: Food and Agriculture Organization, 1953). Also see ANS 1 H 49, "Documentation concernant la santé publique en AOF (1952)," 1.

55. Inter-African Conference on Nutrition, *Conférence interafricaine sur l'alimentation et la nutrition, Dschang, Cameroun, 3–9 octobre 1949* (Paris: Documentation française, 1949). Also see ANS 1 H 49, "Rapport sur la situation et l'évolution de la santé publique en AOF pendant l'année 1949," 24.

56. Commission for Technical Cooperation in Africa South of the Sahara, *Malnutrition in African Mothers, Infants and Young Children: Report to the Second Inter-African Conference on Nutrition Held under the Auspices of the Commission for Technical Cooperation in Africa South of the Sahara (C.T.C.A.) at Fajara, Gambia. 19–27 November 1952* (London: Her Majesty's Stationary Office, 1954), 23.

57. Ibid., 23.

58. Ibid., 17.

59. Ibid., 29.

60. Ibid., 363.

61. "Rapport sur l'activité de recherches (1953)," 57. Also see ANS, 1 H 49, "Documentation concernant la santé publique en AOF (1953)," 5.

62. After independence, ORANA would become even more closely involved with UNICEF. See Organisation de Coordination et de Coopération pour la lutte contre les grandes endémies, Secrétariat Général, *Quelques réflexions sur les activités appliqués de l'ORANA*, no. 6.445/77.Doc.Tech.OCCGE (Bobo-Dioulasso, Burkina Faso, 11–15 April 1977), http://horizon.documentation.ird.fr/exl-doc/pleins_textes/pleins_textes_5/b_fdi_08-09/09149.pdf.

63. "Rapport sur l'activité de recherches (1953)," 8–9, 18, 54.

64. The center was transferred to ORANA after its creation in 1953. Laboratory exams necessary for nutritional evaluation were pursued in conjunction with the Pasteur Institute of Dakar. See ANOM, 2 G 47 (6), C. Durieux, "Rapport sur le fonctionnement technique de l'Institut Pasteur de l'Afrique Occidentale Française en 1947," 5; and ANOM, 2 G 49 (19), C. Durieux, "Rapport sur le fonctionnement technique de l'Institut Pasteur de l'Afrique Occidentale Française en 1949," 7.

65. See J. F. Brock and M. Autret, "Kwashiorkor in Africa," *Bulletin of the World Health Organization* 5 (1952): 1–71; and United Nations, *Special Study on Social Conditions* (1955), 130. By 1955, of 257 UNICEF projects around the

world, 57 were nutrition related, consisting primarily of supplementary feeding programs. See United Nations, *Special Study on Social Conditions* (1955), 9.

66. ANS 1 H 50, OMS, WHO / MCH / 64, "Les activités d'hygiène maternelle et infantile et la formation de personnel qualifié et de personnel auxiliaire: Revue de la situation: Étude présentée à la dixième session du comité mixte FISE-OMS des directives sanitaires, 2–3 mai 1957," 10 June 1957, 129.

67. Food and Agriculture Organization of the United Nations, *Nutrition Conference,* 228. On milk stations in France, see Alisa Klaus, *Every Child a Lion: The Origins of Maternal and Infant Health Policy in the United States and France, 1890–1920* (Ithaca, NY: Cornell University Press, 1993). On similar initiatives in French sub-Saharan Africa (both government sponsored and those run by private associations), see, for example, ANOM 2 G 41 (15), Senegal, health services report, 46; ANOM 2 G 43 (10), Dahomey, 1943 health services report, 33; and ANOM 2 G 55 (49), Dakar, Institut d'hygiène sociale, "Rapport sur l'activité de l'Institut d'hygiène sociale de Dakar (1955), Annexe: Centre de protection maternelle et infantile, rapport sur le fonctionnement général du service en 1955," 5. Also see Food and Agriculture Organization of the United Nations, *Joint FAO / WHO Expert Committee,* 22.

68. United Nations, *Report of the Committee on Information* (1955), 32. On the use of dried skim milk in supplementary feeding programs, also see ANS 1 H 50, OMS, "Les activités d'hygiène maternelle et infantile," 10 June 1957, 46–56.

69. On nutrition for mothers, see ANS 1 H 50, R. Burgess and J. Bierman, "Les bébés commencent à s'alimenter avant leur naissance," Journée mondiale de la santé: "Nourriture et santé," 7 April 1957.

70. United Nations, *Special Study on Social Conditions* (1955), 129–133. On the expansion of UNICEF funding to AOF (including for supplementary feeding programs), see UNICEF, "L'UNICEF ouvre un crédit."

71. See, for example, ANOM, 2 G 49 (18), Dahomey, 1949 health services report, 197; ANOM, 2 G 50 (9), DGSP, 1950 report, 146; ANOM, 2 G 52 (59), DGSP, "Rapport sur le fonctionnement du Service général de l'inspection médicale des écoles (1951–1952)," 14; ANOM, 2 G 53 (65), Upper Volta, Service médicale scolaire, 1952-1953 annual report, 1–2, 4; ANOM, 2 G 54 (75), French Sudan, "Rapport annuel sur le fonctionnement de l'inspection médicale des écoles (1953–1954)," 6; and ANOM, 2 G 55 (60), Côte d'Ivoire, Direction de la santé publique, "Rapport d'inspection médicale des écoles (1954–1955)," 17.

72. Direction de la santé publique, "Rapport d'inspection médicale des écoles (1954–1955)," 39. Also see United Nations, *Special Study on Social Conditions* (1955), 129.

73. United Nations, *Special Study on Social Conditions* (1955), 135. Also see ANS 1 H 50, AFRO / PR / 100, Cambournac, "L'alimentation en Afrique et la santé des enfants," Journée mondiale de la santé, 7 April 1957, Organisation mondiale de la Santé, Bureau régional de l'Afrique (Brazzaville), 3.

74. United Nations, *Special Study on Social Conditions* (1957–1958), 196.
75. "Note au sujet du programme d'aide," 13 February 1952, 3.

Epilogue

1. "Le colloque sur l'allaitment maternel: La femme au foyer, 'une image s'éstompe,'" *Fraternité matin* (Abidjan), 15 November 1972.

2. On the decolonization of Algeria, see Matthew Connelly, *A Diplomatic Revolution: Algeria's Fight for Independence and the Origins of the Post–Cold War Era* (New York: Oxford University Press, 2002); Alistair Horne, *A Savage War of Peace: Algeria, 1954–1962* (New York: Viking, 1977); and Todd Shepard, *The Invention of Decolonization: The Algerian War and the Remaking of France* (Ithaca, NY: Cornell University Press, 2006).

3. On the decolonization of Guinea, see Elizabeth Schmidt, *Cold War and Decolonization in Guinea, 1946–1958* (Athens: Ohio University Press, 2007) and *Mobilizing the Masses: Gender, Ethnicity, and Class in the Nationalist Movement in Guinea, 1939–1958* (Portsmouth, NH: Heinemann, 2005). On West African decolonization more generally, see Tony Chafer, *The End of Empire in French West Africa: France's Successful Decolonization?* (Oxford: Berg, 2002); and Ebere Nwaubani, *The United States and Decolonization in West Africa, 1950–1960* (Rochester, NY: University of Rochester Press, 2001).

4. See, for example, James D. Le Sueur, ed., *The Decolonization Reader* (New York: Routledge, 2003); Martin Shipway, *Decolonization and Its Impact: A Comparative Approach to the End of the Colonial Empires* (Malden, MA: Blackwell, 2008); and L. J. Butler, Bob Moore, and Martin Thomas, *Crises of Empire: Decolonization and Europe's Imperial States, 1918–1975* (London: Hodder Education, 2008).

5. See International Children's Centre, *International Children's Centre: Structure and Activities, Extracts from the Report Presented by Dr. Etienne Berthet at the Meeting of the ICC Executive Board (Paris, 30–31 May 1960)* (Paris: Château de Longchamp, 1960); International Children's Centre, *Activities of the International Children's Centre and Plan of Work for the Years 1962–1966: Report Presented by Dr. Etienne Berthet, Director General of the International Children's Centre, at the Meeting of the Executive Board of the United Nations Children's Fund, June 1961* (Paris: Centre international de l'enfance, 1961); and International Children's Centre, *International Children's Centre: 20 Years of Activity, 1950–1969: A Report Presented by the Director-General at the Meeting of the Executive Board, Paris, 13–14 March 1970* (Paris: Château de Longchamp, 1970). On the broader history of France and Africa after decolonization, see Gregory Mann, *From Empires to NGOs in the West African Sahel: The Road to Nongovernmentality* (New York: Cambridge University Press, 2015).

6. Commission for Technical Cooperation in Africa South of the Sahara, *CCTA / CSA, FAMA: Inter-African Cooperation* (Hertford, UK: Stephen Austin, 1961).

7. Centre international de l'enfance et la Commission de coopération technique en Afrique au sud du Sahara, *Le bien-être de l'enfant en Afrique au sud du Sahara: Colloque organisé à Lagos (Nigéria) du 25 au 31 mars 1959 par le Centre international de l'enfance et la Commission de coopération technique en Afrique au sud du Sahara, sous la présidence de M. le Professeur Robert Debré* (Paris: Centre international de l'enfance, 1959), 3–4.

8. Ibid., 12–13.

9. "Opening Address of Professor Robert Debré," in ibid., 11–12.

10. On the CIE's involvement in postcolonial Africa, see Centre international de l'enfance, *Colloque sur les problèmes de formation du personnel médical et social et l'éducation sanitaire de la population en Afrique, Abidjan 19–23 avril 1960* (Paris: Centre international de l'enfance, 1960); Ika Paul-Pont and Marie Josèphe Bonnal, *Les conditions de vie l'enfant en milieu rural en Afrique: Colloque organisé à Dakar (Sénégal) du 20 au 25 février 1967* (Paris: Centre international de l'enfance, 1968); Centre international de l'enfance, *Les conditions de vie de l'enfant en milieu urbain en Afrique: Colloque organisé à Dakar (Sénégal) du 5 au 12 décembre 1964* (Paris: Centre international de l'enfance, 1966); and Centre international de l'enfance, *Séminaire sur l'éducation en matière de santé et de nutrition en Afrique au sud du Sahara: Pointe-Noire, 5–12 juin 1962, organisé conjointement de l'OAA, l'OMS, l'UNESCO et l'aide du FISE* (Paris: Centre international de l'enfance, 1963).

11. After 1960 the islands of Comoros and Réunion were the only territories in the WHO African region still under French control. See ADLC, NUOI 824, "Rapport de la délégation française à la 11ème session du Comité régional africain de l'Organisation mondiale de la Santé," 1961, 2. French participation in the committee continued for more than a decade after decolonization in French sub-Saharan Africa. See WHOL, World Health Organization, Regional Committee for Africa, twenty-first session, 1971, 4.

12. See Connelly, *Diplomatic Revolution;* and Alanna O'Malley, "Ghana, India, and the Transnational Dynamics of the Congo Crisis at the United Nations," *International History Review* 37, no. 5 (2015): 970–990.

13. ADLC, NUOI 824, "Note pour le cabinet du ministre, a / s Organisation mondiale de la Santé, Bureau de l'Afrique," 12 May 1962, 1.

14. "Rapport de la délégation française," 1961, 6.

15. Ibid., 8.

16. Ibid., 9.

17. "Note pour le cabinet du ministre," 12 May 1962, 2.

18. ADLC, NUOI 824, letter from the French ambassador to Côte d'Ivoire to the Minister of Foreign Affairs (African and Malagasy affairs division), 14 March 1962.

19. "Rapport de la délégation française," 1961, 11.

20. For a much more extreme—and more recent—example of a claim to the "Frenchness" of a strand of scientific inquiry, see Paul Rabinow, *French DNA: Trouble in Purgatory* (Chicago: University of Chicago Press, 1999).

21. Jan C. Jansen and Jürgen Osterhammel, *Decolonization: A Short History* (Princeton, NJ: Princeton University Press, 2017), 105.

22. Geneva [pseud.], "America's Plan for the Colonial World," *American Mercury* 60, no. 254 (February 1945): 140.

23. Sudhir Hazareesingh, *How the French Think: An Affectionate Portrait of an Intellectual People* (New York: Basic Books, 2015), 16.

24. See, for example, Tyler Stovall, *Transnational France: The Modern History of a Universal Nation* (Boulder, CO: Westview, 2015).

25. See, for example, Richard F. Kuisel, *The French Way: How France Embraced and Rejected American Values and Power* (Princeton, NJ: Princeton University Press, 2012) and *Seducing the French: The Dilemma of Americanization* (Berkeley: University of California Press, 1993).

26. Jessica Reinisch, "Expertise Is Always Political," *Reluctant Internationalists Blog*, 31 July 2017, http://www.bbk.ac.uk/reluctantinternationalists/blog/expertise-always-political/

27. On the limited availability of archives for independent Africa, see, for example, Luise White, *Unpopular Sovereignty: Rhodesian Independence and African Decolonization* (Chicago: University of Chicago Press, 2015), xi.

28. For an example of a history of health in Africa that spans that divide between the colonial and postcolonial periods and engages with both European and African expertise, see Sarah Cook Runcie, "Mobile Health Teams, Decolonization, and the Eradication Era in Cameroon, 1945–1970" (PhD diss., Columbia University, 2017).

Bibliography

Primary Sources

ARCHIVES AND LIBRARIES

Archives diplomatiques du Ministère des Affaires Etrangères, La Courneuve
Archives nationales, Paris
Archives nationales d'outre-mer, Aix-en-Provence
Archives nationales du Sénégal, Dakar
Archives du Centre international de l'enfance, Bibliothèque universitaire d'Angers, Belle-Beille
Archives de l'Institut de médecine tropicale du Service de santé des armées, Marseille
World Health Organization Library, Geneva

PUBLISHED PRIMARY SOURCES

"AEF: Brazzaville." *Le courrier colonial illustré,* 15 September 1929.

"Afrique équatoriale—Moyen Congo." *La dépêche coloniale illustrée,* 15 April 1911.

Air France. "Air France en Afrique Occidentale Française et en Afrique Equatoriale Française," *Echos de l'air: Bulletin mensuel* 38 (July 1950): 3.

———. "De Dakar à Brazzaville." *Echos de l'air: Bulletin mensuel* 38 (July 1950): 12.

———. "Richesses agricoles." *Echos de l'air: Bulletin mensuel* 38 (July 1950): 6.

Aubin, Pierre. "A propos des prestations familiales dans les territoires français d'Afrique noire." *Population* 9, no. 1 (1954): 51–60.

Balandier, Georges. *Sociologie des Brazzavilles noires.* Paris: Presses de la Fondation nationale des sciences politiques, 1985.

Belgian Information Center. *The Sacred Mission of Civilization: To Which Peoples Should the Benefits Be Extended?* New York: Belgian Information Center, 1953.

Berthet, Etienne. "Activities of the International Children's Centre." *American Journal of Public Health* 48, no. 4 (April 1958): 458–467.

———. "Problèmes de pédiatrie sociale dans les pays en voie de développement." *Revue médicale du Moyen-Orient* 12, no. 3 (1955): 328–337.

Berthet, Etienne, and Michel Manciaux. *Le Centre international de l'enfance*. Notes et études documentaires 4527–4528. Paris: Documentation française, 1979.

"Les bois de l'Afrique Equatoriale Française." *Le courrier colonial illustré,* 31 December 1931.

Bok, Bart J. "The United Nations Expanded Program for Technical Assistance." *Science* 117, no. 3030 (1953): 67–70.

Bonnenfant. "Treize années de service social rural par l'Association d'hygiène sociale de l'Aisne, 1923–1926." *Revue médico-social de l'enfance* 5, no. 3 (May–June 1937): 168–184.

———. "Treize années de service social rural (suite et fin)." *Revue médico-social de l'enfance* 5, no. 4 (July–August 1937): 283–306.

Brock, J. F., and M. Autret. "Kwashiorkor in Africa." *Bulletin of the World Health Organization* 5 (1952): 1–71.

Bros. "Organisation des services sociaux d'outre-mer." *Les cahiers du Musée sociale* 3 (1955): 78–83.

Buck, Pearl S. "Save the Children for What?" *Journal of Educational Sociology* 17, no. 4 (December 1943): 195–199.

Burns, Alan. *In Defence of Colonies: British Colonial Territories in International Affairs.* New York: Macmillan, 1957.

Centre international de l'enfance. *Colloque sur les problèmes de formation du personnel médical et social et l'éducation sanitaire de la population en Afrique, Abidjan 19–23 avril 1960.* Paris: Centre international de l'enfance, 1960.

———. *Les conditions de vie de l'enfant en milieu urbain en Afrique: Colloque organisé à Dakar (Sénégal) du 5 au 12 décembre 1964.* Paris: Centre international de l'enfance, 1966.

———. *Etude des conditions de vie de l'enfant africain en milieu urbain et de leur influence sur la délinquance juvénile: Enquête entreprise à Madagascar, au Cameroun et en Côte d'Ivoire de 1954 à 1957 par le Centre international de l'enfance, avec l'aide des services sociaux de la France d'outre-mer.* Paris: Centre international de l'enfance, 1959.

———. *Les problèmes de l'enfance dans les pays tropicaux de l'Afrique: Colloque organisé par le Centre international de l'enfance, Brazzaville, 8–13 décembre 1952.* Paris: Centre international de l'enfance, Impr. de Villain et Bar, 1953.

———. *Séminaire sur l'éducation en matière de santé et de nutrition en Afrique au sud du Sahara: Pointe-Noire, 5–12 juin 1962 (Organisé conjointement de l'OAA, l'OMS, l'UNESCO et l'aide du FISE).* Paris: Centre international de l'enfance, 1963.

Centre international de l'enfance et la Commission de coopération technique en Afrique au sud du Sahara. *Le bien-être de l'enfant en Afrique au sud du Sahara: Colloque organisé à Lagos (Nigéria) du 25 au 31 mars 1959 par le Centre international de l'enfance et la Commission de coopération technique en Af-*

rique au sud du Sahara, sous la présidence de M. le Professeur Robert Debré. Paris: Centre international de l'enfance, 1959.
"Les centres sociaux en Côte d'Ivoire." *Informations sociales* 11, no. 8 (1957): 921–925.
Charles, John. "Origins, History, and Achievements of the World Health Organization." *British Medical Journal* 2 (May 1968): 293–296.
Charles-Roux, J. *Exposition coloniale de Marseille, 1906: Compte rendu des travaux du Congrès colonial de Marseille*. Paris: Challamel, 1907.
"Colonial Issue." *Economist* 147, no. 5301 (31 March 1945).
Combes, Raoul. *La recherche scientifique dans les territoires d'outre-mer*. Paris: Université de Paris, 1948.
Commission de coopération technique en Afrique au sud du Sahara. *Coopération scientifique et technique en Afrique au sud du Sahara, 1948–1955*. London: S. Austin and Sons, 1956.
Commission for Technical Cooperation in Africa South of the Sahara. *CCTA / CSA, FAMA: Inter-African Cooperation*. Hertford, UK: Stephen Austin, 1961.
———. *Malnutrition in African Mothers, Infants and Young Children: Report to the Second Inter-African Conference on Nutrition Held under the Auspices of the Commission for Technical Cooperation in Africa South of the Sahara (C.T.C.A.) at Fajara, Gambia. 19–27 November 1952*. London: Her Majesty's Stationary Office, 1954.
"Le Congo français." *La dépêche coloniale illustrée*, 30 November 1908.
Debré, Robert. *Ce que je crois*. Paris: Grasset, 1976.
———. *Hommage au professeur Robert Debré: 1882–1978*. Paris: B. Grasset, 1980.
———. *L'honneur de vivre: Témoignage*. Paris: Stock / Hermann, 1974.
———. *Médecine, santé publique, population: rapports présentés au Comité médical de la résistance et au Comité national des médecins français: Transmis au Comité français de la libération nationale, à Alger, en Janvier 1944*. Paris: Editions du médecin français, 1944.
Debré, Robert, and Alfred Sauvy. *Des français pour la France: Le problème de la population*. Paris: Gallimard, 1946.
De Gaulle, Charles. *Mémoires de guerre*. Paris: Librarie Plon, 1999.
Desprez. "Les maternités rurales en régions libérées." *Revue médico-social de l'enfance* 1, no. 6 (November–December 1933): 418.
Dulphy, G. "Le problème d'enfance outre-mer." *Chronique d'outre-mer* 4 (April 1954): 3–16.
Flexner, Abraham. *Medical Education in Europe: A Report to the Carnegie Foundation for the Advancement of Teaching*. New York: Carnegie Foundation for the Advancement of Teaching, 1912.
———. *Medical Education in the United States and Canada: A Report to the Carnegie Foundation for the Advancement of Teaching*. New York: Carnegie Foundation for the Advancement of Teaching, 1910.

Food and Agriculture Organization of the United Nations. *Joint FAO/WHO Expert Committee on Nutrition, Report on the Second Session, Rome, 10–17 April 1951.* Rome: Food and Agriculture Organization, 1951.

———. *Nutrition Conference, Montevideo, 1948.* Montevideo: Comisión de Alimentación, 1950.

———. *Report of the Nutrition Committee for South and East Asia, Third Meeting, Bandung, Indonesia, 23–30 June 1953.* Rome: Food and Agriculture Organization, 1953.

———. *Report of the Second Conference on Nutrition Problems in Latin America, Rio de Janeiro, Brazil, 5–13 June 1950.* Washington: Food and Agriculture Organization, 1950.

Geneva [pseud.]. "America's Plan for the Colonial World." *American Mercury* 60, no. 254 (February 1945): 135–143.

Goodwin, Ralph R., and William Z. Slany, eds. *Foreign Relations of the United States, 1952–1954.* Vol. 3, *United Nations Affairs.* Washington, DC: US Government Printing Office, 1979.

Gouvernement Général de l'Afrique Occidentale Française. *Instructions du Gouverneur Général Carde sur le développement de l'Assistance médicale indigène sociale et sur la protection sanitaire des travailleurs en A.O.F.* Paris: Librairie Larose, 1931.

Houlet, Gilbert. *Les guides bleus illustrés: Brazzaville, Léopoldville, Pointe-Noire.* Paris: Librarie Hachette, 1958.

Inter-African Conference on Nutrition. *Conférence interafricaine sur l'alimentation et la nutrition, Dschang, Cameroun, 3–9 octobre 1949.* Paris: Documentation française, 1949.

International Children's Centre. *Activities of the International Children's Centre and Plan of Work for the Years 1962–1966: Report Presented by Dr. Etienne Berthet, Director General of the International Children's Centre, at the Meeting of the Executive Board of the United Nationals Children's Fund, June 1961.* Paris: Centre international de l'enfance, 1961.

———. *International Children's Centre: Structure and Activities, Extracts from the Report Presented by Dr. Etienne Berthet at the Meeting of the ICC Executive Board (Paris, May 30–31, 1960).* Paris: Château de Longchamp, 1960.

———. *International Children's Centre: 20 Years of Activity, 1950–1969: A Report Presented by the Director-General at the Meeting of the Executive Board, Paris, 13–14 March 1970.* Paris: Château de Longchamp, 1970.

———. *Statutes of the International Children's Centre, and Addresses Delivered at the Ceremony of Inauguration 18 January 1950 in the Salon de l'Horloge, Ministry of Foreign Affairs.* Paris: International Children's Centre, 1950.

Julien, C. A. "From the French Empire to the French Union." *International Affairs* 26, no. 4 (October 1950): 487–502.

Lahille, Abel. *Mes impressions sur l'Afrique Occidentale Française: Étude documentaire au pays du tam-tam.* Paris: A. Picard, 1910.

"La maladie du sommeil en A. E. F." *La presse coloniale illustrée,* July 1922.

Mathiot, André. *Les territoires non autonomes et la charte des Nations Unies.* Paris: Librairie générale du droit et du jurisprudence, 1949.

Mathis, Constant. *L'œuvre des pastoriens en Afrique Noire, Afrique Occidentale Française.* Paris: Presses universitaires de France, 1946.

Mettler, L. Harrison. "Medical Paris—Notes from My Sketchbook." *Journal of the American Medical Association* 27, no. 9 (1896): 487–490.

Ministère des Affaires Etrangères. *Procès-verbaux de la Conférence sanitaire internationale ouverte à Paris le 27 juillet 1851.* Paris: Imprimerie nationale, 1852.

Nealley, Willis Grafton. "The Caribbean Commission as an International Instrument for Regional Collaboration." PhD diss., Stanford University, 1951.

Némirovsky, Irène. *Suite Française.* New York: Knopf, 2006.

Osler, William. "Impressions of Paris." *Journal of the American Medical Association* 52, no. 9 (1909): 701–703.

Owen, David. "The United Nations Program of Technical Assistance." *Annals of the American Academy of Political and Social Science* 270 (1950): 109–117.

Padmore, George. "'New Deal' for Colored Races." *Pittsburgh Courier,* 29 January 1944.

Pampana, E. J., and P. F. Russel. "Malaria: A World Problem." *Chronicle of the World Health Organization* 9 (1955): 33–100.

"Paris: Reform of Medical Teaching." *Journal of the American Medical Association* 132, no. 12 (22 July 1950): 1110–1111.

"Paris: The New Site for the Paris Faculty of Medicine." *Journal of the American Medical Association* 99, no. 11 (1932): 927–928.

Paul-Pont, Ika, and Marie Josèphe Bonnal. *Les conditions de vie l'enfant en milieu rural en Afrique: Colloque organisé à Dakar (Sénégal) du 20 au 25 février 1967.* Paris: Centre international de l'enfance, 1968.

Piffault, M. A. "Préjugés et superstitions." In *Premier Congrès international d'éducation et de protection,* 127–130. Namur, Belgium: Auguste Godenne, 1905.

Pinard, Adolphe. *La puériculture du premier âge.* Paris: A. Colin, 1919.

Pont, R. L. "Brazzaville." *Air France revue,* Winter 1952–1953, 86–88.

Poole, Bernard L. *The Caribbean Commission: Background of Cooperation in the West Indies.* Columbia: University of South Carolina Press, 1951.

"Prophylaxie de la maladie du sommeil en Afrique Equatoriale Française." *La dépêche coloniale illustrée,* 31 July 1911.

République Française. *Conférence africaine française, Brazzaville, 30 janvier 1944 à 8 février 1944.* Paris: Ministère des Colonies, 1945.

Rouvier, Jules. *Hygiène de la première enfance.* Paris: Doin, 1889.

Savorgnan de Brazza, Pierre Paul François Camille, and Napoléon Ney. *Conférences et lettres de P. Savorgnan de Brazza sur ses trois explorations dans l'Ouest africain, de 1875 à 1886.* Paris, 1887.

Sembène, Ousmane. *Les bouts de bois de Dieu.* Paris: Le Livre Contemporain, 1960.

Sénécal, Jean. "La protection maternelle et infantile en Afrique Occidentale Française." *Bulletin de l'Académie nationale de médecine* 141, no. 34 (December 1957): 780–785.

Sharp, Evelyn. *The African Child: An Account of the International Conference on African Children, Geneva.* Westport: Negro Universities Press, 1970.

Sicé, Adolphe. *L'Afrique équatoriale au service de la France.* Paris: Presse universitaire, 1946.

Soret, Marcel. *Démographie et problèmes urbains en A.E.F.: Poto-Poto, Bacongo, Dolisie.* Montpellier: Imprimerie Charité, 1954.

"South Africa, France Balk on Giving Up Colonies to UNO." *Chicago Defender,* 19 January 1946.

Soyer. "Congo belge: Bien-être familial et équipement sociale." *Familles dans le monde* 11, no. 4 (1958): 299–309.

Tricot-Guisen, A. "Comment faut-il envisager au Congo belge le problème des jardins d'enfants pour les petits noirs?" *Bulletin trimestriel du Centre d'étude des problèmes sociaux indigènes* 34 (1954): 7–35.

United Nations. *Special Study on Social Conditions in Non-self-governing Territories, Summaries and Analyses of Information Transmitted to the Secretary-General during 1955.* New York: United Nations, 1956.

———. *Special Study on Social Conditions in Non-self-governing Territories, Analyses of Information Transmitted to the Secretary-General during 1957–1958.* New York: United Nations, 1958.

United Nations, Department of Public Information. *What the United Nations Is Doing for Non-self-governing Territories.* Lake Success, NY: Department of Public Information, 1948.

United Nations, General Assembly. *Report of the Special Committee on Information Transmitted under Article 73e of the Charter,* Official Records: Third Session, Supplement 12 (A / 593). Lake Success, NY: United Nations, 1948.

———. *Report of the Special Committee on Information Transmitted under Article 73e of the Charter,* Official Records: Fourth Session, Supplement 14 (A / 923). Lake Success, NY: United Nations, 1949.

———. *Report of the Special Committee on Information Transmitted under Article 73e of the Charter,* Official Records: Fifth Session, Supplement 17 (A / 1303). New York: United Nations, 1950.

———. *Report of the Special Committee on Information Transmitted under Article 73e of the Charter,* Official Records: Sixth Session, Supplement 14 (A / 1836). Geneva: United Nations, 1951.

———. *Report of the Committee on Information from Non-self-governing Territories,* Official Records: Seventh Session, Supplement 18 (A / 2219). New York: United Nations, 1952.

———. *Report of the Committee on Information from Non-self-governing Territories,* Official Records: Eighth Session, Supplement 15 (A / 2465). New York: United Nations, 1953.

———. *Report of the Committee on Information from Non-self-governing Territories,* Official Records: Tenth Session, Supplement 16 (A / 2908). New York: United Nations, 1955.

United Nations, *Special Study on Social Conditions in Non-self-governing Territories, Analyses of Information Transmitted to the Secretary-General during 1957–1958.* New York: United Nations, 1958.

United Nations, World Health Organization Interim Commission, *Minutes of the Technical Preparatory Committee for the International Health Conference Held in Paris from 18 March to 5 April 1946.* Official Records of the World Health Organization 1. New York: United Nations, World Health Organization Interim Commission, 1947.

———. *Summary Report on Proceedings and Final Acts of the International Health Conference Held in New York from 19 June to 22 July 1946,* Official Records of the World Health Organization 2. New York: United Nations, World Health Organization Interim Commission, 1948.

US Department of State. *The United States and Non-self-governing Territories: A Summary of Information regarding the United States and Non-self-governing Territories with Particular Reference to Chapters XI, XII, and XIII of the Charter of the United Nations.* Washington, DC: US Government Printing Office, 1947.

van Langenhove, Fernand. *The Question of Aborigines before the United Nations: The Belgian Thesis.* Brussels: Institut Royal Colonial Belge, 1954.

Variot, Gaston. *Comment sauvegarder les bébés: Enseignement de l'hygiène infantile donné à l'Institut de puériculture et à la Goutte de lait de Belleville.* Paris: Gaston Doin, 1922.

———. *La puériculture pratique; ou, l'art d'élever les enfants du premier âge.* Paris: Doin, 1930.

"Voies de transports et moyens de communication en A. E. F." *Les annales coloniales,* December 1933.

Weston, Hugh. "End of Vast French Empire Looms: Full Freedom All Written into New Constitution." *Pittsburgh Courier,* 11 May 1946, 16.

World Health Organization. *Annual Report of the Director-General to the World Health Assembly and the United Nations, 1948.* Official Records of the World Health Organization 16. Geneva: World Health Organization, 1949.

———. *Annual Report of the Director-General to the World Health Assembly and the United Nations, 1949.* Official Records of the World Health Organization 24. Geneva: World Health Organization, 1950.

——. *First World Health Assembly, Geneva, 24 June–24 July 1948.* Official Records of the World Health Organization 13. Geneva: World Health Organization, 1948.

——. "General François Daubenton (Obituary)." *Chronicle of the World Health Organization* 19, no. 10 (1965): 419.

——. *Report on the Malaria Conference in Equatorial Africa Held under the Joint Auspices of the World Health Organization and the Commission for Technical Co-operation in Africa South of the Sahara, Kampala, Uganda, 27 November to 9 December 1950.* Technical Report Series 38. Geneva: World Health Organization, 1951.

Secondary Sources

Akerman, James R., ed. *Decolonizing the Map: Cartography from Colony to Nation.* Chicago: University of Chicago Press, 2017.

Amrith, Sunil S. *Decolonizing International Health: India and Southeast Asia, 1930–1965.* Basingstoke, UK: Palgrave Macmillan, 2006.

Amster, Ellen. *Medicine and the Saints: Science, Islam, and the Colonial Encounter in Morocco, 1877–1956.* Austin: University of Texas Press, 2013.

Anderson, Warwick. "Where Is the Postcolonial History of Medicine?" *Bulletin of the History of Medicine* 72, no. 3 (1998): 522–530.

Bado, Jean-Paul. *Les conquêtes de la médecine moderne en Afrique.* Collection Tropiques. Paris: Editions Karthala, 2006.

——. *Eugène Jamot, 1879–1937: Le médecin de la maladie du sommeil ou trypanosomiase.* Paris: Editions Karthala, 2011.

——. *Médecine coloniale et grandes endémies en Afrique 1900–1960: Lèpre, trypanosomiase humaine et onchocercose.* Paris: Editions Karthala, 1996.

Baldwin, Peter. *Contagion and the State in Europe, 1830–1930.* Cambridge: Cambridge University Press, 1999.

Barnes, David S. *The Making of a Social Disease: Tuberculosis in Nineteenth-Century France.* Berkeley: University of California Press, 1995.

Barnett, Michael N. *Empire of Humanity: A History of Humanitarianism.* Ithaca, NY: Cornell University Press, 2013.

Barthélemy, Pascale. *Africaines et diplômées à l'époque coloniale, 1918–1957.* Rennes: Presses universitaires de Rennes, 2010.

Beigbeder, Yves, Mahyar Nashat, Marie-Antoinette Orsini, and J. F. Tiercy. *The World Health Organization.* The Hague: M. Nijhoff, 1998.

Benton, Adia. "Race and the Immune-Logics of Ebola Response in West Africa." *Somatosphere: Science, Medicine and Anthropology,* 19 September 2014.

Berenson, Edward. *Heroes of Empire: Five Charismatic Men and the Conquest of Africa.* Berkeley: University of California Press, 2010.

Betts, Raymond Frederick. *Assimilation and Association in French Colonial Theory, 1890–1914.* Lincoln: University of Nebraska Press, 2005.

Bonner, Thomas Neville. *Becoming a Physician: Medical Education in Britain, France, Germany and the United States, 1750–1945.* New York: Oxford University Press, 1995.

Borgwardt, Elizabeth. *A New Deal for the World: America's Vision for Human Rights.* Cambridge, MA: Belknap Press of Harvard University Press, 2005.

Borowy, Iris. *Coming to Terms with World Health: The League of Nations Health Organisation, 1921–1946.* Frankfurt: Peter Lang, 2014.

Brogi, Alessandro. *A Question of Self-Esteem: The United States and the Cold War Choices in France and Italy, 1944–1958.* Westport, CT: Praeger, 2002.

Brown, Theodore, Marco Cueto, and Elizabeth Fee. "At the Roots of the World Health Organization's Challenges: Politics and Regionalization." *American Journal of Public Health* 106, no. 11 (November 2016): 1912–1917.

Burke, Roland. *Decolonization and the Evolution of International Human Rights.* Philadelphia: University of Pennsylvania Press, 2010.

Butler, L. J., Bob Moore, and Martin Thomas. *Crises of Empire: Decolonization and Europe's Imperial States, 1918–1975.* London: Hodder Education, 2008.

Chafer, Tony. *The End of Empire in French West Africa: France's Successful Decolonization?* Oxford: Berg, 2002.

Chafer, Tony, and Amanda Sackur, eds. *Promoting the Colonial Idea: Propaganda and Visions of Empire in France.* Basingstoke, UK: Palgrave Macmillan, 2002.

Chakrabarti, Pratik. *Medicine and Empire, 1600–1960.* Basingstoke, UK: Palgrave Macmillan, 2014.

Chorev, Nitsan. *The World Health Organization between North and South.* Ithaca, NY: Cornell University Press, 2012.

Clancy-Smith, Julia Ann, and Frances Gouda. *Domesticating the Empire: Race, Gender, and Family Life in French and Dutch Colonialism.* Charlottesville: University Press of Virginia, 1998.

Cole, Joshua. *The Power of Large Numbers: Population, Politics and Gender in Nineteenth-Century France.* Ithaca, NY: Cornell University Press, 2000.

Coleman, William. *Death Is a Social Disease: Public Health and Political Economy in Early Industrial France.* Madison: University of Wisconsin Press, 1982.

Conklin, Alice. "Faire Naître v. Faire du Noir: Race Regeneration in France and French West Africa, 1895–1940." In *Promoting the Colonial Idea: Propaganda and Visions of Empire in France,* edited by Tony Chafer and Amanda Sackur, 143–155. Basingstoke, UK: Palgrave, 2002.

———. *A Mission to Civilize: The Republican Idea of Empire in France and West Africa, 1895–1930.* Stanford, CA: Stanford University Press, 1997.

Connelly, Matthew James. *A Diplomatic Revolution: Algeria's Fight for Independence and the Origins of the Post–Cold War Era.* Oxford: Oxford University Press, 2003.

Cooper, Frederick. *Africa since 1940: The Past of the Present.* Cambridge: Cambridge University Press, 2002.

———. *Citizenship between Empire and Nation: Remaking France and French Africa, 1945–1960.* Princeton, NJ: Princeton University Press, 2014.

———. *Decolonization and African Society: The Labor Question in French and British Africa.* Cambridge: Cambridge University Press, 1996.

———. "'Our Strike': Equality, Anticolonial Politics, and the 1947–48 Railway Strike in French West Africa." *Journal of African History* 36 (1996): 81–118.

Cooper, Frederick, and Randall M. Packard, eds. *International Development and the Social Sciences: Essays on the History and Politics of Knowledge.* Berkeley: University of California Press, 1997.

Coquéry-Vidrovitch, Catherine. "L'Afrique coloniale française et la crise de 1930: Crise structurelle et genèse du sous-développement." *Revue française d'histoire d'outre-mer* 63, nos. 3–4 (1976): 386–424.

———. "Nationalité et citoyenneté en Afrique Occidentale Française: Originaires et citoyens dans le Sénégal colonial." *Journal of African History* 42, no. 2 (2001): 285–305.

Crapuchet, Simone. *Politique sociale d'outre-mer: Un devoir de mémoire à l'égard des pionnières.* Ramonville Saint-Agne, France: Erès, 1999.

Cueto, Marcos. *The Value of Health: A History of the Pan American Health Organization.* Washington, DC: Pan American Health Organization, 2007.

Curtin, Philip. "Medical Knowledge and Urban Planning in Colonial Tropical Africa." In *The Social Basis of Health and Healing in Africa,* edited by Steven Feierman and John M. Janzen, 235–255. Berkeley: University of California Press, 1992.

Downs, Laura Lee. *Childhood in the Promised Land: Working-Class Movements and the Colonies de Vacances in France, 1880–1960.* Durham, NC: Duke University Press, 2002.

Droux, Joëlle. "L'internationalisation de la protection de l'enfance: Acteurs, concurrences et projets transnationaux (1900–1925)." *Critique internationale* 52 (July–September 2011): 17–33.

Echenberg, Myron J. *Africa in the Time of Cholera: A History of Pandemics from 1817 to the Present.* New York: Cambridge University Press, 2011.

———. *Black Death, White Medicine: Bubonic Plague and the Politics of Public Health in Colonial Senegal, 1914–1945.* Portsmouth, NH: Heinemann, 2002.

El-Ayouty, Yassin. *The United Nations and Decolonization: The Role of Afro-Asia.* The Hague: Martinus Nijhoff, 1971.

Farley, John. *Bilharzia: A History of Imperial Tropical Medicine.* New York: Cambridge University Press, 1991.

———. *Brock Chisholm, the World Health Organization, and the Cold War.* Vancouver: University of British Columbia Press, 2008.

———. *To Cast Out Disease: A History of the International Health Division of the Rockefeller Foundation (1913–1951).* Oxford: Oxford University Press, 2004.

Fassin, Didier. *L'espace politique de la santé: Essai de généalogie.* Sociologie d'aujourd'hui. Paris: Presses universitaires de France, 1996.

Fassin, Didier, and Dominique Memmi. *Le gouvernement des corps.* Paris: Editions de l'Ecole des hautes études en sciences sociales, 2004.

Feierman, Steven, and John M. Janzen, eds. *The Social Basis of Health and Healing in Africa.* Berkeley: University of California Press, 1992.

Fidler, David. *International Law and Infectious Diseases.* Oxford: Oxford University Press, 1999.

Fishman, Sarah. *The Battle for Children: World War II, Youth Crime, and Juvenile Justice in Twentieth-Century France.* Cambridge, MA: Harvard University Press, 2002.

Fox, Robert, and George Weisz, eds. *The Organization of Science and Technology in France, 1808–1914.* New York: Cambridge University Press, 1980.

Gamble, Harry. *Contesting French West Africa: Battles over Schools and the Colonial Order, 1900–1950.* Lincoln: University of Nebraska Press, 2017.

Genova, James E. *Colonial Ambivalence, Cultural Authenticity, and the Limitations of Mimicry in French-Ruled West Africa, 1914–1956.* New York: Peter Lang, 2004.

———. "Constructing Identity in Post-war France: Citizenship, Nationality, and the Lamine Guèye Law, 1946–1953." *International History Review* 26, no. 1 (March 2004): 56–79.

Gildea, Robert. *Marianne in Chains: Daily Life in the Heart of France during the German Occupation.* New York: Picador, 2003.

Ginio, Ruth. *French Colonialism Unmasked: The Vichy Years in French West Africa.* Lincoln: University of Nebraska Press, 2006.

Gordon, Philip H. *A Certain Idea of France: French Security Policy and the Gaullist Legacy.* Princeton, NJ: Princeton University Press, 1993.

Gratien, Jean-Pierre. *Marius Moutet: Un socialiste à l'outre-mer.* Paris: L'Harmattan, 2006.

Hansen, Peo, and Stefan Jonsson. *Eurafrica: The Untold History of European Integration and Colonialism.* London: Bloomsbury, 2015.

Hazareesingh, Sudhir. *How the French Think: An Affectionate Portrait of an Intellectual People.* New York: Basic Books, 2015.

Heaton, Matthew M. *Black Skin, White Coats: Nigerian Psychiatrists, Decolonization, and the Globalization of Psychiatry.* Athens: Ohio University Press, 2013.

Hill, Robert A., and Edmond J. Keller, eds. *Trustee for the Human Community: Ralph J. Bunche, the United Nations, and the Decolonization of Africa.* Athens, OH: Ohio University Press, 2010.

Hitchcock, William I. *France Restored: Cold War Diplomacy and the Quest for Leadership in Europe, 1944–1954.* Chapel Hill: University of North Carolina Press, 1998.

Hochschild, Adam. *King Leopold's Ghost: A Story of Greed, Terror, and Heroism in Colonial Africa.* Boston: Houghton Mifflin, 1998.

Horne, Alistair. *A Savage War of Peace: Algeria, 1954–1962.* New York: Viking, 1977.

Howard-Jones, Norman. *International Public Health between the Two World Wars: The Organizational Problems.* Geneva: World Health Organization, 1978.

Huber, Valeska. "The Unification of the Globe by Disease? The International Sanitary Conferences on Cholera, 1851–1894." *Historical Journal* 49, no. 2 (2006): 453–476.

Hunt, Nancy Rose. *A Colonial Lexicon of Birth Ritual, Medicalization, and Mobility in the Congo.* Durham, NC: Duke University Press, 1999.

———. "'Le bébé en brousse': European Women, African Birth Spacing, and Colonial Intervention in Breastfeeding in the Belgian Congo." In *Tensions of Empire: Colonial Cultures in a Bourgeois World,* edited by Frederick Cooper and Ann Laura Stoler, 287–321. Berkeley: University of California Press, 1997.

Husain, Aiyaz. *Mapping the End of Empire: American and British Strategic Visions in the Postwar World.* Cambridge, MA: Harvard University Press, 2014.

"Introducing *Social Medicine.*" *Social Medicine* 1, no. 1 (February 2006): 1–4.

Iriye, Akira. *Global Community: The Role of International Organizations in the Making of the Contemporary World.* Berkeley: University of California Press, 2002.

Iriye, Akira, Petra Goedde, and William I. Hitchcock. *The Human Rights Revolution: An International History.* Oxford: Oxford University Press, 2012.

Jablonka, Ivan. *Enfants en exil: Transfert de pupilles réunionnais en métropole, 1963–1982.* Paris: Seuil, 2007.

———. *Ni père ni mère: Histoire des enfants de l'Assistance publique, 1874–1938.* Paris: Seuil, 2006.

Jackson, Julian. *France: The Dark Years, 1940–1944.* Oxford: Oxford University Press, 2003.

Jansen, Jan C., and Jürgen Osterhammel. *Decolonization: A Short History.* Princeton, NJ: Princeton University Press, 2017.

Jennings, Eric. *Curing the Colonizers: Hydrotherapy, Climatology, and French Colonial Spas.* Durham, NC: Duke University Press, 2006.

———. *Free French Africa in World War II: The African Resistance.* Cambridge: Cambridge University Press, 2015.

———. *Vichy in the Tropics: Pétain's National Revolution in Madagascar, Guadeloupe, and Indochina, 1940–1944.* Stanford, CA: Stanford University Press, 2001.

Johnson, Jennifer. *The Battle for Algeria: Sovereignty, Healthcare, and Humanitarianism.* Philadelphia: University of Pennsylvania Press, 2016.

———. "New Directions in the History of Medicine in European, Colonial and Transimperial Contexts." *Contemporary European History* 25, no. 2 (2016): 387–399.

Kantrowitz, Rachel. "'So That Tomorrow Would Be Better for Us': Developing French-Funded Catholic Schools in Dahomey and Senegal, 1946–1975." PhD diss., New York University, 2015.

Kent, John. *The Internationalization of Colonialism: Britain, France, and Black Africa, 1939–1956.* New York: Oxford University Press, 1992.

Klaus, Alisa. *Every Child a Lion: The Origins of Maternal and Infant Health Policy in the United States and France, 1890–1920.* Ithaca, NY: Cornell University Press, 1993.

Koos, Cheryl. "Gender, Anti-individualism, and Nationalism: The Alliance Nationale and the Pronatalist Backlash against the *Femme Moderne*, 1933–1940." *French Historical Studies* 19, no. 3 (Spring 1996): 699–723.

Kott, Sandrine. "Les organisations internationales, terrains d'étude de la globalisation: Jalons pour une approche socio-historique." *Critique internationale* 52 (July–September 2011): 9–16.

Krasnick Warsh, Cheryl, and Veronica Jane Strong-Boag, eds. *Children's Health Issues in Historical Perspective.* Waterloo, ON: Wilfrid Laurier University Press, 2005.

Kuisel, Richard F. *The French Way: How France Embraced and Rejected American Values and Power.* Princeton, NJ: Princeton University Press, 2012.

———. *Seducing the French: The Dilemma of Americanization.* Berkeley: University of California Press, 1993.

La Berge, Ann. *Mission and Method: The Early Nineteenth-Century French Public Health Movement.* Cambridge: Cambridge University Press, 1992.

Lachenal, Guillaume. *Le médicament qui devait sauver l'Afrique: Un scandale pharmaceutique aux colonies.* Paris: La Décoverte, 2014.

———. "Le médecin qui voulut être roi: Médecine coloniale et utopie au Cameroun." *Annales, Histoire, Sciences Sociales* 65, no. 1 (2010): 121–156.

Le Sueur, James D., ed. *The Decolonization Reader.* New York: Routledge, 2003.

Levine, Philippa. *Prostitution, Race, and Politics: Policing Venereal Disease in the British Empire.* New York: Routledge, 2003.

Lohrmann, Ullrich. *Voices from Tanganyika: Great Britain, the United Nations and the Decolonization of a Trust Territory, 1946–1961.* Berlin: Lit, 2007.

Louis, William Roger. *Imperialism at Bay: The United States and the Decolonization of the British Empire, 1941–1945.* New York: Oxford University Press, 1978.

Lyons, Maryinez. *The Colonial Disease: A Social History of Sleeping Sickness in Northern Zaire, 1900–1940.* Cambridge: Cambridge University Press, 1992.

Mahood, Linda, and Vic Satzewich. "The Save the Children Fund and the Russian Famine of 1921–1923: Claims and Counter-claims about Feeding 'Bolshevik' Children." *Journal of Historical Sociology* 22, no. 1 (March 2009): 55–83.

Mann, Gregory. *From Empires to NGOs in the West African Sahel: The Road to Nongovernmentality.* New York: Cambridge University Press, 2015.

Manning, Patrick. *Francophone Sub-Saharan Africa, 1880–1995.* Cambridge: Cambridge University Press, 1998.

Marks, Shula. "Doctors and the State: George Gale and South Africa's Experiment in Social Medicine." In *Science and Society in Southern Africa,* edited by Saul Dubow, 188–211. Manchester: Manchester University Press, 2000.

———. "What Is Colonial about Colonial Medicine? And What Has Happened to Imperialism and Health?" *Social History of Medicine* 10, no. 2 (1997): 205–219.

Martin, Phyllis M. *Leisure and Society in Colonial Brazzaville.* Cambridge: Cambridge University Press, 1995.

Martineaud, Jean-Paul. *De Vincent de Paul à Robert Debré: Des enfants abandonnés et des enfants malades à Paris.* Paris: L'Harmattan, 2006.

Massa, Gabriel, and Y. Georges Madiéga. *La Haute-Volta coloniale: Témoignages, recherches, regards.* Paris: Karthala, 1995.

Mazower, Mark. *Governing the World: The History of an Idea.* New York: Penguin, 2012.

———. *No Enchanted Palace: The End of Empire and the Ideological Origins of the United Nations.* Princeton, NJ: Princeton University Press, 2009.

Miller, Carol. "The Social Section and Advisory Committee on Social Questions of the LNHO." In *International Health Organisations and Movements, 1918–1939,* edited by Paul Weindling, 154–175. Cambridge: Cambridge University Press, 1995.

Moreau, Jean-Paul. *Un pasteurien sous les tropiques: 1963–2000.* Paris: L'Harmattan, 2006.

Moulin, Anne-Marie. "The Pasteur Institutes between the Two World Wars: The Transformation of the International Sanitary Order." In *International Health Organisations and Movements, 1918–1939,* edited by Paul Weindling, 244–265. Cambridge: Cambridge University Press, 1995.

Muel-Dreyfus, Francine. *Vichy et l'éternel féminin.* Paris: Editions de Seuil, 1996.

Murard, Lion, and Patrick Zylberman. *L'hygiène dans la république: La santé publique en France ou l'utopie contrariée.* Paris: Fayard, 1996.

Neill, Deborah J. *Networks in Tropical Medicine: Internationalism, Colonialism, and the Rise of a Medical Specialty, 1890–1930.* Stanford, CA: Stanford University Press, 2012.

Nwaubani, Ebere. *The United States and Decolonization in West Africa, 1950–1960.* Rochester, NY: University of Rochester Press, 2001.

Offen, Karen. "Depopulation, Nationalism, and Feminism in Fin-de-Siècle France." *American Historical Review* 89, no. 3 (June 1984): 648–676.

O'Grady, Siobhán. "Colonial Lines Drawn Again for Ebola Aid." *Foreign Policy,* 22 September 2014.

Ollandet, Jerôme. *Brazzaville, capitale de la France libre: Histoire de la résistance française en Afrique, 1940–1944.* Paris: L'Harmattan, 2013.

Olopade, Dayo. "The End of 'the Developing World." *New York Times,* 28 February 2014.

O'Malley, Alanna. "Ghana, India, and the Transnational Dynamics of the Congo Crisis at the United Nations." *International History Review* 37, no. 5 (2015): 970–990.

Ousby, Ian. *Occupation: The Ordeal of France, 1940–1944.* New York: Cooper Square, 2000.

Packard, Randall. "Malaria Dreams: Postwar Visions of Health and Development in the Third World." *Medical Anthropology: Cross-cultural Studies in Health and Illness* 17, no. 3 (1997): 279–296.

———. "Visions of Postwar Health and Development and Their Impact on Public Health Interventions in the Developing World." In *International Development and the Social Sciences,* edited by Frederick Cooper and Randall M. Packard, 93–115. Berkeley: University of California Press, 1997.

———. *White Plague, Black Labor: Tuberculosis and the Political Economy of Health and Disease in South Africa.* Berkeley: University of California Press, 1989.

Parkinson, Charles. *Bills of Rights and Decolonization: The Emergence of Domestic Human Rights Instruments in Britain's Overseas Territories.* Oxford: Oxford University Press, 2007.

Patil, Vrushali. *Negotiating Decolonization in the United Nations: Politics of Space, Identity, and International Community.* New York: Routledge, 2008.

Paxton, Robert Owen. *Vichy France: Old Guard and New Order, 1940–1944.* New York: Columbia University Press, 2001.

Pearson, Jessica Lynne. "Defending Empire at the United Nations: The Politics of International Colonial Oversight in the Era of Decolonisation." *Journal of Imperial and Commonwealth History* 45, no. 3 (2017): 525–549.

———. "O império francês vai a S. Francisco: A criação das Nações Unidas e os limites da reforma colonial." In *Os Impérios do Internacional: Perspectives, Genealogias e Processos,* edited by Miguel Bandeira Jerónimo and José Pedro Monteiro. Lisbon: Almedina, forthcoming.

Pearson-Patel, Jessica. "How Today's Ebola Response Reflects the History of Colonialism in Africa." Interview by Jason Steinhauer. *Time Magazine Online,* 13 February 2015. http://time.com/3707158/ebola-colonialism-history/.

———. "Promoting Health, Protecting Empire: Inter-colonial Medical Cooperation in Postwar Africa." *Monde(s): Histoire, espaces, relations* 7 (May 2015): 213–230.

———. "Remapeando as fronteiras da saúde imperial: A Organização Mundial da Saúde e os debates internacionais sobre a regionalização no Norte de África Francês, 1945–1956." Translated by Luís Domingos. In *Os passados do presente:*

Internacionalismo, imperialismo e a construção do mundo contemporâneo, edited by Miguel Bandeira Jerónimo and José Pedro Monteiro, 295–322. Lisbon: Almedina, 2015.

Pedersen, Susan. *Family, Dependence and the Origins of the Welfare State: Britain and France, 1914–1945.* Cambridge: Cambridge University Press, 1993.

———. *The Guardians: The League of Nations and the Crisis of Empire.* Oxford: Oxford University Press, 2015.

Picard, Jean-François, and William Schneider. "From the Art of Medicine to Biomedical Science in France: Modernization or Americanization?" In *Rockefeller Philanthropy and Modern Biomedicine: International Initiatives from World War I to the Cold War,* edited by William H. Schneider, 106–124. Bloomington: Indiana University Press, 2002.

Pick, Daniel. *Faces of Degeneration: A European Disorder, c. 1848–1918.* Cambridge: Cambridge University Press, 1999.

Pollard, Miranda. *Reign of Virtue: Mobilizing Gender in Vichy France.* Chicago: University of Chicago Press, 1998.

Porter, Dorothy, ed. *The History of Public Health and the Modern State.* Amsterdam: Rodopi, 1994.

———. "How Did Social Medicine Evolve and Where Is It Heading?" *PLoS Med* 3, no. 10 (October 2006): e399.

Porter, Dorothy, and Roy Porter. "What Was Social Medicine? An Historiographical Essay." *Journal of Historical Sociology* 1, no. 1 (March 1988): 90–106.

Rabinow, Paul. *French DNA: Trouble in Purgatory.* Chicago: University of Chicago Press, 1999.

Ramsey, Matthew. *Professional and Popular Medicine in France, 1770–1830: The Social World of Medical Practice.* New York: Cambridge University Press, 1988.

———. "Public Health in France." In *The History of Public Health and the Modern State,* edited by Dorothy Porter, 45–118. Amsterdam: Editions Rodopi, 1994.

Reggiani, Andres Horacio. "Procreating France: The Politics of Demography, 1919–1945." *French Historical Studies* 19, no. 3 (Spring 1996): 725–754.

Reinisch, Jessica. "Expertise Is Always Political." *Reluctant Internationalists Blog,* 31 July 2017. http://www.bbk.ac.uk/reluctantinternationalists/blog/expertise-always-political/.

Roberts, Mary Louise. *Civilization without Sexes: Reconstructing Gender in Postwar France, 1917–1927.* Chicago: University of Chicago Press, 1994.

Rosen, George. "Approaches to a Concept of Social Medicine: A Historical Survey." *Milbank Memorial Fund Quarterly* 26, no. 1 (January 1948): 7–21.

Rosenberg, Clifford. "The International Politics of Vaccine Testing in Interwar Algiers." *American Historical Review* 117, no. 3 (2012): 671–697.

Rosental, Paul-André. *L'intelligence démographique: Sciences et politiques des populations en France (1930–1960).* Paris: Jacob, 2003.

Runcie, Sarah Cook. "Mobile Health Teams, Decolonization, and the Eradication Era in Cameroon, 1945–1970." PhD diss., Columbia University, 2017.

Schmidt, Elizabeth. *Cold War and Decolonization in Guinea, 1946–1958*. Athens: Ohio University Press, 2007.

———. *Mobilizing the Masses: Gender, Ethnicity, and Class in the Nationalist Movement in Guinea, 1939–1958*. Portsmouth, NH: Heinemann, 2005.

Schneider, William H. "The Eugenics Movement in France, 1890–1940." In *The Wellborn Science*, edited by Mark Adams, 70–110. Oxford: Oxford University Press, 1990.

———. *Quality and Quantity: The Quest for Biological Regeneration in Twentieth-Century France*. Cambridge: Cambridge University Press, 1990.

———, ed. *Rockefeller Philanthropy and Modern Biomedicine: International Initiatives from World War I to the Cold War*. Bloomington: Indiana University Press, 2002.

Seay, Laura, and Kim Yi Dionne. "The Long and Ugly Tradition of Treating Africa as a Dirty, Diseased Place." *Washington Post*, 25 August 2014.

Shepard, Todd. *The Invention of Decolonization: The Algerian War and the Remaking of France*. Ithaca, NY: Cornell University Press, 2006.

Shipway, Martin. *Decolonization and Its Impact: A Comparative Approach to the End of the Colonial Empires*. Malden, MA: Blackwell, 2008.

———. "Madagascar on the Eve of Insurrection, 1944–1947." In *The Decolonization Reader*, edited by James Le Sueur, 80–102. New York: Routledge, 2003.

———. *The Road to War: France and Vietnam, 1944–1947*. New York: Berghahn, 2003.

———. "Thinking like an Empire: Governor Henri Laurentie and Postwar Plans for the Late Colonial French 'Empire State.'" In *The French Colonial Mind*, edited by Martin Thomas, 219–250. Lincoln: University of Nebraska Press, 2011.

Sibeud, Emmanuelle. *Une science impériale pour l'Afrique? La construction des savoirs africanistes en France, 1878–1930*. Paris: Ecole des hautes études en sciences sociales, 2002.

Siddiqi, Javed. *World Health and World Politics: The World Health Organization and the UN System*. Columbia: University of South Carolina Press, 1995.

Silver, Marc. "If You Shouldn't Call It the Third World, What Should You Call It?" *Goats and Soda* (blog), NPR, 4 January 2015. https://www.npr.org/sections/goatsandsoda/2015/01/04/372684438/if-you-shouldnt-call-it-the-third-world-what-should-you-call-it.

Simonin, Anne. "Le Comité médical de la résistance: Un succès différé." *Mouvement social* 180 (1997): 159–178.

Staples, Amy L. S. *The Birth of Development: How the World Bank, Food and Agriculture Organization, and World Health Organization Changed the World, 1945–1965.* Kent, OH: Kent State University Press, 2007.

Stovall, Tyler. *Transnational France: The Modern History of a Universal Nation.* Boulder, CO: Westview, 2015.

Terretta, Meredith. *Nation of Outlaws, State of Violence: Nationalism, Grassroots Tradition, and State-Building in Cameroon.* Athens: Ohio University Press, 2010.

———. *Petitioning for Our Rights, Fighting for Our Nation: The History of the Democratic Union of Cameroonian Women, 1949–1960.* Bamenda, Cameroon: Langaa Research and Publishing, 2013.

———. "'We Had Been Fooled into Thinking That the UN Watches over the Entire World': Human Rights, UN Trust Territories, and Africa's Decolonization." *Human Rights Quarterly: A Comparative and International Journal of the Social Sciences, Philosophy, and Law* 34, no. 2 (2012): 329–360.

Thomas, Lynn M. *Politics of the Womb: Women, Reproduction, and the State in Kenya.* Berkeley: University of California Press, 2003.

Thomas, Martin, ed. *The French Colonial Mind.* Vol. 1, *Mental Maps of Empire and Colonial Encounters.* Lincoln: University of Nebraska Press, 2011.

Tilley, Helen. *Africa as a Living Laboratory: Empire, Development, and the Problem of Scientific Knowledge, 1870–1950.* Chicago: University of Chicago Press, 2011.

Tomlinson, B. R. "What Was the Third World?" *Journal of Contemporary History* 38, no. 2 (April 2003): 307–321.

Toungara, Jeanne Maddox. "Inventing the African Family: Gender and Family Law Reform in Cote d'Ivoire." *Journal of Social History* 28, no. 1 (Autumn 1994): 37–61.

Vaughan, Megan. *Curing Their Ills: Colonial Power and African Illness.* Stanford, CA: Stanford University Press, 1991.

Velmet, Aro. "Pasteur's Empire: French Expertise, Colonialism, and Transnational Science, 1890–1940." PhD diss., New York University, 2017.

Webb, James L. A., Jr. *The Long Struggle against Malaria in Tropical Africa.* New York: Cambridge University Press, 2014.

Weindling, Paul, ed. *International Health Organisations and Movements, 1918–1939.* Cambridge: Cambridge University Press, 1995.

Weisz, George. *The Medical Mandarins: The French Academy of Medicine in the Nineteenth and Early Twentieth Centuries.* New York: Oxford University Press, 1995.

White, Luise. *Unpopular Sovereignty: Rhodesian Independence and African Decolonization.* Chicago: University of Chicago Press, 2015.

White, Owen. *Children of the French Empire: Miscegenation and Colonial Society in French West Africa, 1895–1960.* New York: Oxford University Press, 1999.

Wilder, Gary. *The French Imperial Nation-State: Negritude and Colonial Humanism between the Two World Wars*. Chicago: University of Chicago Press, 2005.

Wilsford, David. *Doctors and the State: The Politics of Health Care in France and the United States*. Durham, NC: Duke University Press, 1991.

Zallen, Doris T. "Louis Rapkine and the Restoration of French Science after the Second World War." *French Historical Studies* 17, no. 1 (Spring 1991): 6–37.

Acknowledgments

It is an inescapable reality that book writing is simultaneously a solitary project and a collective endeavor. All shortcomings are my own. All successes are the shared achievement of many people.

My first debt of gratitude is to my teachers, especially Herrick Chapman and my French history family at New York University. Herrick has been an incredible mentor and friend to me for over a decade, and I will always be fiercely grateful for his wisdom, kindness, and indefatigable support. Ed Berenson, Fred Cooper, and John Shovlin supported me and shaped this project over the course of many years. At the Institute of French Studies, Ed created a home for all of us, and Washington Mews quickly became the heart of our lives in New York. In many ways—years after we have all moved on—the IFS remains the core of our intellectual community. At NYU I am also grateful to Karl Appuhn, Laura Downs, Stéphane Gerson, Marion Kaplan, Molly Nolan, and Frédérique Viguier, whose teaching shaped this project in important ways. Before I came to New York, teachers in Minnesota and Michigan inspired my curiosity about the world. I especially thank Charlene Boyer-Lewis, Mary Carberry, Henry Cohen, Amy Elman, Liz Kircher Perona, Mary Kuettner, Kathy Smith, and Jan Solberg.

Colleagues and friends at the IFS and in the History Department at NYU provided crucial feedback and constant companionship over the years. This book would not have been possible without their support. Kari Evanson provided a home for me in Paris when she took a chance on an unknown PhD student and offered to rent me the loft bed over her dining room table. Liz Fink shared her Marseille with me, as well as glasses of rosé and jogs along the Corniche, the Seine, the San Diego waterfront, and—back at home in New York—over the Brooklyn Bridge. Her research on electoral politics in French West Africa during the era of decolonization serves as an important reminder of the myriad ways that Africans mobilized the structures of citizenship to shape their own political destinies. My friendship with Sarah Griswold began in her garden in Paris and traveled back to New York—and eventually to Norman, Oklahoma—where our two-woman French colonial reading group sustained me through my first two years on the tenure track. Rachel Kantrowitz has been my companion through numerous conference adventures, from New Orleans to Pittsburgh. Her work on education and decolonization in French West Africa has encouraged me to think critically about the real and imagined divides between colonial and postcolonial Africa. Evan Spritzer helped me navigate endless bureaucratic tape as I worked to find my own place in Paris. Our annual couscous catch-ups have become one of my favorite yearly traditions. David Weinfeld taught me everything I know about Jewish history and, perhaps more importantly, introduced me to the wonder that is the smoked meat sandwich at Mile End Deli on Bond Street. I would also like to thank Muriam Davis, Valerie Deacon, Thomas Fleischman, Hillel Gruenberg, Nick Hersh, Laura Honsberger, Trina Hogg, Kathryn Kleppinger, Elizabeth Knott, Larissa Kopytoff, Jed Lewinsohn, Phoebe Maltz Bovy, Eva-Maria Muschik, Mary-Elizabeth O'Neill, Reynolds Richter, Alexandra Steinlight, Chelsea Stieber, Emily Teising, George R. Trumbull IV, Aro Velmet, Matt Watkins, Karen Weber, Jerusha Westbury, and Peter Wirzbicki. At NYU, a number of staff members provided vital support. There, I am grateful to Yasmin Desouki, Amy Farranto, Isabelle Genest, Françoise Gramet, and Jennifer Hebert. I could not have hoped for a more supportive first academic home for this project than Washington Mews.

Colleagues in the History Department at Tulane University, where I was a Mellon Postdoctoral Fellow in the Humanities from 2013 to 2014, provided support and encouragement as I revised the manuscript. At the College of International Studies at the University of Oklahoma, I owe an incredible debt of gratitude to Suzette Grillot, Mitchell Smith, Rhonda Hill, and Ronda Martin. My colleagues and students at OU constantly challenged me to think about the world in new ways. There, that world was made brighter by Simon Adenji, Eric Beasley, Moussa Blimpo, Gabe Bonzie, Ana Bracic and Nicholson Price, Jacque Braun, Dante Brooks, Audra Brulc, Laura Brunson, Malin Collins, Rebecca Cruise, Sarah Ex, Jackynicole Eyocko, Jaci Gandenberger, Jeremiah Gentle, Robin and Kevin Grier, Robert Griswold, Molly Hackett, Kati Harris, Aubrey Haverkamp, Nizar Hermes, Katie Hickerson, Khylian Hockett, Jennifer Holland, Kaitie Holland, Aliyah Howard, Blessing Ikpa, Alex Jones, Neira Kadic, Amel Khalfaoui, Andrew Kierig, Hanna Kimpel, Hoi Kipgen, Joshua Landis, Gershon Lewental and Sitora Usmonova Lewental, Catherine Lewis, Dominique Litchfield, Daniel Mains, Afshin Marashi, Heather McGuire, Lindsey Meeks, Sarah Miles, Stefanie Neumeier, Derek Nguyen, Andreana Prichard, Kassidy Quinten, Erika Robb Larkins, Emily Rook-Koepsel, Bala Saho, Carsten Schapkow, Katy Schumaker, Rachel Shelden, Daniel Simon, Nicole Smith, Jamie Tacker, Noah Theriault, Lexi Vermeire Albe, Randee Walck, Solongo Wandan, Katie Watkins, and Christine Williams. The women of the OU History Department were an especially welcoming community, and I am particularly grateful to Kathy Brosnan, Jennifer Davis, Elyssa Faison, Ronnie Grinberg, Miriam Gross, Sandie Holguin, Judy Lewis, Melissa Stockdale, and Jane Wickersham for welcoming me into their group. The Francophone World Workshop filled a France-shaped void, and I am incredibly grateful to have had the opportunity to work with Jennifer Davis and Pamela Genova, as well as Julia

Abramson, Michel Lantelme, and Pete Soppelsa. From the first day I stepped on campus, Monica Goodwin made OU a home for me, and she was a constant companion during my two years there. The hours we spent chatting about French history (and life) over bowls of pho at Coriander Café are my best memories of Norman.

At Macalester College, my fabulous colleagues in the History Department provided much-needed support for the completion of this book. My students, in particular those from my Public Health in Africa course, provided essential insights into the broader stakes of this project. I am particularly grateful to Greg Zacharia and Julia Hirsch for their comments on Chapter 4. It was inspiring to research and write alongside an extremely engaged group of students at Macalester, most of all Rachel Ault, Emma Carray, EJ Coolidge, Morgan Hess, Barbara Kuzma, Sara Ludewig, Kasia Majewski, Sam Manz, Liam McMahon, Mariah Shriner, and Merrit Stüven. Cheese Shop lunches and ice cream outings with Amy Pascoe, my writing assistant, buoyed my spirits in the final stages of manuscript revision. It feels appropriate that the last pieces of this book were completed at a school with such strong ties to internationalism. The ability to catch a glimpse of the United Nations flag waving on Old Main Lawn was a constant reminder of the importance of thinking critically about the ways the world has—and has failed to—come together since 1945.

Workshops and writing groups in New York, Norman, and Saint Paul allowed me to try out new arguments and sharpen old ones. More importantly, though, they provided indispensable intellectual and emotional communities for me at crucial junctures in this project and in my life. I am grateful to the participants of a number of workshops where I had the opportunity to present parts of this work, including the IFS doctoral workshop and the modern European history workshop at NYU. I am particularly indebted to Charlotte Chopin, Sarah Cook Runcie, Claire Edington, Elisa Gonzalez, and Maria John, who read several chapters as part of a joint NYU-Columbia colonial public health workshop. I cannot imagine a group of more supportive or more talented scholars, and I consider myself lucky to have had the chance to work with all of them. I am particularly thankful to Claire, who read and provided feedback on this project since its earliest stages, and was a loyal partner in French colonial history adventures from New York to Paris and Aix-en-Provence to Siem Reap. Jessica Hammerman read several early iterations of these chapters as well and provided feedback and moral support throughout the writing process, usually over coffee and *pain au chocolat* at Dominique Ansel bakery in Soho. At OU, Miriam Gross, Andreana Prichard, and Emily Rook-Koepsel taught me fundamental lessons about the practice of writing. Daniel Mains, Erika Robb Larkins, and Noah Theriault also provided valuable feedback on sections of the manuscript. At Macalester, Amy Elkins, Crystal Moten, and Katie Phillips were a constant source of writing motivation and shared laughter during our regular meetings of the Old Main Awesome Writing Group. Katie, especially, was an indispensable writing partner.

This book has benefited greatly from a number of conversations and collaborations that took place at meetings of the African Studies Association, the American Historical Association, the French Colonial Historical Society, the Society for French Historical Studies, the Society for the Study of French History, and the Western Society for French History. I am particularly indebted to Megan Brown, Melissa Byrnes, Haydon Cherry, Alice Conklin, Liz Foster, Burleigh Hendrickson, Laure Humbert, Emma Kuby, Itay Lotem, Terry Peterson, Andrew Smith, Charlotte Walker-Said, and Owen White for sharing their own work and for their feedback on mine. When I met Deb Neill at a meeting of the Western Society for French History in Banff, little did I know she would ultimately become a member of my dissertation committee, one of my most important mentors, and a dear friend.

In 2013 I had the opportunity to participate in the Eighth International Seminar on Decolonization. This was a life-changing intellectual experience, and I will be eternally grateful to the Andrew W. Mellon Foundation and the National History Center of the American Historical Association for the financial and institutional support that made this seminar possible. Marian Barber guided us through four transformative weeks in Washington, DC, and faculty members Dane Kennedy, Philippa Levine, Roger Louis, Jason Parker, Pillarisetti Sudhir, and Lori Watt provided unparalleled mentorship. One of the most notable—and, indeed, ongoing—strengths of the decolonization seminar is its ability to build relationships across generations of historians and to break down the geographic barriers that sometimes hinder our cooperation. I am indebted to all of my fellow seminarians for their intellectual companionship, but I am especially grateful to John Aerni-Flessner, Marc André, Nicole Bourbonnais, José Pedro Monteiro, Joanna Tague, and Annalisa Urbano. Formal and informal reunions in Geneva, Lisbon, Minneapolis, New York, and Washington, DC, over the past four years shaped this project in critical ways.

Seminarians from earlier cohorts provided mentorship at crucial junctures of this project. Jennifer Foray has been an indispensable companion at annual meetings of the American Historical Association and, more than anyone else, has encouraged me to expand the scope of my work and to think about the global connections between French decolonization and that of other European empires. Miguel Bandeira Jerónimo has been a tireless supporter of my work, publishing two of my essays in edited volumes in Portuguese and English and warmly welcoming me to Lisbon for two different workshops on internationalism and the end of empire. Jennifer Johnson has challenged me to think about the larger political implications of health in the French empire and helped me to situate my work within the broader history of public health on the African continent. The decolonization seminar has also facilitated important conversations between historians working in more traditional academic settings and those serving the government and the general public. Aiyaz Husain and Jason Steinhauer have helped me in myriad ways, encouraging me to think about ways to make my work speak to a broader audience. Although it has reached the end of its ten-year mandate, the decolonization seminar continues to foster the kinds of collaborative endeavors that historians should strive for, and I will be forever indebted to the close-knit community of scholars and friends that it has created.

During the summer of 2015 I had the chance to be part of another transformative collaborative venture. This book owes much to the Reluctant Internationalists research group, envisioned and organized by Jessica Reinisch and generously supported by a four-year Wellcome Trust Investigator Award. As a summer fellow, I had the opportunity to benefit from our reading groups and workshops at Birkbeck, as well as from our animated conversations over tapas and wine at the Norfolk Arms with Jessica, Ana Antic, David Brydan, Johanna Conterio, Brigid O'Keeffe, Francesca Piana, and Dora Vargha. Our final conference, "Outsiders in International Health," gave me an opportunity to think about the ways that intercolonial health ventures both did and did not provide a viable alternative to new global health institutions in the twentieth century.

The time to write and the opportunity to travel to far-flung archives were financially supported by the generosity of several organizations and institutions. Travel funding from New York University, Tulane University, the University of Oklahoma, and Macalester College made the research for this book possible, along with a Jeanne Maradon Fellowship from the Société des Professeurs Français et Francophones d'Amérique and a Mellon Postdoctoral Fellowship in the Humanities from the Andrew W. Mellon Foundation.

In each of the locations I traveled to—Aix, Dakar, London, Marseille, Geneva, Paris, and Washington, DC—numerous librarians and archivists made it possible for me to consult the documents that I needed in order to tell this story. This project would not have been possible without the staffs of the Archives nationales de France, the Archives diplomatiques at both Nantes and La Courneuve, the Archives nationales d'outre-mer in Aix, and the Archives nationales du Sénégal in Dakar. I am especially grateful to Aline Pueyo of the Centre de documentation de l'Institut de médecine tropicale de la Service de santé des armées in Marseille. It was truly a pleasure to have a chance to work in this wonderful archive. I would like to thank France Chabod, of the Bibliothèque universitaire at the University of Angers, who gave me special access to the archives of the International Children's Centre. At New York University's Bobst Library I thank Stacy Williams for her assistance with NYU's United Nations Documents Collection and the interlibrary loan staff for their help in locating rare books and publications that were indispensable to this project. At Macalester I thank Connie Karlen for her help locating the map of the WHO regions included in this book. In Geneva, Tomas Allen facilitated my work at the World Health Organization Library, helping me locate the final missing puzzle pieces for my chapter on the WHO in Brazzaville.

At Harvard University Press, I am incredibly grateful to my editor, Kathleen McDermott, for all of her support and for the direction she gave this project. Stephanie Vyce was instrumental in helping me research the provenance of the images included in this book, and in securing permission for their use. She also provided assistance navigating the use of previously published texts. For their help in the final stages of editing and production, I thank Angela Piliouras and Ashley Moore. Two anonymous readers provided essential feedback, pointed me toward important source material, and helped me to strengthen the book's arguments.

Outside the academy, family—and friends who have become family—provided encouragement for completing what at times felt like an impossible undertaking. This book would not have been possible without the years of support and companionship of Vinay Patel and Books Pearson-Patel. Many friends in New York City helped to make this a truly enjoyable journey, but I am especially grateful to Neda Afsarmanesh, Ya'ir Aizenman and Brookes Brown, Joanna Cohen, Katie and Graham Free, Tim Kleiman, Sara and Jacob Kramer, and Andy Lim and Niki Mahac. This incredible group of friends has brought joy to my life for almost a decade, with jogs in Central Park, Persian feasts in Brooklyn, and spirited games of One Night Ultimate Werewolf in front of the fire at Nauhlakha, Rudyard Kipling's home outside Brattleboro, Vermont. It is perhaps the greatest irony of this project that several parts of this book on the end of empire were written at the very same desk where Kipling—one of the biggest proponents of European colonialism—wrote *The Jungle Book* in 1894. Back in Brooklyn, Steph Anderson and Tieneke VanLonkhuyzen brought the best parts of our days at Kalamazoo to our postgrad life, and I will always be grateful for their company on this journey. During the final months of work on this project, Terence and Monika Murren provided a much-needed haven from the bustle of city life, and our warm dinners and chilly walks in the Hudson Valley were a perfect counterpoint to intense writing sessions in Brooklyn.

When I left New York for other locales, new families adopted me. In France, Pascale Ariñ and Philippe Pillot welcomed me into their home in Nantes. Beautiful dinners of fondue, duck, *bigorneaux,* and *pain aux graines* from the Boulangerie d'Honoré—accompanied by the world's tiniest glasses of wine—were a welcome respite after days spent alone in the archives. Nicolas Clarens, Elisa Kamerze, Guénolé Le Labourier, and Chantal McGowan Oger made me feel at home in France, from glorious breakfasts at La Cigale to weeklong trips exploring the most forgotten corners of Corsica. In Aix-en-Provence, Lindsey Gish and Erica Johnson hiked up mountains and hunted down the best pastry shops. In Paris, Melissa Anderson and Blake Smith helped scout out the best pho and relaxed over glasses of rosé at Verse Toujours. More than anyone else, Kate Thomas has helped me make France my second home. Her love of the world—and of all things French—has inspired me in a way that permeates every page of this book and every aspect of my life. From exploring castles in Périgord to playing *boules* in Kenwood Park in Minneapolis, Kate has helped me build a life in and about France. In New

Orleans, Theresa McCulla and Ashley Young made the culinary history of the city come alive. In Oklahoma, Rob Griswold and Ellie Wisdom invited me as a regular guest to their Italian table in Norman. In Saint Paul, I quickly discovered Herta Pitman to be a kindred spirit. I am thankful for the incredible kindness with which she and Peter Pitman have welcomed me to Minnesota and into their lives. From Minnesota to Washington, DC, Julia and Robert Blizzard provided unwavering support for the entirety of this project.

Decades before I ever began work on this book, my family supported me and encouraged my passion for history. I am especially grateful to my mother, Tina Boden, who always fostered a love of learning in our home. D'Orsay Pearson, my grandmother, imparted to me her own love of the past, from my early childhood when she read *The Canterbury Tales* in Middle English to me as a bedtime story, to my teenage years when she would pass on to me her used paperback copies of the Brother Cadfael murder mysteries. Her determination, her independence, and her hunger for adventure have been an inspiration to me all of my life. I dedicate this book to her.

Ernie Capello has been a source of unflagging encouragement and love, of inspiration to write, and of reminders to take time off from writing to be in the world. In some ways the completion of this book was a solitary endeavor, achieved through countless hours typing alone at our dining room table in Saint Paul. In other ways we finished this book together, over long dinners at that same dining room table, where we talked about history, writing, and everything else under the sun. I count myself incredibly lucky to have the chance to live my life with someone who shares my love of adventures near and far, past and present.

Several sections of this book build on parts of my previously published work. Chapter 2 expands on ideas first discussed in "Defending Empire at the United Nations: The Politics of International Colonial Oversight in the Era of Decolonization," in *Journal of Imperial and Commonwealth History*, 45:3, 525–549, DOI: 10.1080 / 03086534.2017.1332133, published by Informa UK Limited, trading as Taylor & Francis Group, under the terms of a CC BY-NC-ND 4.0 Open Access license. The Introduction, Chapter 3, and Chapter 4 include portions of text from "French Colonialism and the Battle Against the WHO Regional Office for Africa," in *Hygiea Internationalis: An Interdisciplinary Journal for the History of Public Health*, vol. 12, no. 1 (2016), published under the terms of a CC BY-NC 3.0 Open Access license by Linköping University Electronic Press. Portions of "Promoting Health, Protecting Empire: Inter-colonial Medical Cooperation in Postwar Africa," in *Monde(s): histoire, espaces, relations* no. 7 (May 2015) are reprinted in this book's Introduction, Chapter 3, and Chapter 5 with permission. I thank these publishers for the opportunity to publish on topics I address in more detail in my book.

Index